Praise for *The American Way of Poverty*

"Abramsky has written an ambitious book that both describes and prescribes. He reaches across a wide range of issues—including education, housing and criminal justice—in a sweeping panorama of poverty's elements. . . . Abramsky has invited serious rethinking and issued a significant call to action."

—David Shipler, *New York Times Book Review*

"[An] extraordinary book . . . extremely well researched and thorough."

—*Los Angeles Review of Books*

"[A] necessary and important book."

—*Financial Times*

"Abramsky's approach is both heartbreaking in its look at the humans who are affected and inspiring in his explanations of how poverty can be addressed and improved. . . . *The American Way of Poverty* is likely to cause fear—almost no one is exempt from unplanned disasters—but it is also likely to motivate: there are answers; this country can and should improve. Well researched and documented, Abramsky's eye-opening book should be required reading for all US citizens."

—Shelf Awareness

"[A] searing exposé. . . . Abramsky's is a challenging indictment of an economy in which poverty and inequality at the bottom seem like the foundation for prosperity at the top."

—*Publishers Weekly* (starred review)

"[This] portrait of poverty is one of great complexity and diversity, existential loneliness and desperation—but also amazing resilience. . . . Abramsky's well-researched, deeply felt depiction of poverty is eye-opening, and his outrage is palpable. He aims to stimulate discussion, but whether his message provokes action remains to be seen."

—*Kirkus Reviews*

"Abramsky's portraits of the poor illustrate three striking points: the isolation, diversity—people with no jobs and people with multiple jobs—and resilience of the poor. Drawing on ideas from a broad array of equality advocates, Abramsky offers detailed policies to address poverty, including reform in education, immigration, energy, taxation, criminal justice, housing, Social Security, and Medicaid, as well as analysis of tax and spending policies that could reduce inequities."

—*Booklist*

"Sasha Abramsky takes us deep into the long dark night of poverty in America, and it's a harrowing trip. His research and remarkable insights have resulted in a book that is stunning in its intensity."

—Bob Herbert, distinguished senior fellow at Demos and former op-ed columnist for the *New York Times*

"Incisive and necessary, *The American Way of Poverty* is a call to action."

—Lynn Nottage, Pulitzer Prize–winning playwright

"This is a devastating, passionate, and important investigative work."

—Joe Sacco, author of *Palestine, Footnotes in Gaza, The Great War,* and coauthor of *Days of Destruction, Days of Revolt*

"Sasha Abramsky writes compellingly and correctly that poverty is the 'canary' in the coal mine of our democracy. . . . But this is more than a lament! It is a policy roadmap to reclaiming the most vibrant part of our nation: 'We the People.'"

—Sister Simone Campbell, SSS, executive director of NETWORK and leader of the Nuns on the Bus

"This urgent and compassionate inquiry breaks the pact of silence in which politicians refuse to talk about poverty and journalists refuse to investigate it. The spirit of Studs Terkel lives on in Sasha Abramsky. He listens to ordinary Americans speak hauntingly about their struggles to survive in a social welfare system designed by Franz Kafka. Every page reports an outrage, a chord in what might have become a requiem for the American Dream, were it not for Abramsky's conviction that change is possible."

—Raj Patel, author of *Stuffed and Starved* and *The Value of Nothing*

Also by
SASHA ABRAMSKY_____

Hard Time Blues (2002)

Conned (2006)

American Furies (2007)

Breadline USA (2009)

Inside Obama's Brain (2009)

SASHA ABRAMSKY

THE AMERICAN WAY OF POVERTY

HOW THE OTHER HALF STILL LIVES

NATION
BOOKS
New York

www.nationbooks.org

This book is dedicated to
my darling children, Sofia and Leo.
May you always keep your exquisitely
fine-tuned sense of fairness.

Copyright © 2013 by Sasha Abramsky

All photographs © Sasha Abramsky

Published by Nation Books, A Member of the Perseus Books Group
116 East 16th Street, 8th Floor
New York, NY 10003
First paperback edition published in 2014 by Nation Books.

Nation Books is a co-publishing venture of the Nation Institute and the Perseus Books Group.

Books published by Nation Books are available at special discounts for bulk purchases in the United States by corporations, institutions, and other organizations. For more information, please contact the Special Markets Department at the Perseus Books Group, 2300 Chestnut Street, Suite 200, Philadelphia, PA 19103, or call (800) 810-4145, extension 5000, or e-mail special.markets@perseusbooks.com.

Designed by Trish Wilkinson
Set in 11 point Adobe Garamond Pro

Library of Congress Cataloging-in-Publication Data

Abramsky, Sasha.
    The American way of poverty : how the other half still lives / Sasha Abramsky.
        pages   cm
    Includes bibliographical references and index.
    ISBN 978-1-56858-726-4 (hardback) — ISBN 978-1-56858-955-8 (e-book) 1.
Poverty—United States. 2. Poor—United States.
3. Equality—United States. 4. United States—Politics and government—2009– I.
Title.
HC110.P6A54 2013
362.50973—dc23   2013018771

ISBN 978-156858-460-7 (paperback)

10 9 8 7 6 5 4 3

Contents

Acknowledgments

The American Way of Poverty is a book with many benefactors and champions. I wish I could say that I woke up one morning with the concept fully formed in my mind, but I didn't. Rather, there were an array of themes that I was exploring in my journalism and a slew of economic and political issues that, in the years surrounding the 2008 economic collapse, I found to be increasingly fascinating. The unifying concept of the book—the notion that there is something quintessentially American in how we, as a country, think about and experience poverty—emerged over time, with the issues crystallizing as I talked them over with editors; fellow writers; policy analysts and activists; and, of course, hundreds of people experiencing increasingly difficult economic conditions around the country.

The conceit is a large one: that a single book can both paint a vivid, reportage-based portrait of life on the margins of the world's richest nation and, at the same time, develop a blueprint for a set of programmatic and conceptual changes that offer a way to a fairer future. Without a strong network of supporters who believed both that the issue was important and that I had it within me to tell this story, *The American Way of Poverty* would never have been written.

I owe a huge debt of gratitude to Mimi Corcoran and Elise Dellinger, both of the Open Society Foundation's Special Fund for Poverty Alleviation. It was they who initially reached out to me to suggest a large-scale, long-term journey through this hidden America. And it was they who came through with a grant to make this project possible. Their colleague Maria Archuleta was also a source of continual encouragement as the project evolved, from the early days when I first began to build the Voices of Poverty oral history website through the frenetic months of writing this book.

From the beginning, my researcher, Caitlin Buckley, provided invaluable help and extraordinarily speedy responses to my requests for information. Her memo-writing and statistics-collecting skills got me over many a roadblock as the project unfolded. Philip Acosta of Frontside Productions went far beyond the call of duty in the time and effort he and his team put into designing and implementing the Voices of Poverty website. We worked hard, and sometimes under extreme deadlines, to get the website up and running. The result was a testament to Philip's professionalism and dedication to the work at hand. Jessica Bartholow of the Western Center on Law and Poverty ended up serving as an informal member of the team, making herself available for frequent coffees, over which we would discuss complex public policy issues. Her input was crucial for framing the problems at hand. Substitute whiskey for coffee, and Glenn Backes performed a similarly valuable function. From afar, JoAnne Page in New York, Marshall Ganz in Cambridge, Rocky Anderson in Salt Lake City, and Bill Luckett in Mississippi also allowed me to use them as sounding boards.

Once the reporting itself got under way, another circle of colleagues came to play a vital role: the *Nation* magazine's Katrina vanden Heuvel, Mark Sorkin, and Roane Carey all encouraged my work on poverty and spent time both brainstorming with me and editing my articles into a shape fit for publication. At the *American Prospect*, I owe thanks to Kit Rachlis, Harold Meyerson, and Bob Kuttner for their ongoing interest in my reporting on these themes. Other editors who backed this work include Mike Hoyt and Justin Peters at the *Columbia Journalism Review* and Melinda Welsh at the *Sacramento News & Review*. And, of course, I perennially owe profound appreciation to my agent, Victoria Skurnick, and to my book editor, Carl Bromley. A million thanks to you both for your determined belief in the vital nature of this project.

I would be remiss if I did not also give my warmest gratitude to Peter Barnes and the staff of the Mesa Refuge writers' retreat, who provided me the inestimable gift in early fall 2012 of two weeks' residency in the hills above the Pacific Ocean, just north of San Francisco. It was in those two paradisiacal weeks that the scales were lifted and the rough edges of the manuscript made smooth.

Almost always, any list of acknowledgments is incomplete and somewhat arbitrary. Let me, therefore, apologize in advance if I neglect to include individuals who feel they ought to have been included.

With that caveat, I owe particular thanks to the staff of Demos, a think tank at which I have been a fellow for a number of years and which, during that time, has done an extraordinary job of highlighting economic justice themes. My thanks to my colleagues at the University of California at Davis—to my friends in the University Writing Program, who have given me the great opportunity to teach nonfiction writing to always-fascinating, always-changing groups of young students; to the attorneys at the law school's immigration law clinic, who have done so much to highlight the myriad challenges immigrants in America face; and to Ann Stevens, Marianne Page, and the other members of the wonderful team at the Center for Poverty Research, who are helping to put America's poverty crisis center stage. My deepest gratitude, too, to Gary Dymski and A. G. Block, with whom I worked for several years at the University of California Center Sacramento, discussing public policy and economic questions with many of the best and the brightest from within the UC system and the world of California state politics. I owe a debt of gratitude as well to Jacob Hacker, Michael Katz, Katherine Newman, Alice O'Connor, Jim Ziliak, and the many other academics around the country who took the time to explain their ideas to me and to point me in the direction of other people to talk to and additional books to read.

Among my friends, special thanks are due to Eyal Press, Adam Shatz, Theo Emery, Vicki Colliver, Kari Lydersen, Kitty Ussher, Jesse Moss, Danny Postel, John Hill, Steve Magagnini, Ben Ehrenreich, Jessica Garrison, Michael Soller, Rose George, Maura McDermott, Carolyn Juris, Raj Patel, George Lerner, and Jason Ziedenberg. Over the decades, you have acted as an extraordinary politics and journalism brain trust for discussing ideas and methods of telling a story. To my journalism professors and mentors Michael Shapiro and Sam Freedman at the Columbia University Graduate School of Journalism, and to Andrew Graham, Adam Swift, and Alan Montefiore, my tutors at Balliol College, Oxford, I remain forever indebted to all of you for your insights and teachings.

It would, of course, have been impossible to research and write this book without the love, the support, and the enthusiasm of my family. To my parents, Lenore and Jack; to my brother, Kolya, and my sister, Tanya; and to my wife, Julie Sze, and my children, Sofia and Leo, I shout out from the rooftops, "Thank you!" You have helped me ask the right questions and seek out the important answers. To Julie, who not only tolerated but also made possible my extended absences on reporting trips and at writing retreats, I owe my deepest gratitude. To Sofia and Leo, I owe my equilibrium: Your joy in life reminds me how important it is not to sweat the small stuff.

Above all, my thanks go to the many hundreds of men, women, and children in states around the country who let me into their lives and trusted me enough to share their most intimate stories. Sometimes you laughed, many times you cried, always you made clear that your experiences meant something—that the pain, the hardship, and the chaos so many have lived through these past several years were stories worth telling and stories worth listening to. Your words too often humbled me; your dignity inspired me.

A Scandal in the Making

Graffiti at the ruins of the Packard auto factory in Detroit.

Fifty years after the social critic Michael Harrington published his groundbreaking book *The Other America*, in which he chronicled the lives lived of those excluded from the Age of Affluence, poverty in America is back with a vengeance. It is made up both of the long-term, chronically poor and the newly impoverished, the victims of a broken economy and a collapsed housing market.

The saga of the timeless poor, of individuals immersed in poverty for decades, of communities mired in poverty for generations, is something of a dog-bites-man story: It's sad, but it's not new. The tale of the newly poor, however, is more akin to the man-bites-dog story: It is surprising and counterintuitive. It is the narrative of millions of Americans who had economic security, enjoyed something of the comforts of an affluent society, and then lost it. Not since the Great Depression have so many millions of people been so thoroughly beaten down by vast, destructive forces. Yet while the story of the more recent poor has more of a sensation factor to it, in reality the stories of the long-term poor and the newly destitute increasingly blend together, creating a common set of experiences that pummel the bodies and minds of those who live them; that corrode communities; and that, all too often, obliterate optimism.

As with the men and women Harrington wrote about in 1962, too frequently these poor Americans are invisible. "Here are the unskilled workers, the migrant farm workers, the aged, the minorities, and all the others who live in the economic underworld of American life," Harrington wrote in his opening chapter. "The other America, the America of poverty, is hidden today in a way that it never was before. Its millions are socially invisible to the rest of us. . . . The new poverty is constructed so as to destroy aspiration; it is a system designed to be impervious to hope."[1]

Harrington was a Jesuit-educated political activist, born and raised in St. Louis during the years between the world wars. Over several decades he carved out a reputation for himself as a longtime chronicler of the American condition. In the run-up to his book's publication, he had spent years in poor communities as a volunteer with Catholic

Worker and as a left-leaning political organizer—hardly the most fruitful of pursuits in the conservative, affluent era following the end of World War II. In fact, *The Other America* hit a raw nerve at least in part because so many Americans, living comfortably in suburbias miles from the epicenters of hardship, thought their country had already solved the poverty conundrum. With many having a mind-set of out of sight, out of mind, poverty simply wasn't a part of the national political discourse in the 1950s. Indeed, the Harvard Kennedy School of Government lecturer and author Richard Parker, in his biography of the progressive economist John Kenneth Galbraith, noted that when the Joint Economic Committee of Congress commissioned University of Wisconsin economist Robert Lampman to put together "a complete bibliography of postwar books and articles by economists on modern poverty, his typed list required only two pages."[2] That the Gordian knot of poverty hadn't actually been unraveled, and that it could continue to exist alongside the Affluent Society, was a source of tremendous national embarrassment for many. In the wake of *The Other America*'s publication, a critical mass of policy makers doubled down, using Harrington's writings as a Virgil-like guide to America's hidden underbelly and laying the foundations for an all-out assault on the causes and conditions of poverty that would fundamentally impact American social policy for a generation.

Liberal America's belief during the 1960s that with one more great push the scourges associated with poverty could be forever eradicated from America's shores was naïve, possibly even disingenuous. After all, no society in human history has ever successfully banished poverty; and no polity with a modicum of respect for individual liberty has entirely negated the presence of inequality. But it did reflect a confidence in America's innate sense of possibility; in an era of space travel and antibiotics, computers and robots, poverty was just one more frontier to be conquered, one more communal obstacle to be pushed aside. When it turned out to be an order of magnitude more complicated, Americans quickly grew tired of the effort. In 1968, four years after the War on Poverty was launched,

Richard Nixon won election to the White House, in part by stoking popular resentment against welfare recipients. Twelve years after that, Ronald Reagan was elected president on a platform of rolling back much of the Great Society. Today, after four decades during which tackling economic hardship took a distant backseat to other priorities, one in six Americans live below the poverty line, their lives as constricted and as difficult as those of the men, women, and children who peopled the pages of *The Other America* in the Kennedy era. And this is despite the fact that the president, Barack Obama, is a onetime community organizer who understands the impact of poverty on people's lives better than almost any other of his predecessors.

Too poor to participate in the consumption rituals that define most Americans' lives, too cash-strapped to go to malls, to visit cafés or movie theaters, to buy food anywhere other than dollar stores, these men and women live on America's edge. The poorest of the poor live under freeway ramps and bridges in out-of-the-way neighborhoods such as the Alphabet district of northern Las Vegas or Los Angeles's Skid Row. Others live in trailer parks far from central cities. Then there are those living in apartment buildings and even suburban houses, who for a variety of reasons have lost their financial security; their deprivation remains hidden behind closed doors. All of these people share an existential loneliness, a sense of being shut out of the most basic rituals of society.

———

In mid-2011, the Open Society Foundation's Special Fund for Poverty Alleviation gave me a grant to chronicle the faces and voices of economic hardship in America. To do so, I began traveling around the country interviewing and photographing people on the economic margins—Harrington's "economic underworld"—and the environments in which they lived.

As the stories accumulated, three things struck me with particular force.

The first is the sheer loneliness of poverty, the fact that profound economic hardship pushes people to the psychological and physical margins of society—isolated from friends and relatives; shunted into dilapidated trailer parks, shanties, or ghettoized public housing; and removed from banks and stores, transit systems and cultural institutions. The poor live on society's scraps—a few dollars in government assistance or charity, donated food, thrift-store clothes. They can afford neither transport to venture out of their communities nor simple luxuries such as movies or a cup of coffee with friends in a café. They cannot afford to vary the routines of their daily lives. Embarrassed by their poverty, worried about being judged failures in life, and humiliated by that judgment, many told me that they have essentially withdrawn from all but the most necessary, unavoidable social interactions.

The second thing that one realizes in telling this story is the diversity, the complexity, of poverty. Its causes, and therefore its potential solutions, cannot meaningfully be reduced to a pat list of features. There are people with no high school education who are poor, but there are also university graduates on food bank lines. There are people who are poor because they have made bad choices, gotten addicted to drugs, burned bridges with friends and family—and then there are people who have never taken a drug in their lives, who have huge social networks, and who still can't make ends meet. There are people who have never held down a job, and others who hold down multiple, but always low-paying, jobs, frequently for some of the most powerful corporations on earth. There are people who have never had a bank account and use payday loans and other predatory lending sources whenever they need access to extra cash, and there are others who, during more flush times, owned huge suburban houses and expensive cars. There are children whose only hot meals are what they are given at school, and young adults who have nothing now and never really had anything earlier in life either. There are military veterans who have struggled to find a place in civilian life, middle-aged and once-middle-class people falling down the economic ladder as the recession fails to fully lift, and elderly people cascading into destitution as savings evaporate and expected equity in their homes fails to materialize.

Poverty is, in other words, as diverse as the United States itself. What the poor have in common, however, is an increasingly precarious existence in a country seemingly unable—or at least unwilling— to come to grips with their collective despair.

Yet if the lives of America's poor are increasingly desperate, the desire to make something of those lives remains a force to be reckoned with. That leads to the third thing that fascinated me in my travels around the country: the sheer resilience of people who, battered by tough economic times, could be excused for thinking that life never gives them any breaks. Instead, many of the men and women I talked to were doing everything they could to ensure that their futures would look brighter than their pasts. They were going to school, taking job-training classes, looking for any and every source of income, and struggling to make sure that their kids had enough food to eat and little extras to enjoy. It was, in many ways, a humbling, inspiring experience.

WHOSE FUTURE?

The poverty being stockpiled in the early twenty-first century, at the back end of a forty-year stampede toward ever-greater economic inequality, will leave generational legacies affecting current workers, their children, and as likely as not their children's children. What starts off as a temporary hiccup too often results in a permanent downgrading of family prospects.

How we as a society deal with this challenge will determine what kind of a country we become in the years and decades ahead.

As I detail in the second part of this book, we already have the contours outlined for a credible and fair new social compact. That the first Obama administration didn't focus on poverty to the extent that the issue deserved was, I believe, largely the product of a political calculus. Assuming power in the midst of a financial system melt-down, the new administration had to stabilize a collapsing economy early on; they did so, but in so doing they churned up a roiling, ugly opposition. As a result, by the time the free-fall stopped, they had to swiftly start navigating one of the most treacherous political land-scapes in modern history en route to the 2012 election. Now that that election is over, however, in his second term Obama will have to not simply enact technocratic anti-poverty measures but also take the country with him as he explains the moral imperative of a fairer so-cial compact. He will have to employ all of his extraordinary narra-tive powers to craft a new American story in which tens of millions of citizens feel that they have a stake. If Obama accomplishes this, he will secure for himself a legacy as one of the country's great progres-sive presidents. If he doesn't, it will be a serious blot on his tenure in the White House.

Were we as a society to implement this new story in affordable and equitable ways, the result would be a fundamental reimagining of the American economic landscape. We can use four major revenue sources: (1) a public works fund to protect against mass unemploy-ment; (2) a new educational opportunity fund to dramatically expand access to, and affordability of, higher education; (3) a poverty-mitigation fund built up from the introduction of a financial trans-action tax and energy profit taxes; and (4) money to stabilize Social Security and start reducing the national deficit, made available from higher taxes on capital gains, high-end inheritances, and the income of the most affluent of wage earners. I detail the mechanisms of these in Part Two. If we used these revenue sources, we could change both our expectations of society and our long-term financial calculus in a way beneficial to tens of millions of people.

Too often in recent decades, our political leaders have ignored what's staring them in the face and instead enacted policies that make economic hardship worse for those already on the margins or starting the long slide into destitution. As detailed in this book, they do so because America's political process is increasingly beholden to powerful financial interests, its priorities shaped by what used to be seen as Southern mores: a belief not just in the inevitability of inequality, but in the *desirability* of oligarchy as a social structure, in the usefulness of poverty as a social control mechanism, its reaction to that poverty punitive and unforgiving. Increasingly, it is a democracy in which the voices, and the basic economic needs, of ordinary Americans are drowned out by the noise generated by advocates and lobbyists for the well-heeled and already-influential. It is an economy that, to a large extent, revolves not around the making of things but around the shuffling of money—hence the overblown impact of financial sector, insurance, and real estate instability on the broader economic system. And it is one in which, for the last several decades, ordinary Americans have borrowed against home equity, run up credit card debt, and taken out loans to go to school, all just to survive on a daily basis. Data compiled by the Federal Reserve show that just before the financial crash of 2008, the average American household was spending nearly 19 percent of its disposable income servicing debt.[3]

Increasingly, our leaders either ignore the scale of poverty present in our midst—or, tacking to the Southern winds, they seek to blame or to punish those who fail to economically thrive. For proof of the former, witness the fact that throughout the three televised presidential debates in 2012, the plight of the tens of millions of Americans living below the poverty line was *never* meaningfully addressed, nor were the implications of proposed cuts to Medicaid, food stamps, and other safety net programs properly teased out.

That Obama's first administration was unable to fully break out of this mold after 2008, leaving largely untouched the scourge of poverty and inequality that as an insurgent, grassroots candidate he had talked about tackling, was a source of bemusement to many of his supporters. The election of 2012 gave him a new opportunity to so do, which can only be a source of hope. After all, few political leaders are given the sort of second chance to rewrite their story that Obama was granted by the electorate. Unhappy with the status quo, voters nevertheless reelected him as president. One can argue that they did so, at least in part, in the expectation that his second term would deliver on promises never followed through on in the first four years.

THE MINERS' CANARY

Shake a stick in post–financial collapse America, and one hits poverty. It's everywhere: tent cities in municipal parks, under freeway overpasses, along river walks. Food lines stretching down city blocks. Foreclosure signs dotting suburban landscapes. Overstretched free clinics providing a modicum of healthcare to people no longer insured. Elderly people whose pensions have vanished and whose hopes for a decent old age have evaporated. Unemployed men and women looking for clothes for their kids at thrift stores and food for their families at pantries. Mothers begging for free turkeys from churches so they can at least partially partake in the national ritual of Thanksgiving.

By the end of 2010, according to the U.S. Census Bureau, 15.1 percent of Americans were living below the federally defined poverty line, an increase of approximately fifteen million people since the start of the century. Fully 34.2 percent of single mothers and their children were in poverty, up from 28.5 percent in 2000. Some of the poor lived in traditionally deprived communities; many others lived in the suburbs. In fact, according to Georgetown University's Peter Edelman, in his book *So Rich, So Poor*, in the first decade of the twenty-first century, suburban poverty increased by fully 53 percent.[4] Much of that was due to an extraordinary collapse in the worth of assets owned by middle-class African American and Hispanic families. In 1984, the median value of household asset ownership for African

American families was $6,679. By 2009, as the recession destroyed the worth of homes, that number had declined to a mere $4,900— thirty years of asset accumulation vanished. White households, despite suffering during the recession, by contrast still had a median net worth of $92,000.[5]

The disparate impact of the crisis could be measured in soaring regional unemployment numbers and age- and race-specific poverty data. In Imperial County, California, for example, residents were experiencing a collapse on a scale that most of the country didn't witness even at the height of the Great Depression. Nearly one in three workers were unemployed, and for the 68 percent of the working population in the county who had jobs, average income was abysmally low, hovering not far above the poverty line.[6]

In Detroit, more than one-third of the total population was in poverty, and upward of two-thirds of children were in families living below the poverty line.[7] New Orleans fared almost as badly: there, more than four in ten kids were in poverty, and, in the African American community, fully 65 percent of children five and under lived below the poverty line.[8] These numbers were so extraordinary that they made Philadelphia's abysmal data look almost good in comparison: there, a mere one in three children lived at or below the poverty line.[9] In Indiana, nearly one in ten kids lived in "extreme poverty," meaning their family incomes didn't even reach half of the poverty line threshold.[10] In northern St. Louis in 2010, the poverty rate for kids stood at a dispiriting 30 percent.[11]

Not surprisingly, in May 2012, UNICEF reported that of the world's developed countries, the United States had the second highest rate of child poverty, with more than 23 percent of its kids officially poor. Only Romania, still struggling to shed itself of the awful legacy left by Nicolae Ceauşescu's dictatorship, had worse numbers.[12]

We look at the scale of misery unleashed; shake our heads; listen to that inner voice saying sadly, "What a tragedy"; and then, assuming we're fortunate enough not to be poor ourselves, we try to get on with our lives. Yet, if we thought a little harder, we'd realize that what we're witnessing isn't so much a tragedy as a scandal.

It's a subtle difference, but an important one. What turns poverty into a scandal rather than a tragedy is the political landscape out of which it bubbles. "It makes a difference if we treat it as a bug or a feature," argued longtime community organizer and Harvard Kennedy School of Government senior lecturer Marshall Ganz. "Is it a bug in the system for which we provide a safety net, or a *feature* of the system? It's a moral, political, and economic crisis. It's a process of suicide. When countries stratify themselves into a wealthy few and an impoverished many, they go down the tubes."

For Ganz, poverty was akin to the "miners' canary." It was the warning signal of a more general malaise—of school systems in disrepair, healthcare delivery mechanisms that were no longer delivering healthcare to large swaths of the population, a degraded environment, and more. "As long as people think poverty is the problem," Ganz explained, "they're missing the whole point. Poverty is *evidence* of a problem; it's not the source of the problem. They're all based on the weakening of collective institutions—the decline of labor, of common interests. The core question is not about poverty, it's really about democracy. The galloping poverty in the United States is evidence of a retreat from democratic beliefs and practices."

When people go hungry because of, say, drought or a plague of locusts; when thousands die in an epidemic; when natural disasters convert whole countries into wastelands, religious people say these are acts of God—the less religious might say they are acts of nature. But the process of casting around for someone to blame takes a back seat. Tragedy is, somehow, beyond the realm of the deliberate, the product not so much of malign decisions as of confounded bad luck, of happenstance.

By contrast, when poverty flourishes as a direct result of decisions taken, or not taken, by political and economic leaders, and, either tacitly or explicitly, endorsed by large sectors of the voting population, then it acquires the rancid aroma of scandal. It is a corrosive brew, capable of eating away at the underpinnings of democratic life itself.

My aim in writing *The American Way of Poverty* is to shine a light on this travesty; to bring poverty out of the shadows; and, ultimately, to suggest ways for moving toward a fairer, more equitable, and more truly American social compact. For what is caused by human choices can, mostly, be solved by human choices. Tragedies, quite legitimately, tend to generate hand-wringing; scandals, by contrast, ought first and foremost to lead to action.

The American Way of Poverty is a plea for a more morally cogent political approach to poverty, for an acknowledgment of a crisis that existed *before* the 2008 financial collapse and shows every sign of continuing to exist even as the broader economy slowly recovers *from* that collapse. It is more than a technocratic discussion of poverty; rather, it is a portrait of a political system in crisis, of a democracy that has ceased to be able to address the basic needs of a growing proportion of its population.

At the same time, my book also offers a blueprint for change, exploring how a new politics could emerge that prioritizes poverty as a moral challenge, and how once that politics takes root, we could retool our welfare systems; better craft our tax policies; set up new social insurance systems as ambitious as that of Social Security; rethink our strategies on private and public debt; invest more thoroughly in education, housing, healthcare, and other vital parts of the public commons; and set in place wage and pension protections all aimed squarely at providing basic security to the American population.

It is, after all, of little use to identify problems if one doesn't also spend time exploring solutions. The second part of *The American Way of Poverty* details a comprehensive, and creative, set of policies to be rolled out over a period of years, which would not only tackle the consequences of wholesale poverty but would go a long way toward dealing with its underlying causes. I explain how support for such policies can be generated—how many of the organizing methods and outreach used by Barack Obama's campaign team in both 2008 and 2012 lend themselves to just such a mission—and how the rigid anti-government, anti-tax rhetoric popularized by conservatives over the past few decades can over time be successfully neutralized.

Fifty years ago, Michael Harrington warned his readers that unless attention was paid, another journalist decades in the future would end up writing about the exact same conditions that he had chronicled. "After one read these facts, either there are anger and shame, or there are not," he opined. "And, as usual, the fate of the poor hangs upon the decision of the better-off. If this anger and shame are not forthcoming, someone can write a book about the other America a generation from now and it will be the same, or worse." It was, Harrington believed, a moral outrage that in a country as wealthy as America, so many people could be so poor, and so many other people could turn blind eyes to their plight.[13]

Fifty years on, I am chronicling these conditions, as alive today as they were in the early 1960s. For unfortunately, Harrington's prophecy has come true: conditions are again getting worse for a vast number of Americans, yet for millions of others, it is all too easy to downplay, or to simply ignore, these dire straits.

PART ONE

The Voices of Poverty

CHAPTER ONE

POVERTY IN THE LAND
OF THE PLUTOCRATS

Food pantry manager Ginny Wallace opens up an
empty freezer in her Appalachian Pennsylvania pantry.
Demand is up; donations down.

In the fall of 2011, with hunger rearing up across America, the large freezer bins at the Port Carbon Food Pantry (PCFP), in the small, gritty, Appalachian town of Pottsville, Pennsylvania, were empty. The shelves next to the freezers were also largely barren. A few boxes of egg noodles provided about the only sign that this was a place in the business of giving out food to those who could no longer afford to buy it. An adjacent room was doing slightly better, displaying stacks of canned fruit, canned corn, beans, and bags of pasta. But, taken as a whole, these were slim pickings. Clients who walked or drove up the hill, the remnants of an unseasonably early snow storm still on the ground, from the center of town to the two-story building were eligible for six to ten days of food, but that food was all they'd be able to get from the pantry for the next two months.

Three years earlier, explained PCFP's coordinator, Ginny Wallace, the rooms were filled to bursting with food. Then the economy tanked; demand for the free food soared; and at the same time, locals' ability to donate to the pantry crumbled.

Pottsville, and neighboring communities such as Mechanicsville and Schuylkill, made up a bleak region even in the good times. A onetime coal mining hub, it was a center of labor militancy in the early years of the twentieth century. But in recent decades most of the mines had closed down; many of the jobs that replaced the unionized mine work were low-paying, service-sector ones that provided few benefits. Add into the mix rising unemployment and home foreclosures, and an already precarious situation suddenly got a whole lot worse. "The need has increased and the surplus food given has decreased," Wallace explained, holding open the lids of the large freezers to emphasize their emptiness. "The only thing in here is frost building up. Three years ago, we used to have to turn down deliveries."

Many of the men and women who were helped by food pantries such as this were elderly people on fixed incomes who increasingly found they couldn't stretch meager monthly checks to pay all their bills, buy all their medicines, and also feed themselves. People such as 86-year-old widow Mary, a onetime factory worker and bookkeeper of Polish immigrant stock, whose $592 Social Security check didn't come close to covering all her costs. "I manage," she said flintily. "You've got to know how to manage. And if you're a boozer and a smoker, then you don't manage. I live according to my means. That's what life is all about." Yet despite her pride, Mary, who picked up some additional money helping to care for a 102-year-old woman nearby, recently had had to turn to the pantry for help. "Every time you go to the store or turn around," she explained, "the bills are higher."

Other pantry clients were younger, families whose breadwinners lost their jobs during the recession that followed the financial collapse of 2008. Take 53-year-old Luann Prokop, an accountant who was laid off when the local manufacturing company she worked for could no longer stay afloat as an independent business and was taken over, and restructured, by a multinational corporation. "I had to apply for food stamps. Money was really tight. By the grace of God I was able to hold onto my house, but I did have to apply for two deferments during the two years I was on unemployment. I became more introverted, especially after getting rejected [from jobs she'd applied for] over and over and over again. I had a good, solid background; I have fabulous references. I couldn't understand why. It was a difficult, dark period."

Having burned through her savings, her retirement accounts, and her unemployment benefits, and having fallen far behind on her mortgage, Luann realized that unless she started using the food pantry she and her two teenage children would literally go without meals. Then, adjusting her expectations ever downward, she took an accounting job at the center that housed the pantry. She was bringing in about $20,000 per year, whereas a few years earlier she had earned $60,000—not enough to live well, but too much to qualify for many government benefits.

Now, I shop in thrift stores. I live paycheck to paycheck. I make sure my children have necessities before I buy for myself. Fortunately, I don't have a car payment, but my car is on its last lap. I'm barely holding onto the house. I'm on assistance for electricity—a state program, which allows me to keep my lights on. I don't know how I'm going to make it through the winter with heating. I saved up money for oil, but it's a fraction of what I'm going to need to get through the winter. I don't get food stamps. I'm strictly on my own. Last year it was really, really rough—coming up with the money to heat the house. I had to defer my mortgage for three months; they added the interest I would have paid onto my new payments.

When she ran out of food, Luann improvised. "Chicken bouillon plus rice tastes like chicken rice soup," she said, and shrugged. "Of course, there's no chicken in it."

And then there were the pantry denizens escaping domestic violence who had run up against draconian cuts to the shelter system. One client, Wallace recalled, was a woman in her late forties, about to enter a shelter. "We got a request to provide her food because she has to bring her own food to the shelter. The programs that assist the working poor and the poor are in dire straits."

———

Variations on the stories from Appalachian Pennsylvania could be encountered in cities and regions across America. After all, an economic free-fall of the kind that the United States underwent after the housing market collapse and then the broader financial meltdown leaves carnage in its wake. For those born into poverty, the hardship is magnified. For millions of others who thought of themselves as upwardly mobile, with middle-class aspirations and middle-class spending patterns, the crisis flung them down the economic ladder, replacing a precarious fiscal stability with a continuous struggle to survive.

In the working-class, immigrant community of Pomona, a few miles east of downtown Los Angeles, in fall 2008 five eleventh-grade and ten twelfth-grade students in Village Academy teacher Michael Steinman's English classes began compiling their stories of poverty for a video project. "I was aware of the economy, but I wasn't personally affected too terribly," Steinman explained. "But when I asked my students how things were going, in my AP class—we were studying *The Great Gatsby* at the time—every single student had been affected. I wanted them to give testimony to what they had witnessed and they were going through. The concept of the American Dream has either evaporated or gone away. Daily, I work with kids who are very much stressed. They hide it well; there's a certain amount of shame that they carry about being poor or struggling. But I do know they're going through circumstances that definitely impact their studies and their ability to think about the future and be positive." The video footage that they created and put up on YouTube went viral in January 2009. Barack Obama's presidential transition team was shown the video. A couple of months later when he visited Southern California, the newly inaugurated president held a rally in a lot adjacent to the buildings that housed the experimental school—whose student body is overwhelmingly made up of young people from ethnic minority backgrounds, and one ranked by *U.S. News & World Report* as one of California's best educational establishments. Obama also invited Steinman and his students to the White House.

Yet for all the hoopla around their project, nearly a full presidential cycle later, conditions for many of the students at the Village Academy high school remained appalling.[1] Large numbers of the kids lived with parents who had lost their jobs during the recession and either failed to find new employment or were working long hours at jobs that paid only minimum wage. Many had lost homes to foreclosure—either because of variable-rate, subprime mortgages or because of unemployment—or, behind on mortgage or rent payments, lived in constant fear of losing their homes to the banks or to landlords. Almost all of Steinman's students qualified for free school breakfasts and lunches—and, for many of these kids, these were the only hot meals they ate. Evenings and weekends, they either went without or grabbed some dry cereal to stanch their hunger. Several honors students at the high-performing school, who should have been applying to college, were instead thinking of quitting education and getting dead-end work just to help their families pay the bills.

"Sometimes I cry," Oliver Lopez explained as he described his family's struggles—his mother out of work, his father working two part-time minimum-wage jobs, he and his three younger brothers living from meal to meal. "I see how hard my father works; and I'm 18 years old and just come to school. I don't do nothing. Sometimes we don't even have food to eat."

One of Oliver's classmates described how he, his mother, his two sisters, his grandmother, two uncles, an aunt, and her daughter all lived in a one-bedroom apartment, most of them sleeping on the floor, until they fell behind on their rent and were evicted in early 2010. The family had split up, with groups of two or three going off to stay with different relatives. The young man was living with his mother, who in a good week was earning $300 as a housecleaner, and his two younger sisters in a single room in a friend's house. During mealtimes, the mother would eat leftovers off of his and his sisters' barely filled plates. "I'm depressed. I spend most of my time crying alone. My mom tells me I should get a job. She gets mad at me. She works from 6 A.M. to 5 P.M. I'm actually out trying to find a job. But there's nothing."

In the tiny community of Anthony, just outside of Las Cruces, New Mexico, Lorenza and Jorge Caro lived on a piece of scrubby land in the harsh but beautiful high desert. Their living conditions were, to say the least, extraordinary. At the back end of a sandy, cluttered lot, the pastel blues of the New Mexican sky providing a backdrop, they lived in an uninsulated, windowless, cinder-block storage space with an unfinished concrete floor. One half was crammed floor to ceiling with pickings from street fairs and yard sales—they toured the region, buying goods on the cheap and then reselling them at a fraction above what they paid in the street markets of Las Cruces. The other half of the room, divided from the pile by a hung blue tarpaulin, contained a high bed, a propane-fueled stove, huge piles of clothes and bric-a-brac, and a plastic chair with a circular hole cut in its wicker seat. When in use, a chamber pot would be placed beneath the chair. This, said Lorenza in Spanish, her eyes lowered as she talked, was the device on which they performed their morning ablutions.

It was a strange scene, at once theatrical and also deeply depressing. The storage space was dank and chilly, an incubator of germs. Its occupants, wrapped up in heavy layers against the cold—she in lilac sweatpants and a thick white coat, he in workmen's boots, jeans, a wool-lined blue jean jacket, and a woolen hat—were edgy, kind yet skittish, nervous that they were being judged for how they lived.

The Caros lost their mobile home in 2010, when they fell behind on their payments after Jorge lost his job. Now, despite the fact that Jorge had managed to get another minimum-wage job as a cleaner at a local company, and that Lorenza brought in a few dollars from her flea market sales, they lived in the storage room on the land that used to host their home. "We meet our necessities, we don't have beyond our necessities, but we meet our necessities here," explained Lorenza in a soft voice. "It's very, very cold when I use the toilet seat. We have electricity, so we have little heaters right now. But when we run out of gas—the stove is propane and helps to keep the heat—it gets colder. Last January it was very bad for us. We had the freezer, didn't have any water. I had colds. When we need medical care we drink whatever herbs we can, [take] Tylenol."

During the toughest times, they had gotten food on credit from women at the flea market and made do on one or two meals a day. "In the morning we'd have a cup of coffee and a piece of bread; in the afternoon a burrito or gorditas—Mexican sandwiches. Nothing in the evening. Sometimes we had those little instant soup cups out here." On the rare instances they had spare money, they bought potatoes and beans in bulk and made them last for weeks.

The dreams the Caros had were impossibly modest. "I expect things to get better," said Lorenza. "Now that Jorge has a full-time job we hope things will get better. I want to live in a house with an indoor toilet. A nice, big toilet." She laughed, the nervous laugh of someone on the verge of tears. Jorge fiddled with a kettle of water on the propane stove. The sun was starting to go down, and already the mid-December evening was desperately cold.

Residents of the United States increasingly inhabit two economies. Prokop, the kids in Steinman's class, the Caros—they are the denizens of the ill-starred half of this reality, of that "economic underworld" conjured up in Harrington's writing.

Statistics from the Organization of Economic Cooperation and Development (OECD) and the United Nations (UN) show that the United States has the lowest average life expectancy and the highest infant mortality rates of any affluent democracy with a population of more than ten million. "Back in 1987 only seven other countries had longer life expectancies," wrote the UN health economist Howard Friedman in his book *The Measure of a Nation*. "Today we're not even in the top twenty."

Having posted huge increases in life expectancy in the first two-thirds of the twentieth century, the United States rested on its laurels. While other countries extended healthcare to all residents and provided decent antenatal care to all women regardless of income, America in the latter years of the twentieth and first years of the twenty-first centuries witnessed an epidemic of uninsurance, with tens of millions of Americans having no access to routine medical care.[2] The poor health outcomes, Friedman noted, were concentrated in particular parts of the population. Asian American women, he wrote, had a life expectancy twenty years higher than that of African American men, living to nearly 90 years on average.[3] Well-off white women could also expect to live well into their 80s.[4] In stark contrast, several news organizations have reported in recent years that the life expectancy for African American men in New York's Harlem neighborhood is lower than that for residents of Bangladesh.[5] And in August 2012, the journal *Health Affairs* published a paper showing that white women without a high school diploma had seen a catastrophic five-year decline in their average life expectancy since 1990. For white men in the same educational grouping, the decline was slightly smaller, at three years, but still highly disturbing.[6]

The prevalence of low–birth weight babies and of infant mortality was far higher in the South—where a lower percentage of the population had access to healthcare and where, historically, the safety net was weaker—than in the Northeast, and was far more common among African Americans than among whites. Similarly, according to research carried out by a team funded by the Social Science Research Council, the eleven states in America with the lowest life expectancy were *all* in the South.[7] It wasn't that American life expectancy was declining, or that infant mortality was going up; rather, it was that because of the huge inequalities in American society and the well of poverty at the bottom, other countries were now improving at a faster rate than was the United States.

In education, the same trends held. The poorer the family one was born into, the higher the likelihood that a child would struggle in school. Even if he or she did well in the classroom, there was a lower likelihood that the child would be able to attend college. Friedman noted that the most successful eighth graders from poor economic backgrounds had only the same chance of attaining a bachelor's degree as the least successful eighth graders from the wealthiest echelon of society. When the literacy, math, and scientific knowledge of American schoolkids was compared to most other affluent democracies, America performed abysmally. But the numbers weren't evenly distributed. White and Asian American students, especially those from the middle classes, held their own in these international comparisons and as a result were disproportionately able to access many of the world's top universities after finishing school. By contrast, African American and Hispanic schoolkids, and those whites far down the economic ladder, scored very poorly. Once again, the scale of inequity in America, as compared to most other first world democracies, was skewing the country's education numbers downward vis-à-vis other nations.

At the top of the U.S. economy, highly educated, highly skilled professionals are in possession of an ever-greater proportion of the country's wealth. Five percent of Americans live in families with annual incomes in excess of $180,000.[8] That's enough to be very comfortable but not to buy Picassos, fly in private jets, or give tens of thousands of dollars to a political campaign on behalf of a chosen candidate. To get that level of affluence and influence, one has to go even further up the income chain. In fact, it's at the very peak of the economy, among the wealthiest 1 percent, that incomes have truly soared in recent decades. Since the late 1970s, the real income of this group of privileged Americans has almost tripled. As of 2011, *Forbes* magazine found 412 Americans had assets in excess of $1 billion. According to the Credit Suisse Global Wealth Databook for 2011, of the nearly 85,000 people globally with a net worth of more than $50 million each, upward of 35,000 of them live in the United States.[9] Take it down even one more level and the 2011 *World Wealth Report* estimated that the United States had 3.1 million millionaires.[10]

Meanwhile, most Americans—whom the Occupy Wall Street movement, from 2011 onward, took to calling "the other 99 percent"—find their net worth is declining. In 2010, the median annual wage in America fell to $26,364, representing a 7 percent decline over the course of the first decade of the new century and a roughly 20 percent decline from 1973, when, in inflation-adjusted dollars, the median wage was $33,000.[11] What does that mean in practical terms? It means that half of all American wage earners bring home an amount that, at most, is only $4,000 a year over the poverty line for a family of four. If they're lucky, they live in households with more than one earner, the two incomes combined keeping the family afloat; if they're less fortunate, they work full time, and yet their families continue to sink ever closer to the poverty line.

"Our lives are living minute by minute, and we are scared," said 59-year-old Sandy Struznick, describing the life on the margins that she and her husband, John, lived in Des Moines, Iowa. They stood ramrod stiff next to each other as I was introduced to them, looking like the couple in the classic Grant Wood painting *American Gothic*: austere, used to tough times, stoic. "We have no healthcare coverage, very limited income, are underwater with our mortgage. Don't know if we're going to keep our home. It's discouraging on a day-by-day basis. Every program we apply to for help, we get denied." An electro-mechanical worker, John had been in and out of work since the recession hit in 2008. When he found work, it was generally low-paid, and as often as not, the great bulk of his paycheck went to filling up his car's gas tank to drive to jobs outside of town and trying to keep the mortgage payments up-to-date enough to avoid foreclosure. He still owed $27,000 in student loans accrued in midlife while he studied for an electro-mechanical associate's degree.

"We'll probably be without utilities soon," Sandy confided, softly, as if she was imparting a dreadful secret.

We can go to a senior citizens' center and eat lunch. Once a day. That's our main meal. I can't buy things for our grandkids; I can't buy them any gifts. I can't go to see them. We're living in a crunch, feel like we don't have any hope some days. I should be getting commodities, but I can't because we're told his employment is too much income. If I divorce him, I could get commodities. For dinner, we eat cereal or something cheap. We have meat just if they

have it at the seniors' center. No fresh vegetables, no fresh fruit.
That isn't good for my health. I have cancer.

––––––––––

By late-2012, the unemployment rate had significantly declined
from its national peak of considerably more than 9 percent, standing
at 7.9 percent the month that President Obama won reelection. Yet
even so, close to fourteen million Americans remained unemployed.
Millions more were either underemployed—working part-time jobs
in the face of a dearth of better, full-time employment—or they had
simply dropped out of the workforce, convinced that the economy
could offer them nothing. Those who had been unemployed for
years were bumping up against limits on their ability to claim unemployment benefits. And despite Congress's having temporarily extended the benefits at the height of the post-2008 recession, in the
new austerity climate that kicked in after the 2010 midterm elections, political momentum started running strongly against more
extensions. In California and many other big states, hundreds of
thousands of long-term unemployed started losing access to cash
assistance.

In the case of Joyce, an erstwhile Walmart employee in Louis-
ville, Texas, unemployment meant living with nothing. As the 58-
year-old African American lady told me, she had $50 to her name.
In 2012, her economic situation wasn't a whole lot better than that
faced by her family when she was growing up deep in the Jim Crow
South.

> I'll probably have to move in with my daughter and my three
> grandchildren. I have medical bills that are unpaid. I be sick some-
> time, and don't go to the doctor even though I need to go—because
> I have a heart problem. I pray that I don't get sick. If I get a cough,
> I get cough syrup; if I get a sore throat, somebody will buy throat

lozenges for me. I do a lot of prayin' to God; I have a lot of faith
that I'll be able to keep my head above water. How, I do not know.
But I do have a lot of faith in God that He is going to help me
through this.

Like so many others whom I talked to, Joyce sobbed as she told
her story. She didn't speak about her situation often; when she did,
it quickly became overwhelming for her.

I don't like being in poverty, I don't like being hungry. I don't want
to be put out in the streets. I continue to pray that God will hold
me up. I never really asked for much, but if I get a job, I'll be
blessed. I had a heart attack in 2006. I don't want to do any strenu-
ous work, but I have no problem working. Lazy is one thing that I
am not. I was raised by parents and grandparents saying if you want
anything, you have to work for it because nobody ain't going to give
you anything.

Joyce's words seemed to be borne out in February 2012, when
Republicans agreed to back an extension of the payroll tax cut, but
only on the condition that Democrats voted to reduce the maximum
period a person could spend on unemployment insurance after losing
a job from ninety-nine weeks to seventy-three. Because of the length
of the economic crisis, and the difficulties so many erstwhile workers
experienced when trying to chase down new work, huge numbers of
families have been cut off from all access to cash—reduced to living
barter- and-charity-based lives on the margins of American society.
Ironically, in falling so far outside the mainstream economy, these
men and women too often end up locked into a downward spiral.
Around the country, several newspapers have reported on signs put
up at companies hiring new workers: "Unemployed need not apply."[12] Apparently, employers fear that the unemployed will have
to be retrained, their work ethic and their habits of punctuality

relaunched. It is, some worry, too much baggage—far easier, when it's an employer's market, to simply pick from the active workforce.

Millions more are not listed as unemployed because they have long ago stopped looking for work; they are more ambiguously defined as being "jobless." Unable to claim unemployment insurance, they live entirely on savings, on the largesse of friends and family, or on charity.

————

Yet this isn't a story only about those without work. In fact, America's scandalous poverty numbers also include a stunning number of people who actually have jobs. They are author David Shipler's "working poor," men and women who work long hours, often at physically grueling labor, yet routinely find they can't make ends meet, can't save money, and can't get ahead in the current economy. At the bottom of that economy, income volatility is peculiarly high; casual laborers and hourly employees routinely see their hours cut, their wages reduced, or their jobs eliminated during downturns. Oftentimes, their crises are magnified by homelessness, addiction, and mental illness and by involvement with the criminal justice system—from the early 1970s through the early 2000s, America built up the biggest incarceration system in the world, a situation that I discuss in the second half of the book when exploring ways to meaningfully intervene against modern-day poverty.

For these men and women with no rainy-day funds to fall back on, income volatility too often results in instant deprivation. Agricultural laborer Laurentino Loera, a middle-aged man whose life possessions could be carried in a few plastic bags, and who slept nights on the floor of a community center in El Paso, quietly mentioned how a few weeks without being picked by the contractors to work the fields meant having to pawn his one consumer durable item: a small, portable, black-and-white television. For oyster fisherman Byron Encelade, collapsed income meant that he couldn't buy his grandkids Christmas presents. For 30-year-old massage therapist Lauren Kostelnick, meager earnings meant no health insurance and only being able to shop in thrift stores. For Walmart worker Aubretia Edick, low hourly wages combined with her manager allotting her fewer hours each week meant skipping meals and keeping her upstate New York house thermostat on low throughout the long winter months.

———

In his 1971 book *A Theory of Justice*,[13] the influential liberal philosopher John Rawls argued that the moral imperative of a political and economic system was to raise the condition of society's most vulnerable, and that the means to do so were, largely, to be discovered by trial and error. In theory, growing inequality would pass his morality test so long as the condition of the poor was being bettered. In practice, however, because inequality tended to increase during moments when poor people were losing political and economic clout, such developments tended to raise a red flag. Far better to promote policies that have the effect of reducing the divides between the wealthiest and the poorest in any given society, he continued. Rawls wasn't a take-to-the-barricades revolutionary. To the contrary: He believed his goals could be achieved within the framework of modern liberal democracies.

A few years earlier, no less a conservative grouping than the Chamber of Commerce's Task Force on Economic Growth and Opportunity, composed of about one hundred titans of industry and finance, had reached a similar conclusion. "There is every reason to believe that the American economic system will continue to improve the relative position of those on the lowest rungs of the ladder," they cheerfully proclaimed in 1965. "Income differences increase in the early stages of industrialization and decrease in later stages. . . . It is primarily for this reason that the old socialist tradition in discussing income is dying out. Conditions no longer call for deep-seated and widespread social change."[14] As evidence of this, the report cited the fact that in 1963 only 11 percent of families were living on less than $2,000 per year, whereas in 1929 fully 30 percent of families were making do on an income that equaled that amount in 1963 dollar values.[15]

Yet despite the Pollyanna-ish assurances of the Chamber, growing inequality and accompanying upheaval *are* precisely what we are currently living through. By 2009, according to U.S. Census Bureau numbers, more than fifteen million households, totaling approximately 13 percent of all homes in the country, were living on less than $15,000 per year, roughly equivalent to what $2,000 was worth in 1963. And during the years that followed, things only got worse. "The inflation-adjusted average earnings for the bottom 20 percent of families have fallen from $16,788 in 1979 to just under $15,000," CBS News reported in December 2011. "And earnings for the next 20 percent have remained flat at $37,000."[16] In other words, nearly fifty years after the Chamber's declaration that a rising tide was lifting all boats, a considerably larger percentage of Americans were concentrated at the bottom of the economy than was the case during John Kennedy's presidency—not exactly a ringing vote of confidence in its analysis of economic trends.[17] During the boom years of the early part of the twenty-first century, for example, the number of Americans living in poverty *grew* by six million; during the bust years that followed that boom, another nine million people were impoverished, while at the top of the economy the tremendous accumulation of wealth continued apace.[18] The Census Bureau calculated that more than twenty-three million households had incomes of more than $100,000 per year.[19] What was being hollowed out was the middle.

Today, the most affluent 1 percent of the population control fully 40 percent of the country's wealth, the economist Joseph Stiglitz wrote in *Vanity Fair* in 2011.[20] And during the past three decades, the more rarified one's position on the income scale is, the more one has been able to accumulate a disproportionate share of the nation's treasure. Economist Emmanuel Saez of the University of California, Berkeley, and his coauthor, Thomas Picketty, of the Paris School of Economics, have calculated that from the mid-1960s through the early 2000s, the share of national income controlled by the top 0.01 percent of Americans increased from a little more than 0.5 percent to approximately 3 percent, reaching levels last seen during the heyday of the Roaring Twenties. In other words, about 30,000 Americans control one in thirty of the dollars circulating among a population of roughly 300 million people.[21]

During the early years of the recession, the wealth of the top strata of the population *did* decline somewhat, as stock values and other assets took a hit. By 2012, however, income for America's new elites had roared back to at least pre-recession levels. Saez and his colleagues at UC Berkeley estimated that fully 93 percent of income gains in 2010 went to the country's top 1 percent.[22] If you were in that top 1 percent in 2010, Saez calculated, you could expect to see your income increase by 11.6 percent. If you were in the bottom 99 percent, your income would have grown by only 0.2 percent.

Not surprisingly, the further down the income spectrum one goes, the worse one's prospects for economic advance become. In fact, for the bottom 23 percent of earners, real wages, adjusted for inflation, are much lower today than they were in 1979. Even more starkly, according to a 2011 CBS News report, close to half of all Americans at that time were either living at or below the poverty line, or just slightly above it, living off of amounts meager enough to qualify in government surveys as being "low income."[23]

That a country as wealthy, as technologically advanced, and as creative as America in the twenty-first century should be seeing an explosion in the numbers of residents going hungry and homeless; an increase in mortality rates among those at the bottom of the economic ladder (in 2005, the United Nations' *Human Development Report* concluded that America's infant mortality rates had been on

the rise since the beginning of the century);[24] public schools under-
funded to the point of collapse; and plummeting standards of living
for tens of millions of workers has precious little to do either with
the hand of God or the blind forces of nature. Instead, this situation
has far more to do with the emergence of a set of political and economic priorities that privilege wealth accumulation for the few over
the well-being of the many.

We will get far further in understanding twenty-first century
American poverty if we consider how entrenched the new plutocracy, and its economic agenda, has become than if we look solely for
explanations regarding the purported intellectual, economic, and
cultural inadequacies of the poor. It is, after all, surely no coinci-
dence that the United States, the country with the wealthiest elite in
the Western world, and an economy that has averaged 2.2 percent
productivity gains each year since 1947,[25] also has vastly higher poverty rates than its peer nations.

Shortly after the financial crisis hit, the OECD published a table
on income distribution: Even after government benefits were factored in, more than 11 percent of the American population had incomes of only 40 percent of the median income in the country. In
Great Britain, that number was only a little above 6 percent; Germany's number was a little more than 4 percent. In Sweden it was
3.8 percent; and in the Netherlands, 2.7 percent.[26] Even Greece and
Ireland, two countries tottering toward bankruptcy, had a far lower
percentage of their populations living significantly below the poverty line than did the United States.

"What's most striking in the past few years is the absolute absence of discussion of poverty on the public agenda," noted University of California at Santa Barbara historian Alice O'Connor, who
has built her career studying Americans' shifting attitudes toward
poverty over the centuries. "It's just not there. The great shift is that

we've come to accept very high levels of poverty as either inevitable or the way things should be." For O'Connor, the callous approach to poverty wasn't unprecedented in American history, but it *was* something that found equivalents only distantly back in time. "You'd have to cycle back to the Gilded Age," in the latter decades of the nineteenth century, "to find a similarly untroubled acceptance of mass poverty," she believed. These days, said O'Connor, politics has become increasingly reliant on big-dollar contributors, and in so becoming has lost touch with the expectations of the vast majority of Americans who cannot afford to buy access to the political process. "The narrow politics of winning elections," she averred, "has less and less to do with connecting with what people really care about, and more to do with raising money and buying media and these kinds of things."

Increasingly, however, large numbers of Americans *do* seem to be troubled by the political elite's acceptance of wholesale poverty as a normal part of contemporary life. Members of the overwhelming majority—the much-touted 99 percent—who haven't benefited from this epic economic change are realizing the plutocratic implications of this shift. "We're all out here and we all get it," said 26-year-old Thomas Reges, one of the Occupy D.C. protesters camped out in the capital's MacPherson Square, in October 2011. "We're all angry. We all know something is wrong, and we're trying to make it better."

That month, at the height of the Occupy Wall Street protests, an NBC/*Wall Street Journal* poll found 37 percent of Americans supported the protests, and only 18 percent opposed them, with the remaining 45 percent presumably neutral. A couple of weeks later, a CBS News/*New York Times* poll found that 43 percent of Americans sympathized with the protests.[27] Other polls during this period found that more than six out of every ten Americans believed the economic system was rigged in favor of the wealthy; three-quarters felt that things were getting better for Wall Street CEOs but not for ordinary middle-class Americans, and a majority of the population believed that economic inequality was a bigger problem than government overregulation. Sizeable majorities also supported the notion that the administration should pursue policies intended to reduce economic inequality.[28] This was subsequently reinforced by exit polling on November 6, 2012, showing that most voters favored raising taxes on the wealthy to help deal with the country's burgeoning deficits.

When the American Bankers Association held its annual conference in Chicago in 2009, several thousand protesters descended on the event. Three years later, groups such as National People's Action, run by a longtime organizer named George Goehl, trained large numbers of people in what they termed "economic civil disobedience": Protesters would attend shareholder meetings and demand that their economic grievances be heard; often, they engaged in sit-down protests and sometimes blockades.

For many of the protesters, the economic crisis, and the ways in which large banks treated small borrowers, had catalyzed a political response that they didn't know they previously had in them.

Barb Kalbach, for example, was a retired farmer who, in the years following the 2008 collapse, joined an activist group called Iowa Citizens for Community Improvement, began devoting much of her time to protesting economic injustice, and ultimately embarked on campaigns of civil disobedience aimed at putting a spotlight on corporate malfeasance around mortgage foreclosures and other themes. "We ask to meet people like Jamie Dimon [CEO of JPMorgan Chase]," Kalbach explained. "They ignore us, like we are riffraff. That's when we go forward; we go to their places. I call it 'Going to see the person who doesn't want to see you.'" An unlikely direct-action advocate, the elderly farmer had had enough. In all good conscience, she felt she simply couldn't do nothing. Her aim, she declared, was

> to shine light, and now to get corporations to change their tactics. We're trying to get the lawmakers to see that what's happened out in America isn't right, that corporations can't walk all over people. It's

like a pie, and they're pulling all the money they can out of the pie. The homes were a pie, pensions and 401(k)s, that was a pie. They robbed us, and then they took a taxpayers' bailout. Money and power and wealth is being pulled out of America into fewer and fewer hands. It's the same way with wages and salaries and benefits—it's a part of a pie.

Ai-jen Poo, director of the National Domestic Workers Alliance, began organizing low-paid, often undocumented domestic workers in the late 1990s, shortly after graduating from Columbia University. For years, she said, they were considered "shadows," an out-of-sight, out-of-mind pool of caregivers who cleaned up other people's messes, changed other people's soiled bedclothes, and administered other people's medications. In recent years, however, more and more of the people she encountered were finding that their working conditions resembled those of the domestic workers. "Increasingly, the conditions that define the lives of domestic workers—like instability, low wages, low benefits—these are conditions increasingly defining the reality for most American workers. We're in the same boat more than ever."

Yet, while more people *were* making these connections, this hadn't yet translated into mass political movements. Occupy Wall Street garnered much public sympathy, but most people sympathized from the sidelines. They didn't have the time and energy to engage in the sort of all-in protests that came to define the Occupy movement—at least in part because so many people were working such long hours just to keep their families afloat—they didn't like the confrontational tactics and scruffy style of the Occupiers, or they didn't feel that camping out in parks and outside of city halls would actually change a whole lot in their lives. And despite the opinion poll data showing that Americans were becoming increasingly uneasy about the degree of inequality seen in the country, on the whole that unease was more about the shrinking middle class than it was about the conditions of those at the very bottom of the

economy. In fact, politically the country as a whole remained remarkably tolerant of the continued existence of mass poverty and, at
the same time, remarkably reluctant to embrace policies that might
change this dynamic significantly.

"There are essentially two stories over the last forty years," Georgetown Law School's Peter Edelman explained. "The positive story is
there would be forty million more people who are poor if we didn't
have the public policies we have—including Social Security, the
Earned Income Tax Credit, food stamps, and Medicare and Medicaid. They have helped quite measurably in keeping poverty from being even higher than it is. So it isn't that we've been unwilling as a
country to take steps to alleviate poverty." But, Edelman continued,
there's a second, less savory story that runs parallel to the first. "Over
the last forty years, we've increasingly become a low-wage economy.
People in the bottom 20 percent are worse off than they were forty
years ago. Income distribution has deteriorated. The gaps between the
rich and poor have widened spectacularly."

Another way to look at this is to consider that, to a point, America has worked out how to ameliorate some of the consequences of
profound economic hardship—albeit reluctantly and with an increasing number of gaps. Yet it is failing, in ever greater degrees, to
prevent that hardship from arising in the first place—in changing
power relationships in the workplace, the broader economy, and the
political process, so as to stop tens of millions of Americans from experiencing desperate insecurity on a daily basis.

———

That something has gone horribly awry in how we, as a community, distribute our economic goods has to do in part with a breakdown in collective empathy. Witness GOP presidential hopeful Mitt
Romney's extraordinary slip, during the early primary season in
2012, that he wasn't concerned about the very poor. His back-
pedaling a moment later, saying that he meant the very poor were

already adequately provided for by a safety net, only made the statement that much more grotesque. Either a major national candidate was genuinely unconcerned by the plight of the poor—betting that there wasn't political capital to be gained in highlighting the desperately hard times so many millions of families were trapped within— or that same candidate, who at one point in the campaign casually mentioned that his wife drove "a couple of Cadillacs," was so out of touch with daily realities that he honestly believed the poor weren't really that badly off.

It also has to do with a mutation of the country's political discourse, over a period of decades, which today makes it all but impossible for political figures to talk about the needs of the poor—or the societal obligations of the wealthy—without being accused of promoting an almost Bolshevik form of class warfare. In July 2011, as the debate over raising America's debt ceiling risked pushing the country into a default on its obligations, Senator Mike Lee of Utah argued that the president was pitting one class against another. "Class warfare, as much fun as it may be for the president, is not going to solve this problem," the senator told Fox News's Sean Hannity.[29] Representative Paul Ryan, chair of the House Budget Committee (and subsequently Romney's vice-presidential pick), appeared on Fox News in September 2011 to accuse the president of just such a position after he stated that closing the budget deficit would involve both cuts in services and also tax increases on the wealthy: "Class warfare . . . may make for really good politics, but it makes for rotten economics."[30] A couple of days later, Sarah Palin accused Warren Buffett—the billionaire investor who had gone public with his arguments that it was unfair that he paid a lower effective tax rate than did his secretary—of a similarly noxious attempt to "gin up this class warfare rhetoric."[31]

There's an Alice-in-Wonderland quality to much of this. Wealthy individuals who oppose tax increases on the rich are, according to such views, fighting an uphill battle against a vicious conspiracy hatched by a cabal of underachieving but somehow politically all-powerful riffraff. In contrast, other wealthy individuals, such as Buffett, who support such tax increases are, somehow, self-hating billionaires suffering from something akin to Stockholm syndrome. Pushed by their grassroots and wealthy funders, most Republican state and federal lawmakers have signed on to Americans for Tax Reform president Grover Norquist's no-new-taxes pledge, thus inflexibly committing themselves to stripping down government programs no matter what the need or circumstance.

―――――――

In 2010, California state senator Carol Liu, a onetime schoolteacher and longtime anti-poverty activist, pushed SB 1084 to develop a California Economic Security Task Force. Its intent was to reduce poverty and inequality in the state and to explore the connections between different problems that, cumulatively, locked families into hardship. At the time, Liu and her colleagues estimated that more than 13 million Californians were experiencing significant economic insecurity. SB 1084 went nowhere. Investing in broad-based anti-poverty programs wasn't, Liu came to think, "sexy" for many of her fellow legislators, especially in an era in which California's budget-making processes had been hobbled by a minority of legislators absolutely refusing to countenance any tax increases to allow for the continued funding of at-risk social programs.

As she put it, "We didn't used to see families in our homeless shelters. In the last few years we've seen more people needing help. We have tremendous challenges. At the state level we've severely cut back on our safety net programs. As policy makers we're really challenged to do more with less." To Liu's mind, not enough of her colleagues had a grasp of the moral urgency of the issue.

> Some people think poor people want to be poor, they just don't want to work, there are means to lift themselves out of poverty, but they don't apply themselves. I don't think that's true. People are anxious

to improve their lives and especially the lives of their children. But it's hard to lift yourself out of this malaise if it's the only thing you've known, and you're without healthcare and without reliable childcare. In this economy, many have fallen into poverty through no fault of their own. Many of these folks have lived, quote, "middle-income lives," and have found themselves in this economic climate falling further behind.

CHAPTER TWO

BLAME GAMES

Paul Abiley and Cruzanta Mercado, standing in the home that they built for themselves on the edge of the rainforest, on Hawaii's Big Island.

Because we use such simplistic language to explain poverty, we oftentimes find it easier to pile blame on the poor for their plight rather than to look for ways to tackle poverty. After all, it's easy to castigate someone; it's much harder to truly understand his or her circumstances. Both major political parties have been guilty of this sleight of hand in recent decades, though the Republicans, and their talk radio allies, have taken it to new levels—turning verbal denigration of the poor into something of an art form.

In the 1980s, Ronald Reagan sneeringly referred to "welfare queens," Cadillac-driving moochers impudently turning up at government offices to claim their checks. The answer was to ratchet up means testing, drug testing, fingerprinting, and other intrusive checks for welfare applicants. In other words, to *assume* the worst of applicants, to have as a bureaucratic default position the belief that all applicants would cheat the system if they could, rather than that most were simply people who were mired in hard times and needed assistance to survive from one day or one week to the next.

In the 1990s, Bill Clinton pushed a welfare-to-work model that served largely to remove impoverished women from state welfare rolls without first ensuring that they had decently paying jobs to make up for the lost income, and also without creating fallback systems so that welfare recipients who couldn't find work wouldn't be kicked off the rolls during economic recessions. The reform appeared to be a success during the boom times, allowing President Clinton to argue that he had both shrunk the welfare rolls and also reduced the percentage of Americans living in poverty. And to a point, that was true: When Bill Clinton came into office in 1993, approximately 39 million Americans, or 15.1 percent of the country's population, were living in poverty.[1] By the time he vacated the White House eight years later, that number had been reduced to a little higher than 11 percent.[2] That so many people had been lifted out of poverty represented an economic achievement of an order not seen since the Great Society years of the 1960s and their immediate aftermath, when the poverty rate plunged from 22.4 percent to 11.1 percent.[3] But, at the same time, the package of reforms signed off on by Clinton when the economy was booming stacked up a host of problems for the downturns to come, when shrinking welfare rolls and ever-more stringent lifetime limits imposed by states on welfare recipients resulted not in more people employed but in higher numbers living in deep poverty. Just prior to the implementation of welfare reform in 1996, 4.43 million families nationwide were on Aid to Families with Dependent Children (AFDC), the main welfare program for families in deep poverty. In 2010, two-plus years into an economic crisis that had created the worst job market in America since the Great Depression, only 1.86 million families were on Temporary Aid to Needy Families (TANF), the successor program to AFDC.[4]

In the 2000s, George W. Bush talked about "compassionate conservatism" while presiding over a stampede toward income inequality the likes of which America hadn't seen in nearly a century. By 2004, the poverty rate had bounced back up to 12.7 percent, following four straight years in which the Census Bureau reported growing economic hardship for those at the bottom of the economy—falling median wages, despite enormous productivity increases and an expectation that workers would work ever more hours per year,[5] and an increased inability to meet the daily needs of life.[6] By 2008, at the end of Bush's two terms in office, the poverty rate was up to 13.2 percent.[7] At the same time, tax rates were cut for high-end earners, for investors, and for corporations, resulting in a massive expansion in wealth for those at the top of the economic pyramid.

No period since that surrounding the 1929 stock market crash has produced such a vast disparity between rich and poor, a vivid example of Michael Harrington's argument that, in America, poverty exists hidden in plain sight within the crevices and cracks of the affluent society.

More recently, as tens of millions more Americans have come to rely on food stamps to avoid hunger and malnutrition, political figures such as Newt Gingrich and Rick Santorum have accused those on food stamps of no longer possessing the American will to success, of having become permanent charity cases. Barack Obama, Gingrich told audiences around America during the early months of 2012, was a "food stamp president."

Precisely *why* so many tens of millions of people were poor enough to qualify for food stamps—to access the program one has to have a gross income of at or below 134 percent of the federal poverty line in most states, up to 200 percent in other states, and a net income that doesn't exceed 100 percent of the poverty line—didn't concern these presidential hopefuls. What enraged Gingrich, in particular, was the mere *existence* of a safety net, of programs, however inadequate, to break the fall when people lost jobs and incomes, homes and healthcare. That the Supplemental Nutritional Assistance Program (SNAP) was, by 2012, by far the most effective and universally accessible part of a frayed safety net—the number of enrollees expanding roughly in lockstep with the growing need for assistance—made it that much more of a tempting target for those who believed that government should get out of the business of poverty prevention and alleviation.

For Gingrich, poverty represented not a societal failing but an individual one. Twisting the words of Harrington, who had argued that the existence of poverty created a dysfunctional culture in its wake, he decried a culture of poverty that was preventing poor people from bettering themselves. Where Harrington argued that poverty locked in place behaviors that then exacerbated poverty, Gingrich reversed the equation. In particular, he argued, the prevalence of poverty demonstrated a collapsed work ethic. His solution, as advocated during an address at Harvard University's Kennedy School of Government on November 18, 2011, was to relax child labor laws that "entrapped" poor kids, and to put the children of impoverished families to work as school janitors and in similar hourly jobs. "You're going to see from me extraordinarily radical proposals to fundamentally change the culture of poverty in America and give people a chance to rise very rapidly," the ex–Speaker of the House told his audience.[8]

While progressives lambasted GOP candidate Mitt Romney for saying that he didn't care about the poor, conservatives such as Rush Limbaugh jumped on his explanation—that he meant the poor already had a safety net in place, and if that net had holes in it he would fix it—as proof positive that Romney wasn't in fact a true conservative. "'I'm not concerned about the very poor. We have a safety net there,'" Limbaugh repeated in mock astonishment. "The safety net is one of the biggest cultural problems we've got!"[9] Throughout the long recession, Limbaugh used his platform to repeatedly oppose measures such as federal grants to provide meals to hungry children at summer feeding program sites. On November 28, 2011, the talk show host quoted from a *New York Times* article on how Democrats were wooing voters—especially minority voters—who depended on safety net programs, in particular those on food stamps. Limbaugh's response was, "So the Democrat Party and Obama are making it official. We're going after life's losers, and we're going to empower them. We're gonna make them the reason we win. Now, everybody, you should know this, this should not be a surprise. This is what the Democrat Party's been doing for years, they're admitting it now. They're admitting it. They are saying they're not interested in voters who work."[10]

Meanwhile, as the debate over the budget deficit heated up in 2011, Tea Party activists, energized by the 2010 midterm elections, proposed cutting a startling $9 trillion from federal spending during a ten-year period. How would they accomplish this? Among other things, by eliminating the Departments of Education and of Housing and Urban Development, repealing the 2010 healthcare reform, and redesigning Medicaid so that it would cease to be an entitlement for families with children at or below a certain income level and would instead be given out as a block grant to the states—as subject to raiding as welfare funds were once they started being distributed via block grants. Finally, they proposed rolling back *all* discretionary spending—overwhelmingly, moneys spent on social programs for the poor—to 2008 levels.[11] Republicans in Congress also repeatedly called for replacing the entitlement provisions of food stamps with a bloc grant system, one that independent analysts reported would have resulted in millions more Americans being rendered ineligible for food aid and thus being put at risk for going hungry.

The slash-and-burn proposals reached the highest levels of the Republican leadership in Congress. House Budget Committee chair Paul Ryan, soon to be anointed Romney's running mate, called for rolling back Pell Grants, one of the country's most successful methods for allowing low-income people to gain higher education. His proposal, which was ultimately killed off in the Senate, would have eliminated the Pells for up to one million students and reduced the value of the grants allotted to millions more.[12] And South Carolina senator Jim DeMint, hero of the Tea Party, proposed $4.2 trillion in cuts, fully 70 percent of which would have been chopped from safety net programs for the poor.[13]

Absent from all of these discussions were the voices of the poor themselves. What would it mean to cut food stamps?

For 35-year-old Maribel Diaz, a onetime employee of a California-run nutritional program for low-income residents who lost her job when the recession eviscerated the state's budget, it would mean that she and her three young children would no longer be able to afford fresh fruit and vegetables.

Something that's fresh, from the farmers' market, it's something everyone would want access to. If you are consuming your fruits and vegetables on a daily basis, it'll prevent you from getting sick. It's very important to have access to fruits and vegetables. I receive for myself and my kids, Cal-Fresh. If we didn't have those benefits, we'd basically be hungry. I wouldn't be able to feed them. We don't have a lot of access to fruits and vegetables, but we do have some access. If the programs were cut, we'd be hungry, we'd be at food pantries. And they don't give you no protein. They give you two, three, four cans of canned goods, with a box of cereal. We'd be hungry. I don't know what we'd do.

For Marcy Glickman, a widow from Los Angeles's chic West Side whose upper-middle-class lifestyle was destroyed by the medical bills accrued during her late husband's battle with cancer and by the loss of income after they lost his business, the disappearance of food stamps would push her toward outright hunger. As the family's finances imploded, with their income declining from more than $10,000 a month to less than $1,000, "I started collecting coupons for groceries, and I remember cutting down our spending on groceries," said Glickman. Then she began frequenting food pantries, her lean steak and salmon diet replaced by noodles, canned tuna, and beans. "We had to get food stamps. At first I felt embarrassed. But after a while I realized at least we're eating. At least we're able to eat; we just have to cut down on everything."

What would it mean to reduce the services provided by Medicaid? Ask Patty Poole, a Medicaid recipient in the upstate New York town of Endicott, who explained how she underwent surgery to reduce severe swelling in her leg caused by a nasty disease called lymphedema, spent weeks in the hospital, and came out to find that Medicaid in New York would no longer pay for the compression stockings that she needed to keep the swelling from re-emerging. Despite having already been measured for the specialized garment, she was told that due to budget cuts the state was only authorizing the purchase of these stockings for pregnant women or lymphedema sufferers whose skin was so wounded that it had actually broken out in ulcers.

"It made no sense. It would be more expensive to wait till a patient had ulcers," Poole recalled thinking. Desperate to prevent her recently-operated-on leg from filling up again with fluid, Poole embarked on an odyssey of visits to patients' rights advocates and doctors. But she couldn't find a way to get the garment without paying full price, and that price—$900—was quite simply out of her reach. And so, without access to the needed stockings, Poole—who was born with spina bifida and had been disabled her whole life—was reduced to improvisation: spending hours each day carefully covering her own leg with an array of bandages, cotton wraps, and stockings. Some days, it took Poole and her roommate two hours each time her leg needed to be wrapped, and on occasion it would need to be rewrapped three times in a day.

What would it mean to restrict access to Medicaid? Listen to Megan Roberts, whose family ceased to qualify for Medicaid after her husband received a $1 an hour pay raise from the truck mechanics' company that he worked for. The young couple with four children had recently moved from Albuquerque, New Mexico, to a small, impoverished community in California's Central Valley so that her husband could take up a new job with the company. His health benefits were due to begin in January. But, a few weeks beforehand, Megan's appendix ruptured; lacking medical insurance, the family was bankrupted by close to $100,000 in medical bills. Their credit shattered, they resorted to borrowing from one payday loan company after another.

> Five or six days after I was home from the hospital, I got my first hospital bill. About two weeks after that, I got my first failure to pay notice, saying that "you have not paid your $96,000 hospital bill." The dollar pay raise had knocked us off housing benefits; we went from $612 rent to $1,030 rent. Knocked us off food stamps, so we didn't get any food assistance. We had no Medicaid, because the dollar pay raise knocked us off that. He was going to get private health insurance through his work in January. But I got sick. We were left with this bill. On April 16 [2007], we filed for bankruptcy.

In 2008, a year after her husband's company health insurance had kicked in, at the age of only 31 Megan came down with a devastating form of pancreatic cancer. After she survived, against the odds, an extraordinarily brutal regimen of treatments, the family found that even with insurance, and even with anonymous donations from private donors, they now owed hundreds of thousands of dollars in additional bills. Because they had already declared bankruptcy in the recent past, they could not do so again—and, once more, the bills kept piling up. "I want to eventually get a house for my kids. But it ain't going to happen," she said sadly.

Reduce Medicaid services, you get more Patty Pooles. Reduce Medicaid access, you get more Megan Robertses.

In the same way that our political culture lacks the language to adequately confront poverty, so too in recent years it has lacked a vocabulary to explain *why* rampant inequality is a problem. As that inequality grows, and as the political rhetoric and agenda of state and federal politicians increasingly is skewed toward meeting the requirements of the country's new elites, so public infrastructure becomes ever more fragile. An anti-tax, anti-government movement, using the language of populism, and turbocharged in the aftermath of the 2010 *Citizens United* Supreme Court ruling, which allowed outside interest groups to spend freely on attack ads and "independent expenditure" campaigns, claims to represent the little man against Big Brother. In reality, however, it has created a public sector defined by squalor and an insecure citizenry unable to define itself by commonly accessed, and accessible, institutions.

The method is simple: defund public services, ensure that the government only delivers second-rate goods, convince the electorate that long-term societal investments such as Social Security and Medicare are Ponzi schemes unlikely to survive down the generations, and it becomes ever easier to convince ordinary people that taxes are a mugging rather than an investment. There is, after all, a reason that Swedes—who receive quality education, healthcare, childcare, vacation times, and pensions courtesy of their government—tolerate far higher taxes than do Americans. It's not because they have some strange Scandinavian-only pro-tax genes in their DNA. Nor is it because of some bizarre streak of masochism in their culture. Rather, it's because they actually get their money's worth from their taxes. They pay good money and get good quality services. In America, by contrast, increasingly the public receives duds.

Sell enough lemons, conservatives have realized, and you can trigger demands that the whole enterprise be shut down. It is, quite simply, a classic bait-and-switch maneuver.

Able to spend virtually unlimited sums to influence political and judicial races, groups such as the U.S. Chamber of Commerce and Crossroads GPS; and individuals such as the Koch brothers; Newt Gingrich's 2012 primary season backer, Sheldon Adelson; and Rick Santorum's funder, Foster Friess—have seeded a conservative push to undermine what remains of the progressive tax structure and to denude government of its role in providing basic services to the populace. In fact, the push aims to "starve the beast," as anti-tax guru Grover Norquist has piquantly put it—denuding environmental and workplace regulations, protections for trade unions, and broad social safety net programs. Theirs is an attack not only on the legacy of the Great Society, but also that of the New Deal and the Progressive Era. They lead this charge in the name of fiscal probity, but they do so knowing the results will further exacerbate economic divisions within the country. That they didn't succeed in the 2012 elections is an extraordinarily positive thing, but to think that their agenda has somehow dissipated would be naïve in the extreme. They were, after all, remarkably successful in the post-2008 period, especially at the state level, despite being in the political minority in D.C.

Witness one example of the counterproductive impact of this rhetoric: From 2008 to 2011, during the deepest economic crisis since the Great Depression, the number of people able to claim welfare checks (TANF) actually declined in a number of states. Many single mothers, in particular, could no longer access cash assistance, job training, or help with childcare so that they could place their children in safe environments while they looked for employment. Others simply saw the clock run out on them—with many states reducing the number of months a woman could access TANF over the course of her lifetime.

More and more, as a result of the squeezing of government services, those with resources opt out of the public sphere, sending their children to private schools and colleges, protecting their homes and other property with private security systems, abandoning public transit systems, forgoing as many interactions with the public sector and with government agencies as they can. Similar processes have happened in recent years in countries such as South Africa and Mexico. In no instance has such a retrenchment led to a fairer, more equal, or more tranquil society.

————————

The effects of the twin trends of growing inequality and of declining opportunity are particularly apparent the further down the income scale one goes. At the bottom of the economy is a pool of misery in which an increasing number of undereducated, underskilled, underresourced people are being condemned to lives of insecurity, either out of work or working jobs with declining pay in real terms, many of them without access to even rudimentary social benefits—pensions, health insurance, meaningful vacation time, and so on.

In his book *Free Lunch*, the Pulitzer Prize–winning *New York Times* journalist David Cay Johnston estimated that by the early years of the century, most Americans were getting by on about $75 less per week, in real terms, than they and their parents were a generation earlier. He chronicled a hollowed-out middle class, and a resulting chasm between a growing minority of poor people and a sliver of the population in possession of extraordinary and rapidly growing wealth. So great was the economic insecurity experienced by the bottom half and so potent was the concentration of wealth at the very top that, Johnston argued, America now looked more akin to Brazil, Mexico, or Russia than to any Western European society.[14]

Between 1950 and 1975, Johnston calculated, for each additional dollar in income most Americans received as the economy expanded, those in the top 1 percent received $4. From 1960 to 1985, it was $17. "And for 1981 through 2005, it is almost $5,000."[15] For the top 0.01 percent of the economy, that number was a staggering $140,000. In other words, if an average earner took home $100 more one year, it was reasonable to assume that the billionaire living across town had increased his income by roughly $14 million during that same time period. Today, a few hundred billionaires, a new plutocracy, control several trillion dollars in assets—enough to pay median-income salaries for years on end to tens of millions of workers.

The flipside of this wealth concentration is the resurgence of a gritty poverty that decades of New Deal and then Great Society programs had sought to eradicate, a return to a country in which, as Franklin Roosevelt famously noted, "one-third of the nation is ill-housed, ill-clad, ill-nourished." The Census Bureau calculated that not far shy of 50 million Americans in 2011 were living at or below the federal poverty line; included in this demographic were a growing number of children. In many parts of the country, at the height of the post-2008 recession, one-quarter of all kids were living in conditions of deprivation—and when economic measures as a whole started to improve in 2011–12, the poverty numbers remained stubbornly high. If the economy *was* improving, it was doing so selectively, leaving behind millions of families trapped in brutally corrosive impoverishment.

In some of the poorest regions of Appalachia, the Mississippi Delta, and a few other spots of concentrated misery, the number of local children in poverty routinely approached 50 percent. In Detroit, more than 37 percent of residents were living in poverty as of 2012,[16] and nationally approximately six million Americans were entirely excluded from the cash economy, their only formal source of income government food stamps.[17] These men, women, and children were part of a growing subgroup living in what the Census Bureau labeled "deep poverty," their incomes below half that of the federal poverty line. More broadly, a record number of people, upward of 46 million, were receiving food stamps and other nutritional assistance—although even this aid seemed to be increasingly at risk as a budget-cutting mind-set took hold both in Washington, D.C., and in state capitals, with congressional Republicans, in particular, calling for a scaling back of vital safety net programs.

Millions more did not qualify for government aid, yet were poor enough to routinely have to fall back on the charity of food pantries, churches, and other nonprofit groups. These were the people who, in the words of Billye McPherson, found that "the month is longer than the money." McPherson, an 84-year-old woman, and her husband had run a food pantry in California's Siskiyou County since the late 1990s, so she was in a position to know. Able to make their income cover two or three weeks of expenses out of each month, these people were juggling which bills to pay, which services to let be cut off, which meals to skip, and which medicines to do without come the end of the pay cycle.

Billye's husband, a World War II veteran suffering from bone cancer when I interviewed him in late 2011, put it this way:

> When we were younger, and we had moved up here from the Bay Area, we had some really hard times raising our family. I remember, we got to say "we lived on stone soup." Pancakes sometimes—with syrup on 'em as long as we had syrup, sometimes pancakes without anything. We struggled simply just to feed our family. So we understand what it is to be hungry. I've worked pretty hard all my life; never taken any workmen's compensation or unemployment insurance or money from charitable things. Like I said, we understand what poverty is, what it is to be hungry.

Jim Ziliak, a Lexington-based University of Kentucky economist and director of his campus's Center on Poverty Research, called it the "eat or heat" conundrum, in which people are reduced to making an elemental calculation: Feed the kids when they're hungry and not have enough money to heat the house in winter, or heat the house when the cold gets too much and have to listen to the kids bawl for food.

———————

When it comes to healthcare, millions of Americans find that that too presents appalling dilemmas, with one illness having the potential to plunge a family into poverty, even into bankruptcy. And why not? After all, with the political classes piling blame on the unemployed for being out of work, on families reliant on welfare for being destitute, and on the hungry for needing food stamps, it makes perfect sense that those who cannot afford insurance can be asked to pay a devastating financial price for daring to need medical care when they get sick.

Despite the passage of healthcare reform in 2010, a growing number of Americans either lack access to health insurance; have to pay more out of pocket to remain insured; or despite having basic coverage, are receiving increasingly substandard and constricted healthcare. Fifty million Americans don't have any health insurance—when they get sick, they go into debt, sometimes to cataclysmic effect.

This happened to 61-year-old grandmother Marta Montano, a night porter in a nonunion casino in Las Vegas, who racked up medical bills paying both for the hospitalization of a young niece she was caring for and also for her own medical treatments. Montano ended up owing $18,000 and had to file for bankruptcy. She lost her credit and was reduced to borrowing from payday loan companies to make her monthly rent—loans that, when we met more than a year after she took them out, she had not been able to make a dent in repaying. On her feet all night every night, Montano couldn't afford new shoes; those she had were worn down and worn through. When she came home in the early morning and removed her broken shoes, her legs ached, and the nerves in her back shot fire up her spine.

For Joe, who lived in a small town in a onetime mining region in Appalachian Pennsylvania, the breaking point came when he had a massive heart attack at the age of 54. Uninsured, he found himself having to sell his house just to cover his medical bills. Years afterward, he'd spent all his assets and, isolated and lonesome, was living on just a little more than $600 a month in federal disability payments. "I just sat home now. I just sat home. I can't even afford to go out. Like I said, I couldn't even afford toilet paper if it wouldn't be for my boys helping me out," he said in a deep, slow voice, the words rolled out over a mellifluous Appalachian accent.

> They help me out with toilet paper, soap, dish detergents, wash detergents. I couldn't even afford that. By the time I'm done with my bills, I'm lucky if I have ten dollars a month. Now if a person can go out and have a social life on ten dollars a month, I'd like to know how they do it. I have no luxuries, buddy, no luxuries whatsoever. I can't afford luxuries. I'm lucky if I go shoppin' twice a month; and that's the best I go anyplace. It makes me feel worthless. My whole life's worthless. What are you going to do about it? You can't do it if you ain't got to do it with; and I ain't got to do it with. If I didn't have my TV to watch and my bird to talk to, I don't know, I'd probably go nuts. And that's about the extent of my life. That's about it for my great lifestyle.

Further fueling America's poverty epidemic are two other trends. The first is the breakdown of pension systems, be they private systems into which employers have stopped paying contributions or state and municipal systems teetering on the edge of insolvency. Elderly men and women who have worked for decades, have paid into their pension plans, and have been promised certain monthly payments upon retirement are now finding those promises have been voided, with companies blaming high pension costs rather than mis-management for their fiscal difficulties. In Longview, Washington, for example, hundreds of middle-aged aluminum workers lost their union pensions and their promised healthcare benefits after the company they worked for filed for bankruptcy. Men who worked for decades as skilled smelters were reduced to begging for casual work as landscapers, porters, or supermarket baggers. One of the workers ended up sleeping in his car in mall parking lots; another got a job at Walmart, earning half of what he had earned at the foundry. Another took to drinking, one man ended up institutional-ized, and yet another took his own life.[18] More recently, the small towns of Prichard, Alabama, and Central Falls, Rhode Island, have filed for Chapter 9 bankruptcy protection, the financial collapse tak-ing down not only pensions promised to current workers but also those already being paid to retirees. Pennsylvania's state capital, Har-risburg, has entered insolvency. And larger cities, such as Stockton, California, and Providence, Rhode Island, were also brought to the brink of the financial abyss by the financial collapse and its after-math. Stockton was forced into bankruptcy in mid-2012; Provi-dence, to date, has narrowly avoided bankruptcy. In 2011, there was a flurry of media speculation that this trend might even reach up to state level, with Rhode Island's entire state pension system thought to be at risk.

The second trend is the problem of the ongoing housing bust and a political response that has seen large numbers of politicians blaming the poor for taking out loans they could not afford rather than the financial institutions that marketed such dubious products in the first place. For tens of millions of American families, savings painstakingly accumulated during the years have been wiped out since 2006 as property values plummeted. More homes went under-water—the owners owing more on the mortgages than the homes were now worth—and millions of homes were foreclosed on. Be-tween 2006 and 2012, three million homes were repossessed by banks, their owners left either homeless or living in downscale rentals. Realty experts predicted that, despite a federal settlement with the five largest banks intended to provide $26 billion of mortgage relief to homeowners, and notwithstanding state-level efforts by attorneys-general in California and elsewhere to protect homeowners from foreclosures, another three million homes could be repossessed before the crisis burned itself out, with as many as three million seniors at risk of losing the houses they lived in, according to an AARP study.[19]

These are not simply abstract numbers. They are lives shattered.

"It's hard because it's like you were begging the bank to go ahead and give you something, so you have a house to come back home to," recalled 50-year-old Matthew Joseph, a sheet-metal worker and church deacon in the hard-hit California Central Valley town of Stockton, who lost his job after the 2008 crash and spent the years that followed struggling mightily to keep his home.

In my neighborhood where I live now, the saddest sight is to realize half your neighbors aren't there. There're empty lots; the grass is growing up above the For Sale signs. Houses look as if they've been abandoned, windows broken. Western Ranch at one time was one of *the* prime areas to live. In the last few years, all you see is people losing their houses. I cannot tell you how many U-Haul vans I've seen coming into our neighborhood, moving people out; people losing their houses.

I bought my house for $245,000. My house, at one time, went up to $575,000, and then it nosedived down to $171,000. When I called my bank, my bank went ahead and told me I was in an upside-down situation. My house is going down, and I'm looking at unemployment only. My wife, Celia, had been through quite a few medical procedures, operations on her shoulders—she had worked at Toys "R" Us warehouse; and doing repetitive pulling put her in a situation where she couldn't work. I went ahead and took it upon myself to say, "What am I going to do? Am I going to lose my house? Am I going to look for another job—when there is no job?" The bank puts you through so many hoops, saying they're doing something for you; but they're really not. They're not giving the normal guy a hand to be able to go ahead and save his house.

In some poor neighborhoods, schools are now inundated with homeless students, some of them street kids, but many of them children whose families have either lost their homes to foreclosure or have been evicted after the parents lost their jobs.

"We have 150-plus homeless students," said Angela Urquiaga, the full-time advocate for kids without places to call home at Rancho High School in a deeply impoverished part of North Las Vegas.

One child, she's 14 years of age, a freshman. She was very hurt because her father had lost his job; the mother threw the father out, and the child said she was going to go with him. The mother said, "You both leave." They were staying in a car three or four days. I got him in a church—they're staying in a church right now. The child comes and sits with me at lunchtime and talks with me. She's 14 years of age, wears a size 12 little girls. She was hungry. The father came and talked with me. He cried. We both cried. My goal is for them to continue with education, so they become somebody in the future. I have lots of heartbreaking stories—children who've been molested, been refused their families' love, they've been on drugs.

Urquiaga had been a homeless advocate at Rancho for the past eleven years. When she started there, she was working with ten to fifteen kids each year. Then the numbers exploded. "After 2009 it became a hundred; 2010, 120 or 130; 2011, over 200 students. This year we've been in a few months, and I've already got over 130 students. Two families living in cars, families the community brought them in to sleep in their garage. These are very, very hard things for kids who deserve a room of their own, a TV, and an atmosphere where they can do their homework in peace and have a meal."

The men, women, and children caught in these traps of poverty—whether made homeless by economic collapse or rendered bankrupt by medical bills—came from all corners of America and virtually all walks of life. Suffering the indignities of poverty, they also suffered the shame of stigma, of being blamed for their plight and ignored by those lucky enough to still have resources to fall back on. Their presence complicated the American story, and as with the presence of paupers in the nineteenth century or sharecroppers, tenements, and ghettoes in the twentieth, made the rosy, oftentimes complacent, national self-image harder to maintain. The presence of wholesale poverty was a societal embarrassment and, as with all embarrassments, it was one the broader community could bear only if the victims themselves were made blameable for their condition.

AN AMERICAN DILEMMA

Immigrant rights advocate Carlos Marentes on the U.S. side of the border with Mexico. Immigrant farmworkers' possessions are left in bags hanging from trees.

For America, a country that presumes to measure itself against high ideals codified in its founding documents—the Declaration of Independence, the Constitution, and the Bill of Rights, in particular—balancing the demands of individual freedom with those of economic justice has, historically, been especially challenging. What if untrammeled economic liberty for some ends up in a diminution of happiness for others? What if the right to flourish implies as well the chance that many others will flounder? And what if those who prosper the most then turn around and rig the game against their fellow citizens? What if the political rights enshrined in the Constitution aren't always in harmony with the economic rights so embedded in the country's psyche?

In the early twentieth century, the German sociologist Max Weber theorized in *The Protestant Ethic and the Spirit of Capitalism* that Protestantism generated a unique set of traits that promoted thrift and capital accumulation. Threaded through his ideas was a complex psychological theory: Calvinism, he argued, preached a doctrine of predestination, the idea that some people had been marked by God for salvation and others for damnation. There wasn't a whole lot in practice that one could do to alter one's status, but there *were* signs one could interpret as suggesting that one was among the chosen ones. Among those was secular success, achievement in the realm of business being a core part of this.

For Weber, this helped explain why and how England came to thrive economically during the first Industrial Revolution. From Henry VIII's time on, the country had been majority Protestant, and, argued Weber, it had placed a premium on capital accumulation that had created huge momentum toward economic growth, and by extension, scientific accomplishment and expanding military and political influence on a global scale. By the same rationale, that ethic had played a role in defining America's extraordinary economic success down the centuries. You want to be saved, so you work hard in order to acquire a sign of God's approval—wealth—that justifies the assumption that you are indeed one of the lucky ones. And when enough people buy into this, the country's economy flourishes.

Intellectually, this is gibberish; it's a classic circular argument, a cause and a consequence defined in terms of each other. But psychologically, it's powerful, providing a reassuring rationale for affluence and the pathologies of privilege that too often prevent a clear-eyed understanding of complex social problems: "I am rich because I am a good person; I am a chosen person; I am a person marked by God for greatness. You are poor because you can't cut it with the Creator; you aren't destined for salvation; and your poverty is a sign of your cosmic failing." By extension this becomes, "My country is thriving because we are a virtuous people; yours is sinking because your culture is delinquent."

That poverty was a sign of moral failing—of drunkenness, sexual promiscuity, laziness, and lack of ambition—was an idea hard-baked into British politics from the Tudor period onward. Poorhouses, and later workhouses, were carefully structured around principles of "less eligibility," designed to be as unpleasant as possible in order to avoid being seen as somehow attractive options for a slothful underclass. When churches stepped in to fill the void left by a largely absent state when it came to helping the poor, they, too, generally did so in ways that provided barely subsistence relief offered up in tandem with large doses of religious moralizing, admonitions to temperance, and warnings about the spiritual dangers of depravity.

In his classic turn-of-the-century exploration of poverty, *Life and Labour of the People in London*, the late-Victorian British journalist Charles Booth gently noted of one church actively fighting poverty: "This church has a large and very aggressive temperance society. 'If they scent a drunkard they are always at him.' But as to the people at large it is not temperance, nor lantern lectures on current topics, nor anything of that sort in which interest is found. The 'little things they care about,' and about which information is provided by the cheap newspapers, are betting and sport of every kind."[1]

Until well into the twentieth century, America's approach to poverty relied largely on religious charities and, to a point, do-good social workers stepping in to keep poor people from absolute destitution. When progressive social workers in late-nineteenth-century American cities set up settlement houses, modeled on community centers established in England in the preceding decades, they brought a charity vision to the problems of poverty rather than a belief that government should step in to solve the great problems of urban poverty generated by industrialism.

From Teddy Roosevelt's presidency onward, however, a series of reform bursts—in the pre–World War I years, during the Great Depression, and in the 1960s and early 1970s—created the infrastructure for a modern, bureaucratic welfare state. And yet, for all the energy invested in this century-long project, today that infrastructure remains fragile—in many ways more vulnerable to political and economic vagaries than at any time since its founding. Today, the language used by conservatives to discuss poverty and its perceived pathologies, and the charity-based solutions offered up by conservatives to deal with its rawest manifestations, is more akin to that of the nineteenth-century English vicars than to the ideas developed by generations of twentieth-century welfare reformers.

SOUTHERN MORES, THE GREAT UNWASHED, AND A FARMER FROM IOWA WITH A GOOD IDEA

That the pillars of America's welfare system remain so unstable, despite a century of construction, is largely a result of how they were built and of the federal/state compromises made during that process. Federal systems *were* created, but unlike in, say, Germany, France, or the United Kingdom—all of which began the long process of building modern social insurance systems and central government-funded welfare programs in the last decades of the nineteenth and first decades of the twentieth centuries—they were frequently left to the states to fund and administer. And many of those states, especially the more conservative and religious amongst them, were peculiarly hostile to the poor in their midst. Baseline anti-poverty yardsticks *were* created, but local and state governments could choose whether or not to go beyond these minimums.

Aspirations generated by federal reformers to curb economic hardship too often rubbed up against either local indifference or tax revolts that denuded programs of the dollars needed to make them effective. As a result, in some states, namely in the Northeast and upper Midwest, benefits have historically been fairly generous. In others, in particular the Old South and, increasingly, parts of the West, those benefits have been miserly at best. In states such as Mississippi and Alabama, anti-tax sentiments, combined with extreme racial and class stratifications, have made the creation and expansion of safety net systems for the poor all but impossible. A slew of welfare benefits in these states are, on a good day, only bare-bones. On a bad day, they are practically nonexistent. Because more than 40 percent of the nation's poor live in the Old South, more than five million of them children, southern resistance to implementing decent welfare programs has had, and continues to have, dire implications for the nation's overall ability to tackle poverty.[2]

Witness the story of 71-year-old Clara Joseph, a onetime supermarket clerk, theater usher, and elevator operator in southern Louisiana, who had spent a lifetime working minimum-wage jobs and whose house was flooded with five feet of water during Hurricane Katrina. The victim of four strokes, she had been forced to retire a few years before I met her. Her income consisted only of $579 a month in Social Security. She didn't receive other top-up assistance from the state and routinely found her basic monthly bills were unaffordable. Her way of bridging the gap between that income and her expenses: turning up at food pantries four hours before they opened every weekend so that she'd be near enough to the front of the line that she might actually get some fresh meat and a few fresh vegetables. Come much later, she averred, and the pickings were slim.

Clara would drive up in her little old white sedan, a woolen hat rolled down over her head, her eyes small and watery behind horn-rimmed spectacles. She would park her car, slowly get out from behind the wheel, make her way to the sidewalk, and sit and wait. It seemed an awfully long time to wait for a bag of food. But Clara didn't seem to mind. Most of her friends, she announced, were now also using the pantries.

In the face of regional animus, particularly from southern politicians, the central institutions of America's social safety net—a welfare system for destitute families, unemployment insurance, food stamps, Social Security, nutritional programs for pregnant women and for children, redistributive taxation policies, subsidized housing, Medicaid and Medicare—emerged in fits and starts throughout the twentieth century. From the Progressive Era at the start of the 1900s, through the New Deal, into the postwar years, the Great Society programs of the 1960s, and finally the Nixon era, government agencies were created and policies promoted to mitigate the ravages of poverty. "It was an issue that had to be focused on," argued UC Santa Barbara's Alice O'Connor. "It had a moral tug on the public consciousness." Then, qualifying her comment, she quickly added, "But compassion only goes so far; it leads to charity, which people do when they're comfortable, and they don't have to give up a whole lot to be charitable. If you don't have the strong politics behind it, it's not going to go very far."

Even an incomplete system implemented with half-hearted enthusiasm, however, requires huge amounts of money to function. As government obligations grew, so the need to raise revenue increased, and a host of taxes were used to garner this money: federal and state income taxes—first used, to great effect, by the Union during the Civil War years, made a permanent part of the landscape four decades later, during Teddy Roosevelt's presidency—state property taxes, state and local sales taxes, corporate taxes, a slew of industry-specific taxes, so-called "sin taxes," and for many decades the infamous southern poll tax. When all of that wasn't enough to make ends meet, governments borrowed money and issued bonds.

Within the federal system, as the infrastructure of modern governance evolved, so richer states, New York and California for example, came to contribute more in taxes to the federal government than they received back in benefits; conversely, poorer states paid far less into the system than they got back. Resources were thus at least partially redistributed within the fifty states of the nation. Paradoxically, the most federal largesse went to the impoverished, anti-tax, and ostensibly anti–big government South, which by 2010 was getting back $1.40 in federal assistance for every dollar in taxes that it contributed to Washington. Even with this assistance, however, since its own tax base was so extraordinarily low the South had neither the ability nor the willpower to create the sort of comprehensive safety net system aimed at by the more liberal northeastern states.[3] And thus, in that part of the country in particular, even in the heyday of federal liberal activism, deep poverty continued to fester and state responses to lag.

From Georgia, a man posted an entry on my Voices of Poverty website explaining how he and his wife had been unable to afford a doctor because the low-wage jobs that he worked never provided health insurance. She had, he wrote, died of untreated pneumonia at the age of 50. Shortly afterward, he had been hit by a car. "Only by the grace of God was I able to survive the next six years. But now, I am going down slow. Every month, I have less and less and I am falling farther and farther behind. I pray that things will improve, but my horizon seems to have a picture of my losing my home, and then slowly starving to death."

As of 2012, Georgia was one of twenty-five states that provided no medical coverage to low-income, childless adults. Partly because of this, more than one in five Georgians had no health insurance as of 2009, according to Census Bureau data.[4] In fact, of all the southern states, only Arkansas and Tennessee provided some, albeit very limited, healthcare coverage for this part of their population.

The South's aversion both to taxes and to mandated government safety net structures had a long, and somewhat surprising, pedigree. In the late eighteenth century, popular radical writers such as Condorcet in France and Tom Paine in England had called for the creation of comprehensive social insurance systems based around universal pensions, child allowances, and education for all. Neither, however, managed to successfully alter prevailing political and moral doctrines. In France, after the frenzy of the revolutionary years the counterrevolution of the post-Napoleonic period put a halt to radical social experiments for decades. And in the United Kingdom, at least partially in response to the violence unleashed by revolutionaries in France, the early nineteenth century saw a tide of conservative reaction. Give money to the poor, the theory went, and you were encouraging indolence, dependency, and ultimately societal chaos. In 1834, after the publication of the Poor Law Report, "outdoor relief"—the giving of state moneys to the able-bodied poor in a non-workhouse context—was banned. For most of the rest of Queen Victoria's near-seventy-year reign, "the great unwashed" were either left to find their own ways through terrain of hunger, homelessness, and disease, or were corralled into the sorts of ghastly workhouse settings made infamous by the writings of Charles Dickens.

In America, the South in particular took the Victorian lesson to heart, though to a lesser degree so too did the rest of the country. As did most of Europe. After all, Great Britain was the dominant power of the age, its economic prescriptions as hard to avoid as, say, the Washington consensus's emphasis on opening up markets to international trade, privatizing public services, and deregulation a century and a half later. Coercive poor law politics, shaped around workhouses, poor houses, and other near-prison-like conditions for confining and attending to the subsistence needs of the poor was, as a consequence, the dominant response to poverty on both sides of the Atlantic throughout the middle decades of the nineteenth century.

A couple generations later, however, as the rise of industrial societies in Europe created huge economic dislocations and massive political unrest, Europe revisited the issue. Between 1883 and 1889, Otto von Bismarck's Germany created a slew of social insurance programs. In England, at about the same time, social reformers such as Arnold Toynbee began calling for the creation of a government-funded safety net. And in 1908, Parliament passed the Old Age Pensions Act—part of a two-year spasm of social reform that culminated in the fabled People's Budget of 1909. French reformers preached voluntary mutual assistance schemes and increasingly urged the government fund universal assistance programs out of a general tax base. After decades of agitation, the French Parliament enacted a state pension system in 1910.

In the United States, though, support for such reforms remained more tenuous. True, an array of progressive political groups supported workers' compensation laws by the early twentieth century. And by 1917, with the Supreme Court having upheld the constitutionality of these laws, thirty-seven states had systems in place, most of them compulsory. In fact, as a region, only the Deep South had completely neglected to implement compensation schemes for at least some categories of injured workers. But in contrast to this, enthusiasm for social insurance systems didn't take off prior to World War I. True, several states in America created their own very limited pension plans during these years, especially for widows and for teachers—who at the time were mainly women—and several also seeded their own unemployment insurance systems. Yet not until the New Deal did the idea of a federal system gain traction. Before then, even the American Federation of Labor and the left-wing *Nation* magazine opposed mandatory Social Security.[5] Hence the paradoxical fact that when, in 1912, Teddy Roosevelt's Progressives came out in support of social insurance, including a form of compulsory medical insurance, an alliance of conservatives, socialists, trade unionists, and federalists combined to defeat it. Opponents argued that the imposition of mandates on working Americans, forcing them to pay into a system to support the elderly and to provide medical coverage for the sick, was foreign to the country's founding principles. What was happening in Europe was, they argued, too paternalistic, too coercive. Moreover, in a land of great social mobility and endless opportunity such systems were unnecessary. Keep them for the ossified Old World—keep them for places where one's station in life was determined by one's parentage.

Thus, while America's peer nations across the Atlantic were experimenting with forms of universal old age pensions and healthcare coverage—to tackle the extremes of poverty that had driven so many Europeans to migrate to the United States in search of higher living standards—when it came to the creation of nationwide safety net protections America stalled. Hobbled by the South's antipathy to any form of welfare, and by a broader national reluctance to corral citizens into insurance programs against their will, advocates for the sorts of reforms occurring in Europe ran up against a brick wall. It would take the Great Depression, and the collapse of both the working and the middle classes' sense of stability and burgeoning economic possibility, to shift public opinion behind the establishment of Social Security and government aid in the arena of housing and employment. In fact, it wasn't until 1935, six years after Wall Street's catastrophic collapse, that Congress legislated into being Social Security, disability and unemployment insurance, and Aid to Families with Dependent Children. And it was not until 1937 that Congress would take the lead on funding large-scale public housing.

As for healthcare reform, long a holy grail of social reformers, attempts by Franklin Roosevelt before World War II and Harry Truman at the end of the war to create universal healthcare foundered on the rocks of opposition from the American Medical Association, as well as more general hostility from the same political wellspring that had opposed Social Security's creation. Truman's proposal for a 4 percent payroll tax to cover a national health insurance system, which he proposed in a special message to Congress on November 19, 1945, was denounced as being an attempt to "socialize medicine." It was a critique that would crop up repeatedly over the decades, when Presidents Truman, Kennedy, Johnson, Nixon, Carter, Clinton, and finally Obama proposed significant overhauls to the country's dysfunctional and inequitable healthcare systems. Ultimately, it would take the upheavals of the 1960s to partially get around this critique and pave the way for Medicaid and Medicare—though in the case of Medicaid, Congress gave the states considerable leeway as to whom they covered and what services they provided. And it would take the 2008 financial collapse to create just about enough momentum for President Obama to get Congress to pass a watered-down version of universal healthcare. Even then, the backlash was massive, the acrimonious debate creating a climate in which the conservative Tea Party movement could flourish.

So, too, it would take the calamity of 1930s-era deflation, and the threat of wholesale bankruptcy for America's millions of farmers, for the federal government, at the urging of Secretary of Agriculture Henry Wallace, to start providing food aid to the country's hungry. It would take the work of Michael Harrington and others a generation later to prod Washington to set up a national food stamps system and then to expand vital nutritional programs such as school breakfasts and lunches and WIC, the Women, Infants, and Children program run by the U.S. Department of Agriculture.

At first, this food assistance to the poor was, essentially, a way of propping up agricultural prices by having local counties buy up surplus crops and thus preserve market buoyancy. "We must adjust downward our surplus supplies until domestic and foreign markets can be restored," Wallace, who had grown up on a farm in rural Iowa, declared in his first radio address on March 10, 1933.[6] The strategy worked for the farmers, and to a degree it alleviated hunger for a portion of the indigent population. It was, however, massively incomplete. Too few people received the aid; too many regions and categories of poor were left unhelped.

In 1961, a generation later, newly inaugurated president John F. Kennedy signed an executive order creating a pilot food stamp program, funded by the federal government, in eighteen states. After Kennedy's death, President Johnson pushed Congress to pass a Food Stamp Act that allowed counties across the country to choose to opt into the food stamp system, with poor families paying a percentage of their income to access food stamps worth considerably more—the stamps, in other words, were not free but were heavily subsidized. In the late 1960s, the voluntary nature of the system was replaced. Over several years leading up to 1974, *all* counties would have to opt into the system. By the mid-1970s, food assistance paid for by the feds, to the tune of billions of dollars a year, had become the country's single most effective intervention against poverty; by the end of the decade, food stamps alone had expanded to the point that the program was costing the government more than $20 billion (in 2012 dollar values) annually.[7]

In fact, even while President Richard Nixon rhetorically tilted rightward—talking of a Silent Majority enraged by lax criminal justice codes, a mollycoddling welfare state, and the presence of a seemingly permanent underclass—in reality he presided over significant expansions of the welfare state, especially when it came to anti-hunger programs. He also sought to create a universal healthcare system that in many of its particulars looked strikingly like the one ultimately implemented under President Obama nearly four decades later.

Three years after Nixon left office, Congress eliminated the requirement that poor families had to buy into the food stamp program; thenceforth, the cost of the food stamps was fully borne by the federal government. "The most important accomplishment of this period was the elimination of purchase prices as a barrier to participation," wrote the social scientist Dennis Roth in a history of the food stamp program commissioned by the Economic Research Service of the U.S. Department of Agriculture.[8]

LYNDON JOHNSON'S UNFINISHED WAR

Although far from perfect, at its acme this inelegant safety net developed in the first three quarters of the twentieth century and, given a peculiar impetus by Johnson's War on Poverty, *did* serve to limit hunger's reach. In the early 1930s, when real per capita income in America had fallen by a third and when tens of millions of people had literally no income, New York City reported more than one hundred residents a year dying from hunger and related causes.[9] Elsewhere, similar tales of starvation could be easily found. In cities throughout the South, the unemployed received *no* assistance,[10] and around the country, soup kitchens were all that stood in the way of famine for those without work, without homes, and without incomes. By 1980, after decades in which the federal government had taken an ever more active role in both reducing the cost of food and in subsidizing food purchases for the poor, low-income Americans could access food stamps, WIC, free breakfast and lunch programs in schools, Meals-on-Wheels for the elderly, and a slew of other well-funded systems. "In a few years this nation basically eliminated hunger as a problem," wrote the authors of the 1985 Harvard University School of Public Health–sponsored report *Hunger in America*, as they examined the extraordinary demise of hunger in the postwar period and bemoaned its woeful and entirely unnecessary reemergence during Ronald Reagan's presidency. "The success was relatively swift and not difficult to see," they continued. "We have enough food to end hunger in this land. All that remains is the political will."[11]

Johnson's expanded safety net yielded results in other arena too. As recently as 1959, for example, upward of 35 percent of the elderly were living in poverty—much of it caused by high medical bills. Once Medicare was passed in the 1960s, however, that number plummeted. By the year 2000, the government was reporting that only 10 percent of the country's elderly residents were living at or below the poverty line.[12]

The Progressive Era had introduced a number of workplace protections for Americans but had shied away from tackling broader conditions of hardship. The New Deal had begun to roll back poverty in America. The Great Society, of which Medicare for the elderly was a core part, set itself the peculiarly high ambition of actually ending it.

From the presidential bully pulpit on down, national resources were mobilized in what President Johnson, in his first State of the Union address on January 8, 1964, would, with a somewhat utopian flourish, term a "War on Human Poverty." This phrase was later improved upon by the deletion of the word "human."

Johnson, who had assumed the presidency a mere six weeks earlier, following John Kennedy's assassination, urged Congress to think big and to think holistically.

> Let this session of Congress be known as the session which did more for civil rights than the last hundred sessions combined; as the session which enacted the most far-reaching tax cut of our time; as the session which declared all-out war on human poverty and unemployment in these United States; as the session which finally recognized the health needs of all our older citizens; as the session which reformed our tangled transportation and transit policies; as the session which achieved the most effective, efficient foreign aid program ever; and as the session which helped to build more homes, more schools, more libraries, and more hospitals than any single session of Congress in the history of our Republic.[13]

According to such a line of reasoning, science would render poverty and the tangled web of hardship associated with economic want as quaint, as obsolete, as the horse-drawn carriage.

The speech ranks as one of the most ambitious State of the Union addresses ever delivered; it is worth quoting at length, for it represents one of the few times in American history that a president has so wholeheartedly prioritized the problems of the poor and the destitute:

This administration today, here and now, declares unconditional war on poverty in America. I urge this Congress and all Americans to join with me in that effort. It will not be a short or easy struggle, no single weapon or strategy will suffice, but we shall not rest until that war is won. The richest nation on earth can afford to win it. We cannot afford to lose it. $1,000 invested in salvaging an unemployable youth today can return $40,000 or more in his lifetime. Poverty is a national problem, requiring improved national organization and support. But this attack, to be effective, must also be organized at the state and the local level and must be supported and directed by state and local efforts. For the war against poverty will not be won here in Washington. It must be won in the field, in every private home, in every public office, from the courthouse to the White House.

The new president laid down a new measure of success: "Our aim is not only to relieve the symptom of poverty, but to cure it and, above all, to prevent it." For Johnson's vice president, the liberal Minnesotan Hubert Humphrey, the clarion call to defeat poverty marshaled all the can-do instincts of the American spirit. "We can afford it," he wrote of the War on Poverty in the foreword to the 1965 book *The Shame of a Nation*, a collaborative effort between photographer George de Vincent and writer Philip Stern to chronicle the lives of America's forgotten poor. "We have the wealth, the energy, yes, and the daring and imagination to defeat poverty in America, to relegate to the history books the sad and somber portraits in this volume."

———

It didn't happen.

Yes, Medicare and Medicaid expanded access to healthcare. Yes, an expanded food stamps program cut down hunger. Yes, job-training programs, drug rehabilitation clinics, and federal dollars for schools and housing all flooded into poor communities. But for all of the investments, poverty remained part of the national landscape. Some of the symptoms of poverty were indeed alleviated, yet the grand goal of the Great Society to actually eradicate poverty—to pull it up by the roots and erase all evidence of its existence—proved to be a bridge too far.

Three years after Johnson had launched the War on Poverty, with the country's attention largely having shifted to the war in Vietnam rather than the domestic "war," Senator Robert Kennedy would tour the Mississippi Delta and be shocked to see barefoot, malnourished, sickly children living in shanties with no indoor plumbing. By early 1968, as Kennedy campaigned for the Democratic Party's presidential nomination, his take on poverty's unrelenting grip on much of America had gone from surprise to shuddering, incandescent horror.

> I have seen children in Mississippi starving, their bodies so crippled from hunger and their minds have been so destroyed for their whole life that they will have no future. I have seen children in Mississippi— here in the United States—with a gross national product of $800 billion—I have seen children in the Delta area of Mississippi with distended stomachs, whose faces are covered with sores from starvation, and we haven't developed a policy so we can get enough food so that they can live, so that their children, so that their lives are not destroyed, I don't think that's acceptable in the United States of America and I think we need a change.

As the senator told an audience at the University of Kansas on March 18 of that year, "I have seen Indians living on their bare and meager reservations, with no jobs, with an unemployment rate of 80 percent, and with so little hope for the future, so little hope for the future that for young people, for young men and women in their teens, the greatest cause of death amongst them is suicide."

In full oratorical flight now, Kennedy continued, borrowing heavily from Harrington's imagery of a few years earlier:

> I run for the presidency because I have seen proud men in the hills of Appalachia, who wish only to work in dignity, but they cannot, for the mines are closed and their jobs are gone and no one— neither industry, nor labor, nor government—has cared enough to help. I think we here in this country, with the unselfish spirit that exists in the United States of America, I think we can do better here also. I have seen the people of the black ghetto, listening to ever greater promises of equality and of justice, as they sit in the same decaying schools and huddled in the same filthy rooms—without heat—warding off the cold and warding off the rats.

For Kennedy, campaigning on a platform far more radical than the one on which his brother had won election eight years earlier, ongoing poverty of this nature represented a staggering, existential challenge. "If we believe that we, as Americans, are bound together by a common concern for each other, then an urgent national priority is upon us. We must begin to end the disgrace of this other America."[14]

For Martin Luther King Jr., the continued existence of desperate hardship throughout America rendered as hollow victories much of the civil rights achievements of the mid-1960s. In his 1967 book *Where Do We Go from Here: Chaos or Community?* the civil rights leader called for radical measures. "I am now convinced that the simplest approach will prove to be the most effective—the solution to poverty is to abolish it directly by a now widely discussed measure: the guaranteed income," King wrote. "Two conditions are indispensable if we are to ensure that the guaranteed income operates as a consistently progressive measure. First, it must be pegged to the median income of society, not the lowest levels of income. To guarantee an income at the floor would simply perpetuate welfare standards and freeze into the society poverty conditions. Second, the guaranteed income must be dynamic; it must automatically increase as the total social income grows." No longer in a mood to compromise, King argued that "the curse of poverty has no justification in our age. It is socially as cruel and blind as the practice of cannibalism at the dawn of civilization, when men ate each other because they had not yet learned to take food from the soil or to consume the abundant animal life around them. The time has come for us to civilize ourselves by the total, direct and immediate abolition of poverty."[15]

King and Bobby Kennedy were the two public figures best able to articulate the moral importance of dramatic anti-poverty interventions in late 1960s America. With King's assassination in April 1968 and Kennedy's two months later, the last best chance for America to embrace systemic anti-poverty policies, and the moral language accompanying them, vanished. A slide began, slow at first, later more rapid, away from understanding poverty as society's problem and toward redefining it as a problem of individuals and underperforming communities.

Even while President Nixon expanded access to welfare programs, proposed minimum income guarantees, and gave his support to efforts to create universal healthcare access, he built a political base largely centered around Middle America's resentments toward the poor, the black, the brown, and the different. There was something of a schizophrenia to his politics, a residual desire to ameliorate the plight of the poor, on the one hand—he had, after all, made his way in life from humble beginnings—and a competing urge to denigrate the weak, on the other. Nixon sought the support of the Archie Bunkers of the country, people frustrated both by the speed of cultural changes taking place around them—from the rise of the anti–Vietnam War movement to the emergence of Black Power, hippie culture, and feminism—and also by the shifting contours of the economy. He played to the dyspepsia of a Silent Majority and—like few other mainstream politicians of the late 1960s but all too many of the decades to come—correctly gauged the potency of scapegoating when it came to building a political machine.

In such a milieu, the ideas posited by a New York academic named Daniel Patrick Moynihan flourished. Moynihan had held positions in both the Kennedy and Johnson administrations—as an assistant secretary of labor under Kennedy, as one of the architects of the War on Poverty under Johnson—and had shot to fame and notoriety during these years after writing a report that decried the emergence of a "culture of poverty." This culture, Moynihan believed, existed among the country's urban African American population and was characterized by dependency, sexual profligacy, lack of ambition, violence, and other dysfunction. Harrington, a few years earlier, had also written of a culture of poverty. Yet where for him that culture was largely the product of hardship, for Moynihan it was a primary causal factor explaining poverty's iron grip on so many millions of Americans' lives. It wasn't enough to change material conditions, Moynihan averred; government also had to figure out a way to change poor people's behavior. It was an argument tailor-made to gel with the concerns of Nixon's Silent Majority, and the newly elected president realized as much. In 1969, Moynihan was appointed counselor to the president for urban affairs.

Gradually at first, then with increasing rapidity, American popular opinion shifted. We became more impatient, less forgiving, in our attitudes toward the poor and the pathologies that all too often accompanied harsh living environments. In the post–World War II years, polls suggested that fewer than one in four Americans wanted to reduce public expenditures on welfare. By the early 1970s, solid majorities favored cutting back welfare dollars for the poor. And by 1977, more than 90 percent of respondents believed welfare recipients should be working.[16]

From the 1970s on, as misery and hardship stubbornly refused to vanish from the national landscape, America's commitment both to reducing income inequality and to mitigating the effects of that inequality began to wane. Both rhetorically and in terms of practical policies, America's leadership class began a long march away from redistributive liberalism. Tax policy became more regressive. And the tax code came overwhelmingly to benefit the wealthiest Americans, with a falloff in the progressive nature of the tax bands and the near-complete emasculation of the estate tax system. Huge companies such as GE found ways to avoid paying any corporate taxes,[17] and billionaires such as Warren Buffett, who made most of his money from capital gains, ended up paying a smaller percentage to the government in taxes than did their secretaries.

Cumulatively, programs and wage protections developed over the better part of a century came under tremendous pressures as the great unraveling of public infrastructure picked up pace.

––––––––

That this unraveling could pick up such speed was at least in part due to the fact that such policies had never had the sort of across-the-board political support seen for welfare systems in most other modern industrial democracies. In fact, taken as a whole, America's welfare system has always been an uneasy balancing act between the federal government and the states. Its access has been more or less tied into employment, its availability very much influenced by the direction of the political winds both federally and on a state-by-state basis, as well as by shifting religious and cultural values. Historically, it has been more generous to women than to men, its political process more open to giving aid, and wage protections, to women than to the "free agents" thought to make up the male populace. Thus, by 1923 fifteen states had enacted minimum-wage laws designed to protect low-paid women working in what were known as the "sweated" industries. But it wasn't until the Fair Labor Standards Act of 1938, passed as a cornerstone of the second part of the New Deal, that men received the same protection.[18] Historically, also, its union movement—a movement that in other countries was an integral part of Labor or Socialist parties, which sought to bind the interests of all parts of the working class—was more limited, both in its aspirations and its political achievements. Despite a militant history in the nineteenth and early twentieth centuries, in the decades after the 1935 Wagner Act paved the way for the mass unionization of the industrial professions, unions increasingly came to lobby for skilled workers, forgoing the hard work of organizing the unorganized, and leaving the mass of day laborers and unskilled workers as badly off as ever. There were exceptions, of course—Cesar Chavez and California's farm workers, and more recently the Justice for Janitors campaign. But, across the postwar decades, unions taken as a whole did a dismal job of moving beyond their traditional bases. As a result, many of the benefits accrued by labor in such industries as auto and mining never trickled downward. At the bottom of the economy, poverty remained pretty much untouched, its victims—living largely outside of trade union culture—voiceless and overwhelmingly without political muscle.

From the late 1970s onward, as unions were dramatically weakened, that hardship and insecurity welled upward once again like a chronic infection never quite tamed. By the 2000s, workers even in top-tier professions such as auto manufacturing were seeing their wages pushed downward and their benefits packages eviscerated. An auto worker signing on in 2012 could expect to earn far less, in real terms, over the course of a lifetime of hard work than could his father or grandfather working in the same industry in bygone decades.

As for the quality pensions fought for by previous generations of trade unionists, increasingly they were being relegated to the history books. In 2005, Hewlett-Packard began dismantling its pension plan for existing employees and announced that new hires would simply have no pensions. The intent? To save $300 million a year for the tech giant. Having narrowly avoided bankruptcy in 2009, in the years following the large automakers all began pushing their retirees to accept lump-sum buyouts in lieu of lifelong pensions. It might have been a good deal if you weren't planning to live to a ripe old age; it was a far riskier proposition if you anticipated you still had several decades left in you. In 2012, the airplane manufacturer Boeing pushed its unions to accept 401(k)s in lieu of defined benefit pensions for newly hired engineers and technical professionals.

And the list goes on.

That the unions found it so difficult to fight back at least in part had to do with the past sixty-plus years of history. In the late 1940s and 1950s, when Western European nations were distributing a range of social benefits to their populaces, America's progressives fell victim to a McCarthyite political culture that denounced comprehensive federal safety net systems as being somehow "Communist." McCarthyism ended in the mid-1950s, but it left a toxic rhetoric in its wake, one that was particularly hostile to big-picture safety net reforms. From debates around full employment policies during the Truman years to debates over universal healthcare in the Obama years, large-scale attempts to smooth out the market's rough edges have routinely been denounced as somehow anti-American.

Hence the kluge-like, makeshift nature of the American safety net. It existed, but it was neither uniform nor elegant. Rather, it was something that had managed to eke out a survival against the odds, that had managed to weather McCarthyism and a series of successor movements, and that somehow continued to exist despite the vibrancy of the notion that a country of "free men" didn't need or want large-scale government interventions in the economy. It was, wrote historian Michael Katz, a "rickety, uncoordinated welfare state."[19]

––––––––

That this welfare state was rickety didn't, however, minimize its significance. In fact, over the decades, many millions of lives were bettered by its existence.

In the 1930s, the federal government, drawing on progressive ideas that had been percolating on both sides of the Atlantic for at least half a century, created viable templates to stimulate employment, to keep people from starvation, to provide the elderly with Social Security, and so on. The economist John Maynard Keynes provided a theoretical justification for governments to borrow money during downturns to plow back into the economy via public works programs, infrastructure investments, and the like. He argued that the best way to revive a stagnant economy was to boost consumer spending, and that the most effective way to do that was to use the tools of the government to circulate money back into corners of the economy that weren't thriving. Give poor people money, Keynes realized, and they would spend it. And that would increase companies' revenues, stimulate employment, and ultimately boost the government's ability to raise taxes. Keynes's intellectual successor, John Kenneth Galbraith, went further. Even in flush times, he theorized, a vibrant safety net—a welfare system that served to keep the unemployed out of destitution—and a tax structure that functioned to limit income inequality would help create virtuous circles in which more money circulated, more people flourished, and fewer people at the bottom of the pyramid fell through the cracks.

Keynes had argued that government spending, and in some circumstances borrowing, was good. His prescriptions, considered heretical by many conservative critics at the time, had enabled America to find its way out of Depression in the 1930s, and, after World War II, into decades of broad-based economic growth. In fact, by the 1950s, wrote Richard Parker in his well-received biography of Galbraith, so widely diffused was American affluence that the overwhelming majority of economists were focused on how to grow the economy even more rather than how to distribute its fruits more fairly. Poverty was something old, a thing of the past, an unpleasant reminder of the long-gone Great Depression. When a government-commissioned academic tried to generate a complete list of publications in which contemporary economists wrote about American poverty and inequality, he found it impossible to make his bibliography stretch more than two pages.[20] Galbraith wasn't buying it. Throughout the 1950s, he was one of the few curmudgeonly voices warning Americans that poverty was still very much alive, albeit hidden, in their midst. Armed with this insight, he set about issuing prescriptions as to how the government ought to spend money in order to tackle economic hardship.

In 1964, Galbraith's work paid off when he was appointed to the White House Task Force in charge of putting down the basic template to fight the War on Poverty. As a result of his work, combined with the journalistic writings of Harrington, poverty once again took center stage in the national discourse. By 1970, that flimsy two-page bibliography of works related to poverty had exponentially grown to more than 440 pages as economists around the country started rediscovering narratives of economic hardship.

In the 1940s, the government had created a healthcare system for military veterans. In the 1960s, in an attempt to tackle one of the great sources of poverty in America, the government expanded access to medical coverage for the destitute and the elderly. In the 1970s, food stamps were made a critical part of the safety net, as were a raft of other nutritional assistance programs, and, at the same time, the nation's network of food banks, backed by USDA surplus, took off.

Some of this was simply about responding to the ongoing memories of the Great Depression, assuring a generation that had grown up in the hardest of hard times that the government had their back. Much of it, though, was about mediating the worst excesses of markets—excesses that left significant sectors of the population at risk even absent the conditions of a Great Depression—and about recognizing that complex modern societies had needs that transcended the profit motive. "Within the nation," wrote Karl Polanyi in 1944, in his book *The Great Transformation*, "we are witnessing a development under which the economic system ceases to lay down the law to society and the primacy of society over the system is secured." A Hungarian-born sociologist living in exile in London at the end of the war, Polanyi pondered the new world that, he hoped, would emerge out of the ashes of the old. The refugee-historian saw a future in which regulations would be carefully used to buttress the well-being of workers. Such codes of conduct, he argued, far from limiting freedom, as was claimed by theorists such as free-marketeer Friedrich Hayek, could be used to increase freedom for the great majority of laborers. "Not only conditions in the factory, hours of work, and modalities of contract, but the basic wage itself, are determined outside the market; what role accrues thereby to trade unions, state, and other public bodies depends not only on the character of these institutions but also on the actual organization of the management of production," he noted in the final chapter of *The Great Transformation*.

Polanyi believed that unfettered markets had a tendency to destroy the cultures and institutions out of which they grew—a process that, he believed, had led to World War I and then to the disastrous chain of political events and economic crises that had culminated in the rise of Fascism and the catastrophe of another world war. Rein markets in, Polanyi warned, or risk collapse. By all means, nurture and preserve the dynamism that markets injected into society, the theorist argued, but don't for one minute be fooled into thinking that all societal problems, all of the tensions generated by poverty, upheaval, hunger, or uncertainty, would, *or even could*, disappear as markets expanded into all corners of life.

Polanyi's ideas would have been familiar not only to liberal American presidents such as Lyndon Johnson, but also to conservative leaders such as Richard Nixon, men who came of age during the Great Depression and the run-up to world war, who served in that war, and who knew firsthand the horrors that had been unleashed by economic chaos. In the halls of power in the postwar decades, a broad consensus held that one of the state's core functions was to either slow down the destruction of markets unfettered or to subsidize the incomes and benefits of those whose livelihoods had been irrevocably damaged, or stunted from the get-go, by sweeping market changes.

Skip forward forty years, however, and in many political circles that concern with addressing the needs of the worst-off, and with wrestling with markets' imperfections, had largely vanished.

In the post–Cold War world—a triumphalist environment that the political scientist Francis Fukuyama notoriously labeled "the end of history"—there were, quite simply, few to no breaks placed on the machinations of markets. The result was both a philosophical and practical breakdown in many of the networks of laws, regulatory agencies, and cultural practices designed to tame markets. The crisis that ensued is as much an existential one—of identity—as a practical economic mess. Increasingly, we have lost the language to explain exactly *why* market-generated inequality is a problem—and, by extension, why widespread poverty poses a challenge to the body politic.

WALLING OFF THE POOR

In part, America's poverty epidemic is a failure of imagination—we haven't invested enough energy into understanding the causes and the manifestations of poverty in today's United States, or into imagining alternatives. In part, though, it's a failure of empathy—we haven't as a society worked out *why* we should care. Too many people either believe they have no obligations to the broader community or do not understand the consequences that follow when public infrastructure is allowed to crumble. That is the point raised by then–Harvard Law School professor Elizabeth Warren, whose work led to the creation of the U.S. Consumer Financial Protection Bureau, in her critique of businesspeople who didn't want to pay their fair share of taxes and who didn't believe that the state played any role in their success. Even a self-made man, she explained to an audience in 2011—at the start of her successful campaign for the U.S. Senate—used publicly funded roads to truck his goods to market, hired workers educated in publicly funded schools, and relied on publicly funded police forces for security and firefighters for putting out fires. "Part of the underlying social contract," she continued, "is you take a hunk of that [profit] and pay forward for the next kid who comes along."[21]

This point should be easy to grasp. But too often those connections aren't made. The sense of a community bound together both in good times and in bad eludes us. Tom Costanza, executive director of the Office of Justice and Peace at the Catholic Charities chapter in New Orleans, commented on the dispiriting poverty data routinely generated by the Big Easy, explaining of poverty's growth, "it should ring alarms all over New Orleans, and the nation really. We've had systematic poverty before, here in New Orleans. But poverty is increasing nationwide."

Costanza talked of low-income communities inundated with returning prisoners and drug dealers, of neighborhoods swamped by violence, of huge numbers of kids whose mothers and fathers were behind bars. And he also spoke of the desperate need for more investment in the people and infrastructure of these neighborhoods, in mentoring programs for children, and in job training and education, rather than simply in the building of more prisons.

You might have heard of the term "the checkerboard neighborhoods." In a lot of ways, New Orleans is strong that way. We've lived together. But we absolutely have pockets of poverty—and now it's spreading more to suburban areas—to Jefferson Parish, to the suburbs. Also rural poverty; we have a fairly large diocese. The percentage of poverty is higher in the rural counties and parishes. It's a serious concern for us, say, in Washington Parish, where there's not much economics driving things. We have challenges geographically. It's spreading; it's not just an urban phenomenon. We see the homeless population increasing; food banks run low. If you talk to our food bank directors, they'll tell you it's a continuing challenge to keep the banks stocked.

In our imagination, we hermetically seal off this kind of saga from the broader American story. We like to think that the "pockets" of poverty referred to by Costanza are just that: isolated pockets in a land of plenty. That sense of the poor being somehow "different" probably had a lot to do with how the food pantry worker outside of New Orleans could answer my query for people to interview with the disclaimer that too many minorities were coming to her pantry from New Orleans, were taking food and clothes, and were then selling them in flea markets in the Big Easy. Alternately, she believed, they were taking clothes only to ship them to relatives in

Latin America. It was, she informed me bitterly, a journey, dealing with racial minorities on a daily basis. They were manipulative, untrustworthy, out to make a quick buck. She wanted to introduce me to the *right* kind of person—which I got the strong impression meant the *white* kind of person—not to any old riffraff. And yet, despite her distrust of racial minorities—her fear that black and brown people just wanted to rip her, and her community, off—day after day she returned to volunteer at the pantry. At some subconscious level she realized that the stories of the people she worked with just couldn't be hermetically sealed off from her own life experiences. The poverty she saw terrified her and stoked up a host of bigotries and stereotypes. But at some level she recognized how intricately her own story was tied up with that of the destitute people of whom she was so scared.

Nowhere is the attempt to wall off the poor as having, somehow, separate narratives from the rest of us more overt than in the roiling politics around illegal immigration. Many observers have noted that starving public institutions of cash is a pastime that state electorates sign off on during times in which populaces are in flux. Smaller, more homogenous populations rarely vote to defund social safety nets and educational infrastructure that they see as benefiting mainly people culturally, linguistically, and racially more like themselves. When, by contrast, public goods are seen mainly as benefiting "others," people who are blacker and browner, who don't speak English well, and who have a different set of cultural references, then support for the public sector wobbles.

That's a theme well developed by the California journalist Peter Schrag in books such as *California: America's High-Stakes Experiment*. Schrag describes something akin to a breakdown in collective empathy, and a growing sense, based more on illusion than reality, that the taxes paid by one group are going to fund the benefits received by others. No accident, this analysis goes, that social democratic systems emerged in historically homogenous countries such as Sweden; no accident, either, that as those countries have absorbed more immigrants in recent years, more "others," so support for the comprehensive welfare state has shown signs of stress. It's an issue that Harvard University's Richard Parker also deems to be critically important. Large pools of undocumented immigrants and transient workers, he says, make it that much harder to generate mass support for institutions seen as somehow illegitimately rewarding these families for their illegal entry into, or stay within the borders of, America. And as with southern Louisiana parishes and the racism of some of their residents, oftentimes the most extreme politics on immigration comes from people who live in close proximity to, and experience the daily presence of, undocumented populations.

FIGHTING TALK

In a televised debate in 2010, Arizona state senator Russell Pearce, author of the nation's toughest anti–illegal immigration law, argued that the Constitution "does give the federal government the responsibility to protect the states from invasion. But it's right also in the Constitution, it says, when there is an invasion the states have a right, even—even to declare war if you will, you know, they have a right to protect. And again, we're sovereign states, I mean, just like everybody here. We're not citizens of the United States. We use that term, well, we're actually citizens of one of the several sovereign states."[22] Pearce, who strongly felt that Arizona was, indeed, suffering an invasion, believed that there ought to be a moratorium on all forms of immigration into the country, be it legal or illegal; that the right to citizenship for those born in the United States should be modified to exclude children of illegal aliens; and that such children should be barred from all state benefits—including access to education and healthcare. His bill gave police in Arizona the power to demand residency papers of anyone they suspected of being in the country illegally—a vague criteria that, not surprisingly, immediately ran into a barrage of litigation—and was specifically crafted to scare large numbers of immigrants into moving away from Arizona. It was a clumsy law, unsubtle in its requirements, and likely to lead to almost as many problems, almost as many run-ins with law enforcement, for "legitimate" immigrants as for their undocumented neighbors. But for Pearce, a onetime sheriff's deputy in Maricopa County, it was a call to arms. "I will not back off until we solve the problem of this illegal invasion," Pearce averred during a National Public Radio interview in 2008. "Invaders, that's what they are. Invaders on the American sovereignty and it can't be tolerated."

For Fox News pundit Glenn Beck, "If there's a reason to suspect that you're in the country illegally, why wouldn't I ask? Citizenship is valuable; the Statue of Liberty says I hold my torch before a golden door. You don't put a golden door on an outhouse. You put it on someplace special. Citizenship is something to be cherished. We're not citizens of the world; we're citizens of the United States. At least right now, we still are."[23]

Life, though, is rarely as black-and-white as men like Russell Pearce and Glenn Beck make it out to be. Like it or not, the reality is that many millions of undocumented migrants consider America to be their home; that no deportation program could possibly deport so many people; and that unless their children are schooled and provided healthcare and other vital assistance, the effects will be felt throughout society over the decades to come. Any meaningful anti-poverty movement will, therefore, have to first convince a majority of Americans that the undocumented ought to be worthy of help; and, second, ensure that immigration reform—through moves such as the DREAM Act—is a core part of its strategy. For whatever one's theoretical take on immigration—whether one favors a route to legalization, or an emphasis on border control and the deportation of the undocumented; whether one believes that the initial act of illegal entry into the United States renders all subsequent actions moot, or whether one judges the undocumented by how they act and live once in the country—in reality many millions of undocumented residents will likely continue to live in America for the foreseeable future. And thus, for the foreseeable future, any discussion of American poverty is going to, in part at least, overlap with discussions on immigration.

Talking about the events that led to her arrival in the United States as one of the millions of undocumented immigrants fleeing violence and economic devastation south of the border in the 1990s and 2000s, Maria explained, "I came because my daughter died," speaking in Spanish, via a translator, in a community center in downtown Albuquerque. "My youngest daughter and myself were threatened with our lives." In Albuquerque, Maria eventually found work caring for an elderly person as a live-in help. She and her teenage daughter Yasmin found themselves on call pretty much around the clock.

> I worked to have a place to live and for food. The church, the family I worked for, gave me clothing, articles I needed. Sometimes the service providers who came to the person's home, the nurses, would bring gift certificates, things they bought at Walmart. I don't speak English, have education. I don't have a grand thing that I can say is mine. I don't have a house. I don't have a bank account. I don't have any money saved. There's not enough. I'll keep working while I can. My life scares me. I look at the people I work for and think about how I have seen some people treat them. I worry, because what will happen to me when I'm old? I want to study; I want to be a nurse. That's my biggest dream.

Dotted through the West and Southwest, illegal immigration encampments have been built up in recent years. Cumulatively, many hundreds of thousands of men, women, and children now live in these communities. The buildings are basic: third-hand trailers; wooden, cardboard, and tin shacks. The amenities are improvised: some are hooked up to the power grid, water delivery systems, and sewage lines after the fact—a de facto acknowledgment by local counties of their existence, even absent zoning permits and ownership titles. Others are more haphazard; pirated electricity, water trucked in from miles away, septic tanks in place of sewage pipes, kerosene stoves in place of gas pipes. They are desolate places, overcrowded and underserviced, as rife with sickness and despair as the tenement slums of New York photographed by Jacob Riis more than a century ago.

Living in abject poverty, America's undocumented are peculiarly susceptible to disease, to criminal victimization, to workplace exploitation, to living in shanties and colonias. And ultimately, none of the problems that percolate in these environments long remain sealed off within the world of the undocumented. Crime, disease, economic dislocation—all eventually percolate out from their epicenters. When sociologist Katherine Newman, a widely published author on poverty in America, and dean of the Zanvyl Krieger School of Arts and Sciences at Johns Hopkins University, analyzed data about states with the highest tax burdens on poor families, she found that not only did these states also have higher poverty rates, but most of them had higher crime rates as well as a larger percentage of their population incarcerated. Higher crime rates affect not only poor neighborhoods but entire regions; higher incarceration rates—even if, as many conservative analysts have concluded, disproportionately accounted for by the numbers of undocumented immigrants who end up behind bars—have to be paid for by all taxpayers. And, as anyone who has studied incarceration can tell you, locking people up doesn't come cheap. In fact, in most states, it costs about as much money to keep someone in prison for one year as it would cost to send that person to an Ivy League university.

For broad public health and safety reasons, as well as simple budgetary math, any twenty-first-century movement to tackle poverty will have to propose solutions not only to the ingrained hardship of the Lower Ninth Wards of America, but also to the problems of the undocumented. In the same way as those in New Orleans marginalized by the wider society present a set of specific challenges to those interested in tackling poverty in America, so too the undocumented need to be unmarginalized. That is not just a matter of altruism; rather, because of the financial impacts of problems that originate in impoverished communities, it is a matter of profound self-interest for the wider population. The undocumented must be integrated as much as possible into the broader economy, while at the same time the country works out ways to regain control over its borders, so as to prevent a reemergence down the line of the entrenched poverty of today's undocumented populations.

Such is the political balancing act around immigration that a modern-day war on poverty must engage in. It isn't easy, but it *is* vital.

"We have thousands of people crossing into the United States to look for agricultural work in this region. It's something historic, not created from one day to the other," said Sin Frontera's Carlos Marentes in El Paso, Texas, as he walked along the lonely, early morning, detritus-strewn streets lining the U.S.-Mexican border.

On a day here, we have hundreds of workers coming to this area next to the international border looking for work, and labor agents coming looking for workers. By one or two in the morning, you have many workers looking for work and many employers looking for the most productive workers. In general, the wages of farm workers in the United States are bad. Here, in particular, they are *really* bad. A farm worker who wakes up at midnight and sets off for the fields at one or two in the morning, and returns to El Paso at four or five or six P.M. It's so many hours, and they bring in from the fields $20 or $30. They get paid on a piece-rate basis.

Most of the farm worker families lack a permanent place to live. The farm workers' center is a place where farm workers can spend the night; during the summer we have whole families using the center as a shelter. They don't have access to health. Their children don't have access to education. Most of the farm workers quit school at a very early age, to work in the fields and add to the income of the households. In March of this year, we did a survey, where we were developing a plan for our kitchen—because we cook every day for the farm workers when they are coming back from the fields. We did a survey of three hundred farm workers; the first question was, "How many days of the week do you not have food in your home?" The majority answered that during the winter they are having problems to feed their families. When we asked, "How many times a day do you have something to eat?" the answer was once a day.

The twenty-first-century farm workers in Southwestern border towns have much in common with immigrant sweatshop workers or meatpackers living in tenements in New York or Chicago a hundred years ago. In their hand-to-mouth existences, they live lives similar to those of sharecroppers in the post–Civil War South. In the anger hurled at them by men such as Russell Pearce are echoes of the rage and contempt directed against migrants from the 1930s Dust Bowl along the highways leading westward. Rage mixed with fear: fear of impoverished immigrants bidding down the wages of local workers; of diseases brought into communities by malnourished, nomadic migrants; and of crimes carried out by young, hungry desperadoes.

The faces of those living along society's margins have changed over the decades, but the stories behind those faces remain fundamentally the same. The moral challenge posed in Jacob Riis's documentation of tenements is similar to that captured by Dorothea Lange's camera and to that articulated by Bobby Kennedy in describing hunger in the Mississippi Delta. And it is essentially the same as that detailed by Carlos Marentes in El Paso or Tom Costanza in New Orleans today.

It is a challenge that cries out for government intervention. Yet too often, that intervention is either lacking or unsuited to the great needs of the moment.

CHAPTER FOUR

THE FRAGILE SAFETY NET

Burned out high school in North Philadelphia.

For Jessica Bartholow, a Sacramento-based legislative advocate for the Western Center on Law and Poverty, the stories of dysfunctional or inadequate government systems failing to raise people out of poverty, as well as of public opprobrium toward the poor, had become a dime a dozen. No matter how hard her organization worked on anti-poverty initiatives the need for help seemed to grow on a daily basis.

Put simply, America's safety net, never particularly munificent to begin with, was showing itself unable to adequately meet the cascading needs triggered by the rolling collapse, over several decades, of wages at the bottom of the economy; the post-2008 unemployment crisis; and the massive loss of assets so many families lived through as the housing market disintegrated.

Welfare systems in states with a social safety net exist to mitigate the worst excesses of poverty. That's the theory, anyway. The post–World War II Keynesian state was crafted on the understanding that markets required management. The components of that state were supposed to act counter-cyclically, increasing in availability during those months, or years, when the economy hits the skids, serving to iron out the kinks in inherently volatile, dynamic, market economies, and thus providing something of a firewall against a growth in severe poverty during downturns.

In practice, that's never really been the case. While the countries of Western Europe, during the austere post–World War II years in which welfare systems were fully developed, embraced the notion of cradle-to-the-grave security for citizens, America chose not to go down that path. Southern and rural politicians, in particular, stood as blocks in the way of comprehensive reforms. As a result, what progress *has* been made toward securing government benefits to the needy as a right of citizenship—during the New Deal years, and in the 1960s, in particular—was made in the face of southern and rural opposition rather than with their blessing, and was left permanently vulnerable to conservative political winds. In recent years, those winds have torn gaping holes in the safety net.

Bartholow herself, the daughter of a Vietnam veteran who suffered from severe posttraumatic stress disorder, had grown up in chronic poverty. She had carved out for herself a career working at the center of California state politics on issues that she passionately cared about. Ideally, her group lobbied to increase resources for nutritional assistance for the poor, to make welfare benefits more accessible, to expand subsidized healthcare, the network of affordable housing units, community mental health clinics, and so on. In practice, in recent years, the work had been all about preventing more cuts rather than increasing resources. In a particularly discouraging encounter, she recalled, the Republican Party's House minority leader had blasted the safety net as a "hammock with cute little drinks with umbrellas." Presumably he meant this opaque comment to reflect his belief that welfare recipients were simply having sun-drenched vacations at state expense. Ironically, Bartholow noted, he came from Tulare County, the poorest county in California, with, she said, 12.9 percent of the population on the CalWORKs welfare program.

A disabled state employee had phoned Bartholow to tell her that she was losing her job, was about to lose her home, and needed help finding transitional housing until she could find a more affordable place to live. "There wasn't a place to send her other than the Salvation Army shelter," said Bartholow. "There isn't anywhere in between. That's the current state of our safety net program right now. If we keep food in the refrigerator for three weeks out of the month, we've achieved what we can right now. We force people to become very, very poor before we are able to help them."

FINGERS IN THE DIKE

In the post-2008 milieu, and especially in the conservative, budget-cutting environment prevailing after the 2010 midterm elections, many parts of the country's welfare system have actually ceased to have any real impact on poverty numbers. President Obama's administration, in the years following 2008, did a good job of protecting what remained of the safety net for those who lost jobs in the recession; it did a far less solid job, however, of protecting both the long-term poor and the very poorest of the poor at the bottom from budget cuts.

Hence the fact that, once American Recovery and Reinvestment Act dollars dried up in 2011, job training programs were decimated; many food programs ended up running on fumes; many community health and mental health clinics, drug treatment centers, and homeless shelters had to shutter their doors or limit their clientele to those already on their rosters.

For advocates such as Ed Shurna, executive director of the Chicago Coalition for the Homeless, the trends were dispiriting. In 2012, his organization had had to fight to reverse a 52 percent cut in funding for the state's emergency shelters, implemented as a part of a package of cuts to deal with Illinois's catastrophic budget deficit. They had succeeded, but the numbers of homeless were growing so astronomically that he felt his organization was, at best, always playing catch-up. "It's just been cutting and cutting and cutting, and there's no end in sight," Shurna explained. "There's very few stories of people we have who are able to leave homelessness, get a decent job, and pay for rent without some kind of assistance." And yet, adequate levels of assistance weren't forthcoming.

> People accept homelessness as just a condition of modern society; "Yeah, people are going to fall through the cracks." And then we blame the individuals for that failure. We don't think there's a problem with the system itself. But the mark of who's homeless is just somebody who's poor. And in Chicago, it's people of color— primarily African Americans, and secondarily Latinos. It would take a sea change over the next twenty-five years in thinking in this country to turn around the idea that government doesn't have a role to play in protecting needy people.

Absent that sea change, Shurna worried that his organization was simply putting fingers into a broken-down dike and watching the floodwaters surge around the plugged hole and through the nearby gaps. No matter how hard he worked to counter homelessness, the need grew. It was an endless, Sisyphean battle against chronic, hardcore poverty. Shurna felt, he said, like the man in the fable who threw one beached starfish, out of hundreds, back into the sea, and humbly said, "At least that one starfish got help."

Ninety-two thousand Chicagoans could expect to be homeless during the course of a year, and on any given night fully 21,000 would be sleeping in improvised accommodations. "You have to create more affordable housing for working poor people," Shurna argued, sitting behind his desk on the seventh floor of a large office building in the heart of Chicago's Loop. "The other solution is the service jobs have to be paying more than they're paying now." To really tackle homelessness, he knew that "you'd have to have a massive jobs program that paid decent wages." He also knew that wasn't about to happen.

In 2010, Chicago authorities had calculated that 14,000 school kids would be homeless in the city at some point that year. By 2011, that number had increased to 16,000—more than 3,000 of whom weren't even living with an adult. In fact, the advocate fretted, every year from 2005 onward the number of homeless kids in his city had dramatically risen. Nothing suggested to him that trend was about to be reversed.

WELFARE, WEIGHT LOSS, AND THE INVISIBLE WORKING CLASS

In 1965, the author Philip Stern had written about America's priorities before the onset of the War on Poverty, excoriating the country for spending "more for the care of migrant birds than for the care of migrant humans," and for a culture in which it was acceptable that 98.5 percent of new homes built were unaffordable for low-income Americans. Forty years later, after decades of underinvestment in affordable housing, one in twenty Americans, and one in six families who rented homes, were living in what the government described as "worst case" housing situations, with incomes at less than half the local median income, and having to pay more than half of that paltry income toward housing.[1]

As for what the country was spending on fripperies: at a time when vital social services were being slashed, Americans in 2007 spent $41 billion on their pets. "More than the gross domestic product of all but 64 countries in the world," the Business Week journalists Diane Brady and Christopher Palmeri dryly noted. Four years later, with the country mired in the after-effects of the financial collapse, and with the number of desperately poor Americans skyrocketing, that number had risen to $51 billion, nearly double the total federal and state expenditures on Temporary Aid to Needy Families.[2] Americans spent more than $40 billion per year on maintaining their garden lawns[3] and another $40 billion-plus annually on weight loss products.[4] Close to half a million cosmetic liposuction surgeries were being performed annually by the early twenty-first century.[5] And according to ABC News, as of 2011 more than 2,000 Americans were signed up to be cryogenically frozen, at a cost of $30,000 per person, after their deaths.[6] In 2003, Business Wire estimated that Americans were spending $12 billion annually on tanning salon visits and tanning products.[7] That's roughly the same as the amount that was being spent annually on renting and purchasing porn movies at the time.[8]

The result of all these changes in the national mood, and in the spending priorities that accompanied it: a social structure that in many ways had more in common with India than with other first-world industrial democracies, with joblessness, homelessness, and lack of access to healthcare becoming simply a part of life for millions of Americans, even while those at the top of the economy built ever bigger homes, spent ever more on luxuries and absurdities, and accumulated ever more capital. The most unequal states, according to American Community Survey data put out by the Census Bureau in 2011, were New York, California, Connecticut, Louisiana, Mississippi, Texas, and Alabama, along with the District of Columbia. Throughout almost the entire South, by 2009 upward of 17 percent of the population, and 23 percent of children, lived in poverty.[9] Many large urban areas, including New York; Washington, D.C.; Atlanta; and Dallas also saw the rise of particularly skewed income distributions.[10]

By the time the economy had the rug pulled out from under it in 2008, the plight of America's poor had become something of a political footnote. Lacking money, the poor tended to lack political clout; lacking organization, they tended to become invisible. Even as the numbers of poor soared, a political commitment to tackling poverty remained elusive. Democrats tended to simply ignore the scale of the problem, defending the largest safety net programs (Social Security, Medicare, Medicaid) while turning a blind eye to the dismantling of other parts of the system, touting relatively small declines in unemployment while only half-heartedly defending extended unemployment benefits for those millions who still couldn't find work. Republicans, as the party swung rightward, increasingly took gleeful swipes at programs aimed at the poor. In Maine, a newly elected Tea Party governor, Paul LePage, set out an agenda to dismantle much of the state's anti-poverty infrastructure; among other destructive policies, his budget proposals went after free medical coverage for thousands of low-income residents and shattered the state's preventive health systems for the poor. In South Carolina, GOP leaders in early 2012 pushed through legislation requiring applicants for unemployment benefits to pass a drug test, and then requiring them to "volunteer" sixteen hours per week to access these benefits.[11]

———

For 50-year-old Raquel, a mother of two who was laid off from her data-entry job in a working-class suburb of Los Angeles during the recession, navigating the increasingly coercive welfare system had become a desperate endeavor.

Raquel's employer hadn't paid into the unemployment insurance program, and so she wasn't eligible to receive unemployment benefits. She ran through her savings, borrowed what she could from almost equally hard-pressed relatives, applied for food stamps, and ultimately managed to qualify for the CalWORKs program. Cal-WORKs is the state's version of TANF, and at the time Raquel accessed it, it had already gone through years of budget cuts. Recipients were limited to forty-eight months on the program; but, increasingly, there was talk of cutting this to twenty-four. Moreover, the amount they received during these months kept being reduced. Every four weeks, Raquel was sent a check for $317, $200 of which immediately went to the rent she paid to stay in her brother's house, the rest of which vanished buying household necessities.

Raquel had applied for dozens of jobs; but, caught in the vise of recession, she had ended up with nothing. To stay eligible for that CalWORKS money, Raquel now had to spend hours a week doing community service jobs—mainly interviewing clients who came to a nearby community center, MEND, in the gritty town of Pacoima, to see if they would qualify for charitable assistance.

It was, in a way, lucky that she was there. The CalWORKS payments were so small that she never had any cash left over for food—which meant that she had to make the $300 she got in food stamps last an entire month. And because her two sons were both going through puberty and eating her out of house and home, that was never possible. Each month, about a week before she received her next installment of food stamps, Raquel would have to shamefacedly ask her MEND employers for a box of food to tide her over. For three or four days, the family would have just about enough to eat; no meat, but enough canned goods to throw together a few meals. For the last few days of the month, however, they'd frequently go hungry. No matter how she scrimped and saved, it was, said Raquel, "a struggle trying to make the meal."

By the winter of 2012, when I met her, Raquel had been out of work for close to eighteen months. There was talk of ending CalWORKs as a way of plugging California's vast budget hole; there was more talk about keeping the program but reducing the number of months people could receive benefits and chopping even more dollars from those benefits. Both scenarios filled Raquel with terror. If the program was cut, she worried, "I don't know what all of us would do. They want us to work, but if there is nothing out there how are we going to do it?"

HOW MANY HOLES CAN YOU POKE IN A NET BEFORE IT'S JUST A HOLE?

In recent years, as the political climate has grown more conservative, and government finances have worsened, the American welfare system has increasingly shed itself of what were once considered key obligations. Accessing core benefits such as TANF has been made ever more difficult, in terms of the severity of the means tests imposed, the work requirements, and the add-on difficulties that some states tack on, such as drug-testing applicants and charging fees for the application. What does this mean in practice? Let's look at a few examples: in Arkansas, despite unemployment increasing from 68,700 in December 2007 to 107,200 three years later, the number of families on TANF dropped by 100 families. In Missouri, unemployment increased by more than 75 percent, but TANF enrollments also fell slightly. In Florida, the TANF caseload went up by about $10,000, but the number of unemployed in the state increased by nearly 700,000. Moreover, total TANF expenditures in Florida in the ten years preceding 2011 had declined by well over $100 million.[12] The same trends held true around the country. At the same time as it became harder to access TANF, the value of the benefits for those who *did* manage to access them declined. In all but two states, benefit levels as of 2012 were below what they were in 1996 (and by 1996, most states had already been cutting the real value of their welfare benefits for a quarter century); and in no state in the country did the maximum TANF benefit get a family above 50 percent of the federally defined poverty line.

Let's stick with this a bit longer. At the height of the recession, throughout most of the South TANF benefit levels declined to a mere one-fifth to one-tenth of the poverty line. In Mississippi, that meant that a family of four was averaging less than $200 a month in benefits. Tennessee, Arkansas, Alabama, South Carolina, Louisiana, Texas, Kentucky, North Carolina, Arizona, Georgia, Indiana, Missouri, Oklahoma, and Florida didn't do much better; all had combined benefits that came to less than 20 percent, or, for a family of four, $4,500 annually, of the federal poverty guideline.[13]

Perhaps not coincidentally, in many of these states tax systems were peculiarly regressive, with income and property taxed at very low rates, and with sales taxes—which take a disproportionate percentage of the cash available to low-income Americans—filling in the revenue gaps. In other words, the meager benefits available to poor Alabamans or Mississippians, say, were rendered still more meager by the fact that staple goods such as food, purchased with these benefits, were made more expensive by the imposition of state taxes.

During the recession unleashed by the housing market collapse and fiscal meltdown of 2007–08, unemployment more than doubled in many states, yet, to reiterate the point, in most states the number of TANF enrollees increased either by a few percentage points only or actually decreased. Tiny Rhode Island's welfare rolls went from 10,900 at the start of the recession to a mere 6,800 by the end of 2010. In a two-year period, Indiana saw the number of unemployed in the state more than double, from the end of 2007 through the end of 2009, while its welfare rolls were reduced by 10 percent. In Georgia, while the number of unemployed increased from 245,200 at the end of 2007 to nearly half a million by the end of 2010, TANF rolls during this period went down from 22,700 to 20,700. Nebraska also reduced its welfare rolls during these hardscrabble years, as did North Carolina, North Dakota, and several other states.[14]

"In 1994–95, for every 100 families with children in poverty, the AFDC program served 75 families," researchers from the Center on Budget and Policy Priorities (CBPP) concluded in September 2011. "In 2008–09, only 28 families with children participated in TANF for every 100 families in poverty." In Arkansas, that number was a mere 9 percent by the end of 2009; in Mississippi, 12 percent; in Alabama, 15 percent.

In California, the most populous state in the union, the Western Center on Law and Poverty estimated that 22 percent of kids were living at or below the poverty line in 2012, but only 3 percent were on TANF, and only one in five within that 3 percent actually received the maximum level of benefits. Many of these kids' families, having nowhere else to turn, ended up on food lines. They were a mixture, said Jessica Jones of the Los Angeles Food Bank, of "the people who did everything right and had the rug pulled out from under them, and the people who were already struggling [and] are struggling even more. When I first started [working at the food bank] in December 2008, we served 39 million pounds of food. In 2010, we did 62 million pounds of food. The number of people we serve has gone up by 73 percent since the recession started."

By the end of 2011, the real value of TANF was lower than it was in 1996 in every state except Maryland and Wyoming—which had preserved the value of the benefits it awarded but had made it almost impossible for families to enroll in the first place. In the entire state, only a few hundred people were on TANF as of 2012. Moreover, the nationwide fall-off in benefits post-1996 didn't tell the full story: in the quarter century prior to the creation of TANF, AFDC benefits had also fallen across the country—by more than 20 percent, according to CBPP, in all but one state; by more than 40 percent in two-thirds of the states.[15] By 2012, benefits had, as a result, been in a state of steady decline for four decades.

Even in the state of New York, which had preserved more "generous" welfare payments than any other state, a family of three could access a maximum of $753 a month in TANF, far shy of what was required to get such families even close to the federal poverty line. And in New York City, to access that money, a series of "reforms" pushed by Mayors Rudy Giuliani and then Michael Bloomberg, meant that even in the depth of the recession a recipient had to spend approximately thirty-five hours per week in what was ambitiously termed a "back to work" program. In reality, argued welfare rights advocates, despite its offices supposedly being equipped with numerous computers to help people on their job searches and staffed by numerous counselors to help people navigate the often-intimidating terrain of the employment market, this was little more than a sit-on-your-hands-and-twiddle-your-thumbs holding area. It was, said Barbara Zerzan, a woman who had worked on poverty-related themes in the city since the 1970s and who, in 2012, was an employee of a group called the East River Development Alliance, "like the rubber room. People lose it and just stop going. There's insane fall-off." People who were clearly poor enough to qualify for cash assistance instead were going without rather than enduring the humiliation of this process. "So most people end up not getting public assistance, even though they've applied and are eligible for it. They get Medicaid and food stamps, but not cash assistance. So they do things, commit crimes, fall behind on their rent. It's a real disaster."

If, somehow, they made it through several weeks of sitting on their hands seven hours each weekday, then they were channeled into WEP, New York's version of workfare. In that capacity, they'd end up doing jobs such as park maintenance and street cleaning that in bygone years would have paid decent salaries to unionized workers.

For Zerzan, it was one of the most discouraging cycles that she had seen in all her years working on poverty in the Big Apple. "You're either at WEP or in the room doing nothing for your entire work week," she explained of the men and women her organization campaigned on behalf of. "You're not allowed to look for a job or go to your kid's school or anything. It's so insane." It was, she felt, little more than a shell game: an expensive, bureaucratic system that claimed to encourage poor people to look for employment but that, in reality, made it extremely hard for them to do so, and, in so doing, oftentimes pushed them away from cash aid that they were legally entitled to. "I told my kids recently: 'My goal is to eliminate poverty and to work on social justice. I'm a complete failure.' It's gone from bad to worse. There's no humanity."

A similarly dispiriting situation existed in Michigan, home to some of the country's most depressed Rust Belt communities. In towns such as Flint, unemployment was rife, drug addiction and involvement with the criminal justice system was commonplace, and undereducation was a daily part of life. Illiteracy rates were stunningly high—in Genessee County, of which Flint was a part, about one in five adults were functionally illiterate, and amongst the welfare population estimates ranged as high as 70 percent. Tied in with that, many workers, left unemployed by the closure of auto factories and other heavy industries from the 1970s onward, didn't have the skills needed to find new employment. What jobs there were tended to pay in the $8 an hour range, despite the fact that the Michigan League for Human Services estimated that for a family of four both parents would have to be working full time and earning at least $10.71 per hour in order for that family to have a modicum of economic security. Few workers in the area had the skills needed to secure them decently paying jobs.

And yet, said Alicia Booker, an employee of the Mott Foundation whose mandate was to focus on work issues, the state's workfare system didn't allow people to study for a GED or receive other basic education training in lieu of hours worked. Private foundations such as Mott and the Open Society Foundation pumped significant sums of money into programs such as Earn and Learn, which subsidized the wages of workers hired by local companies in Flint in exchange for those individuals committing themselves to job retraining. But those programs only ever were Band-Aids, providing jobs and training to a few hundred people in a community with thousands of desperate, out of work laborers.

For those who didn't get into such programs, prospects were increasingly bleak. In the 2011–12 fiscal year, the state's Workforce Investment Act funds were cut by 21 percent, or $4 million. One consequence: During the years in which federal dollars from the American Reinvestment and Recovery Act flowed to Flint, 1,100 teenagers were provided with summer employment; in 2012, by contrast, with federal funds having dried up and with state cuts having kicked in, summer jobs for at-risk teens were all but eliminated. "In Flint, the murder capital of the world," Booker caustically stated, "giving 1,100 kids employment makes a difference."[16] She continued: "One of the things the TANF community in our area needs is literacy." But because GED training wasn't considered to count toward hours worked, there was no incentive built in for the recipients of this aid to get more education. "What they need the most is considered non-core, nonessential. And so the cycle repeats."

Increasingly, the poorest of the poor have found that they cannot access educational programs, or they have discovered that in pursuing education and not working the required number of hours to qualify for TANF they are excluding themselves from access to the cash economy.

RUNNING UPHILL

This is not merely a kink in the system, but a fundamental flaw in the design of the modern-day American safety net. Caught at the intersection of politics and economic malfunction, millions of American families are now almost totally excluded from the cash economy.

For many of them, simply getting up to the poverty line is an impossibility; they live in what the government terms "deep poverty," accessing cash and cash-equivalent benefits that don't even bring them up to half of the poverty threshold. Nearly 3 million children now live in households in which each person has less than $2 per day to spend.[17]

As Jessica Bartholow of the Western Center on Law and Poverty puts it, this is a grievous state of affairs. "Below 50 percent of the poverty line, we're putting kids in extreme danger—they're going to the hospital more often, missing school, missing opportunity at a great rate." At that level of poverty, the basic realities of daily life become so difficult to navigate that people end up facing not just temporary hardships but permanent handicaps. They are more susceptible to life-threatening food-borne diseases such as cysticercosis, and, because of the poor housing and sanitary conditions that they face, are more likely to become infected by, and to have to live with, insect-borne sicknesses such as dengue fever and Chagas disease.[18] Exposed to deep poverty as a child, a person is likely to grow into adulthood burdened with poor health, lower life expectancy than their wealthier peers, inadequate education, possibly low self-esteem. For people born and raised in deep poverty, the playing field has not been leveled; they are, quite simply, left to run uphill throughout their often-truncated lives.

It's the opposite of a virtuous circle. Witness, for example, the trajectory described by community organizer Gloria Dickerson, who had returned to her hometown of Drew from the state capital of Jackson to work with impoverished residents on bettering their lives. The Mississippi Delta town that she worked in, said Dickerson, looked like

> neighborhoods with a lot of blight; people who are feeling hopeless; people stuck in their place; a place where the educational levels are very low because the schools are not performing well. The infrastructure is deteriorating—the roads: potholes. People want to do

better, but people feel like they don't have a way out. They find ways to accept the way they live. They're stressed, because of a lack of money to pay the utility bills, water bills, put food on the table. A lot are dependent on low-income housing, food stamps. It looks like children who are probably more hopeful than the adults, but they're looking for someone to help them succeed. They want good schools; they want to be able to be successful.

In Drew, half of the kids didn't graduate high school—and the schools themselves had been taken over by the state. "There are no extra-curriculum activities in the school. The kids are feeling like they're not learning what they need to learn; the teachers aren't doing what they are supposed to be doing; the administrators aren't doing what they are supposed to be doing; the adults aren't taking care of the kids in terms of education; the parents aren't involved in the schools. The schools are lacking in funding and lacking in resources." Many of the kids simply dropped out, ran the streets, ended up in trouble with the law.

"We have a lot of lockup of children in the Drew area. If they're not going to Parchman, a state penitentiary seven miles north of Drew, they're being locked up in town jails, county jails. A lot of it is for drug use. The parents have really given up. They say 'We don't know what to do, how to help these children.' They are unemployed; they're trying to find some ways to enjoy life. They enjoy parties and coronations and basketball games. However, when you talk about things that affect their lives—like politics and community organizing—most of them talk about '*They* should do this,' or '*You* should do that,' rather than coming together as a community."

Most of it, said Dickerson, was "generational poverty; the attitudes have been handed down from generation to generation. 'I can't.' 'It's too hard.' 'Nobody's going to hire me.' Until people start to have hope and know that things can change, nothing's going to change. Nothing's going to change. So my part is working on the hope, and showing them that things *can* be possible in this town.

We all have to come together in terms of people coming together and talking about 'how can we turn this little town around?' It takes work to turn this thing around. It's a long-term process, but we just gotta keep working on it. We're still fighting."

———

Overwhelmingly, in the aftermath of 2008 politicians of both major parties downplayed the struggles experienced by those such as Raquel, or by the rubber-room WEP workers in New York—those truly at the bottom of the economy. Instead, they declared their concern for the struggling middle classes. It was a turn of phrase that, while being imprecise and elastic enough to include the majority of Americans, couldn't really be interpreted to include those out on the far margins: the long-term unemployed, the homeless, residents of trailer parks and shanty towns, patrons of food pantries and overcrowded free medical clinics.

How, for example, could one consider 43-year-old Frank Nicci, a onetime chef who, in 2008, lost his leg to an infection related to his diabetes, his job because of his ill health, and his home in the hotel at which he worked once he lost his job, part of the middle class?

In the fall of 2011, Nicci was back in the hospital, in the small town of Lewisburg, Pennsylvania, in the Susquehanna Valley, with another diabetes complication, the stump of his amputated leg hidden beneath the thin white hospital sheets. He and his wife, Julie, didn't seem in any hurry to go home; after all, home was now a run-down trailer, and cash was so tight that Frank no longer even had the gas money to go see his 8-year-old son, who lived with his ex an hour or so drive away. Julie worked part-time in a store, Nicci got disability payments. Between the two of them, they brought in under $20,000 a year. "It's very hard, from anyone's standpoint, to make it from week to week, let alone from month to month. She has three children and I have a son. We try to get them once a month, per our custody agreements. But we can't do that, because we don't have the money to get them. Try telling an 8-year-old you can't get them because you don't have the money. It's very devastating, very frustrating."

For Frank and Julie the most basic parts of daily living had become a constant battle. "We don't have the money to put gas in the car. Some months we get behind, you use money for food that you should be using for bills; then your bills get behind and you get shut-off notices. We've got shutoff notices on our electric. It's very hard. We found a place cheaper than what our subsidized housing was, a two-bedroom trailer, and we pay $350 a month in rent. I get discouraged a lot."

Even if he managed to reenter the workforce, Frank would likely spend the rest of his life hobbled by unpayable medical bills and the loss of credit that he experienced because of his inability to get on top of these obligations. For despite being on Medicaid, because he had no secondary coverage he had to pick up 20 percent of his medical expenses.

I'd say over the past four years I probably have $200,000 in health-care bills since I lost my leg. I haven't been paying on them. I have no credit. I don't borrow money. You do without. I skip at least one meal a day. I usually don't eat breakfast, which, for me, is very important. That's probably the most important meal of the day for a diabetic. When I don't eat breakfast I eat more for lunch; it messes with my sugar levels. That's probably part of the reason why I am in the hospital right now. I'm in the hospital because I hadn't been eating properly. I don't eat the right kinds of food, because I can't afford the right kinds. I eat pasta, things that are cheap, things that are easy for my wife to make, that are cheap and easy to buy, and it's not the best food for you. If I had more money I'd eat the right kind of diet, more meat, more protein, cut out some of the foods that I shouldn't be eating. If I had money to buy better foods I would.

Girshriela Green was another person who in no way, shape, or form could be considered a member of the struggling middle class whose collective plight has been the focus of so much political rhetoric in recent years. A onetime Walmart worker from South Central Los Angeles, Green injured her shoulder on the job and ended up on disability, struggling to house and feed herself and the three of her six children who still lived with her, on approximately $1,000 a month in disability and a few hundred dollars worth of food stamps.

Green got her job in 2009 after spending time in California's welfare-to-work program, CalWORKs. She earned slightly over the minimum wage and never managed to build up any savings. Once she had to go on disability, her life became a constant struggle, not to get ahead but simply to avoid falling too far behind on her monthly financial obligations.

"I am surviving, from check to check. I make ends meet. And I substitute or take away what's not necessary. All I can afford are the necessities of taking care of my children and having a roof over their head," explained Girshriela, sitting on a bench outside a small bookstore in her neighborhood as she talked. When she first got the job, she recollected, she earned $8.20 an hour.

> I was a sales-floor associate, I mixed paint in hardware, was in the sporting goods department, cut fabrics, was a cashier in electronics, and I took care of our customers. After tax, I was bringing home $400-and-something every two weeks, barely enough to get by. I had to stay on county healthcare and dental, because in my first six months I was not eligible to get benefits. Walmart would not allow benefits if you're a part-time associate. So I took the initiative to earn more so I would be able to climb that ladder. My first six-month evaluation, I did get a twenty-cent raise. I tried harder. I was promoted to photo technician, got a raise as a photo specialist. It gave me a forty-cent raise. So now I operated in maybe eight different jobs. I got promoted to health and beauty manager. I started supervising other associates, actually running a store within a store.

Overworked, the Walmart employee's health started to decline. She damaged her shoulder, tried to work around the pain, and ended up with a serious injury. "One day, I picked up something and my whole left side just paralyzed, it just froze. They rushed me to the company doctor. I was asked if I had reported it. Well, I did. I had several witnesses that I'd reported it for three months straight and they didn't give me the help I needed. I had an MRI; they found out that with me compensating with the rest of my body that I was injuring other parts of my body. I had to have surgery on a bone in my neck."

Unable to work, Girshriela went onto workers' comp. "Five hundred and eleven dollars every two weeks. God only knows how I survive with three girls. Sometimes I go without eating just to feed them. Probably drink a cup of coffee and some chips, when I go to visit friends. I often sacrifice to take care of my girls, to where they don't have to suffer. My church often helps a lot; I haven't been to a food pantry before, but I can see that coming with my bills accumulating. I had to drop our life insurance, so we're not covered. If something happened to my children today, would I be able to bury them? I don't know. A whole bunch of cutbacks. Life insurance. Healthy food versus noodles. I'm about to cry." She stopped and started to snuffle.

My family just got together and actually bought me the outfit I have on, because I was accepting an award and they wanted me to look nice. I only own two pair of tennis shoes, a couple of pair of pants and a few T-shirts. We don't watch TV often because I can't afford electricity to run like that. I don't have a bank account. I live from check to check. I don't do luxury. I just do what is absolutely necessary. I don't take rides around in my car, take my kid to school, go to movies, eat romaine lettuce, have chicken versus noodles. Once a month I get $6 from WIC for fresh fruit and vegetables.

WANTON LITTLE WAIFS AND SERFS

But for Green and others like her, as conditions grew worse—as the numbers of those out of work or in work that paid so little that it couldn't bring families out of poverty increased—so the dominant political narrative when it came to the poor became increasingly harsh. Many states reduced the number of months a woman could access welfare over the course of a lifetime. In California the limit was reduced from sixty to forty-eight months, with some budget proposals calling for that number to be cut in half again, to a mere twenty-four months, Arizona cut its limit to twenty-four months; politicians in Oregon proposed reducing their state limit to a mere year and a half.[19] States that provided general assistance to childless adults began rolling back these mandates, and counties in states that continued to mandate such assistance began reducing the number of months out of the year that they would give aid to these individuals. In many locations, childless adults could now only receive aid, amounting to a couple hundred dollars per month, for three months out of the year.

In a desperate attempt to save money, states also began cutting back the number of weeks in the school year, one unintended consequence of which was that hungry children, whose main meals came through free school breakfast and lunch programs, spent more of each year hungry. This problem was exacerbated by the fact that states also began slashing the number of "summer feeding sites" that they operated in poor neighborhoods, meaning that already-hungry children had even fewer options, during the elongated school breaks, for accessing hot meals.

When federal grant money from the Department of Agriculture was used to try to shore up such sites, conservative cheerleaders such as Rush Limbaugh were shrill in their opposition. In a tirade against such a plan for Kansas City, Missouri, that was aimed at feeding 10,000 low-income kids, Limbaugh called the children who received such free food "wanton little waifs and serfs dependent on the state.

Pure and simple." Children in school lunch programs, he argued, had had their independent impulses bred out of them. "If you feed them three square meals a day during the school year, how can you expect them to feed themselves during the summer? So they *demand* to be fed during the summer, or their acolytes *demand* that they be fed. Because we've conditioned them to not feeding themselves."[20]

Back in Pomona, California, some of these young waifs and serfs were clinging onto their dreams against almost impossible odds: "At our highest financial point, we had all the bills paid and $30,000 in the bank. Life was easy compared to what we have now. Now all the bills are late, and we owe $10,000 in credit and like $15,000 in home equity. Now we're just trying to get by," said Juan, in Michael Steinman's AP English class.

> Ever since I was introduced to the idea of college, I've been want-ing to go—especially to the U.C. I have three goals; one to get a college diploma, the other to buy my parents a house, and third to have a son and see my dad play with him. During this time in No-vember, when we're supposed to be applying to college, I am, but I'm not putting as much care or attention as I thought I would. Whereas I'm putting more care into my résumé, looking out for jobs, talking to people; I write cover letters, talk to the manager, but I don't get a call back. It just really sucks. I really wish I could get a job. College has sadly become a second priority. That's how things are right now.

Another student, Nielli, talked about how her mother tried to hide the family's financial crisis from her, "because she wants me to go to school." And she, wanting to please her mother, pretended not to know. Only through such double bluffs could she continue with her education.

Fighting to save his immigrant parents' home, a boy spent hours trying to translate legal documents from the bank for his mother and father to read. "I couldn't understand what it was saying. I'd have a sentence with huge words, foreign, alien words to me. I'd type it up, use Google Translate; it isn't that good for really long documents. Whenever we couldn't understand what a letter from Chase Bank was saying, we saw bold letters, red marks, so we knew it was important. If I couldn't help, we'd go to someone who could. That's how we got through stuff."

————

Three years after the nation's financial catastrophe unfolded, in the summer of 2011, the poor were once again being blamed for the sorry plight of the nation's finances, and being asked to bear the burden of fixing those finances. "So let me be as clear as I can be. Without significant spending cuts and reforms to reduce our debt, there will be no debt limit increase," House Speaker John Boehner told an audience at the Economic Club of New York on May 9, in the early days of the debate about raising the country's debt ceiling—a debate that took America to the very precipice of defaulting on its debt obligations. "And the cuts should be greater than the accompanying increase in debt authority the president is given. We should be talking about cuts of trillions, not just billions. They should be actual cuts and program reforms."[21]

Cut entire federal programs, especially those aimed at ameliorating the conditions of America's poor, the men and women who made up Boehner's majority warned, or they would shut down the government. Said Michele Bachmann, the Minnesotan congresswoman whose opposition to raising the debt ceiling briefly propelled her into the front tier of GOP presidential hopefuls, "The 'Great Society' has not worked and it's put us into the modern welfare state. If you look at China, they don't have food stamps. If you look at China, they're in a very different situation. They save for their own retirement security. . . . They don't have the modern welfare state and China's growing.

And so what I would do is look at the programs that LBJ gave us with the Great Society and they'd be gone."[22] Programs, it should be noted, that include Medicare and Medicaid.

Bachmann might have been slightly franker than many of her peers, but she wasn't alone in her basic beliefs. Thus, for example, despite the fact that there's an abundance of evidence that enrolling poor people in Medicaid saves society money in the long run—by emphasizing preventive health measures, by cutting down the number of emergency room visits, and by enabling the medical system to monitor emerging health crises before epidemics develop—an increasing number of politicians urged replacing right-of-access to programs like Medicaid with block grants to the states. Such a plan was at the heart of Representative Paul Ryan's budget proposals in April 2011, a change supported by conservative governors such as Virginia's Bob McDonnell and Mississippi's Haley Barbour, both of whom argued that their states couldn't afford to keep doling out Medicaid to all those currently entitled to it under federal laws.[23] What was perhaps most disingenuous about all of this, about the implication that this was a system weighted down by freeloaders, was the notion that accessing Medicaid was either easy or pain-free. To qualify for Medicaid, most states mandate that applicants have first sold off almost all of their assets; homes, cars beyond a bare minimum value, retirement accounts, and so on. It's a program that *does* provide a basic level of service, argued Jessica Bartholow, of the Western Center on Law and Poverty, but at the cost of "eviscerating the assets of the working class." Instead of making it harder to qualify for Medicaid, a genuine anti-poverty strategy, she believed, would make it easier, allowing the temporarily out of work and cash-poor to access medical coverage without stripping themselves of the assets that they would need, down the road, to pull themselves back into a condition of economic security.

In the budget-cutting environment of 2011, however, such arguments received short shrift.

While the Obama White House held the line against the most savage of these cuts, in exchange they ceded ground on a raft of other issues. Job-training programs were slashed; monies used by states to fund counseling for sexually abused children shriveled, services available to the mentally ill were curtailed, and budgets for drug and alcohol treatment programs were reduced. At best, as the election neared, the administration was willing to play defense, fighting to preserve what it could of the legacy of the New Deal and Great Society. Absent was the sense of offense, the sense that epidemic levels of poverty merited the creation of *new* programs, *new* benefits, *new* investments specifically targeted at tackling the underlying causes of poverty. Absent was the language of a new social compact that could build public support for such programs. "Liberals, at the end of the day, their solutions maintain poverty," Jim Wallis, CEO of Sojourners, concluded, sitting in his book-lined study in a northern suburb of Washington, D.C. "And conservatives, they want to abandon poor people." Absent was any real commitment to a wide-ranging, holistic approach to poverty. There simply wasn't gas in the tank to allow the body politic to rev up and launch a new, twenty-first-century War on Poverty.

Marshall Ganz believed that there was a "need for a whole counterargument. There's intellectual work that's not been done, political work. The whole post-war Keynesian welfare state was designed to create automatic stabilizers. It was understood that markets required management. We have been savaging the political and cultural and social institutions that emerged from that order—and we're paying the price right now."

That price was being seen in the form of programs cut, benefits slashed, and social infrastructure corroded. A form of public squalor was becoming the norm in contemporary America, girded by an expectation that the government could only deliver below-par services, and by a belief that those who utilized such services were illegitimately sucking off an overutilized public teat. It wasn't that America didn't have the resources to care for its poor or to nurture its great public institutions. Rather, in many ways, it seemed to be suffering from a crisis of will, its collective moral imagination no longer quite up to the task of understanding the impact of poverty on the lives of the poor and the necessity of solutions big enough to meet this existential challenge.

CHAPTER FIVE

THE WRONG SIDE OF THE TRACKS

Darren McKinney sits on a vacant lot that used to be houses and businesses before Katrina obliterated the Lower Ninth Ward.

On any Saturday morning, hundreds of people, of all ages, and of all colors, can be found snaking along the sidewalk of West LeHigh Avenue, toward the entrance, sunk several steps below street level, to a large community food center. The pantry is in the basement of a local public library. Down the street from the center the fire-gutted stone-and-brick shell of a huge high school dominates the landscape, looking more like a ruined medieval monastery than a modern-day American urban academy. The smaller side streets are pocked with hundreds of boarded-up houses, and hundreds more in such disrepair that one can only marvel at how people manage to live in them.

This is North Philadelphia, one of America's poorest urban neighborhoods. In 2011, researchers with Pew Charitable Trusts estimated that citywide Philadelphia's poverty rate stood at 25 percent, with a median household income of barely $37,000. But those numbers hid huge disparities. Some suburbs were as leafy, as affluent as any in America. Meanwhile, in the eastern part of North Philadelphia, the city's poorest district, the poverty rate stood at above 56 percent, and the average household income was only $20,896. In 2008, the median home price in this blighted neighborhood was $33,000; by 2010, it was a mere $10,000.[1]

Sitting on the curb, waiting for the food pantry to open, in the chill of a late fall morning, was Vicenta Delgado. She was bundled up in several layers, had a walker resting on the sidewalk beside her, and wore a dark head scarf to cover her bald head.

Vicenta was 61 years old and undergoing chemotherapy to treat a brain tumor. Originally from Puerto Rico, she had lived on the mainland since 1967, first in Trenton, New Jersey, then in Philadelphia. She suffered from depression and an array of other mental health ailments, problems that went from bad to worse after her oldest son was shot dead in Trenton several years earlier.

Vicenta's husband received a little more than $1,000 a month from Social Security; with almost no work history of her own, she qualified, she said, for just $27 a month in SSI. The couple also qualified for $34 per month in food stamps. On a multitude of medications, the prematurely aged lady paid a $3 copay each time she filled a prescription. While that might not sound like much, it quickly added up, eroding what little financial security the couple enjoyed. Medicaid didn't cover the nutritional supplement shakes that she needed because of her cancer, and so she had to buy those out of pocket.

Priced out of the food market like so many of her neighbors, Vicenta was reduced to spending each Saturday morning waiting in line for several hours until the pantry opened its doors for shoppers. She tried to stay warm, but feared picking up a cold—because the chemotherapy had undermined her immune system.

When the pantry doors finally were unlocked, Vicenta slowly, painfully, made her way down the stone steps, went under the heavy arched entryway, signed in with the volunteers sitting behind bulletproof windows, and was admitted into the large food supply room to choose her weekly groceries. It was a demoralizing ritual, but at least it kept her fed.

"Right now, I'm fighting cancer, I'm really sick," Delgado said, speaking slowly, her voice a little slurred. "I need fruit, vegetables, all different things I'm not able to buy. That's why I come to this place to get it. I get $34 a month [in food stamps]. You can buy hardly nothing. You go to the store with $34, you can't buy nothing." Coming to the pantry made her feel "sad, depressed. You know. 'Cause nobody do anything for you. The people [in the line] don't care." Delgado couldn't afford her nutritional supplements and went without some of her medicines. "If I can afford it, I buy it; if I can't, I do without it. I'm on four medications for my depression. I have high blood pressure, diabetes, a chronic bad back. I have to walk with a walker. I can't drive. If I need somebody to drive me, I have to pay for gas. Nobody take you anywhere if you can't pay for gas."

RUINS PORN

Bill Clark was used to all of this. As the executive director of a huge nonprofit food distribution organization named PhilAbundance, he

oversaw 450 pantries throughout the Delaware Valley that, cumulatively, helped support 650,000 families per week. Some of the
communities PhilAbundance served—Camden, New Jersey; North
Philadelphia—counted among the very poorest in the country. The
congressional district in which this area was located came in as
America's fourth hungriest. Across the Philadelphia region, approximately one in three children were living in poverty.[2]

Like Ginny Wallace at her pantry in the Appalachian Mountains
off to the west, Clark had had to navigate a minefield since the economic collapse of 2008. PhilAbundance was receiving less surplus
food from the USDA and at the same time was also getting less salvaged foods. Dented cans, for example, that in the recent past had
been donated by food producers to the pantries, were now winding
up in dollar stores, where they were sold at discount rather than
given away. For the working poor, this might have been a blessing;
for those too poor to even afford discounted food, however, it was
more akin to a curse. The amount of salvaged food ending up in
PhilAbundance pantries had fallen off a cliff, down 85 percent from
2008 to 2011. At the same time, the numbers attending the centers
each Saturday morning had skyrocketed, leaving pantry administrators scrambling to plug the gap—canvassing the community for food
donations and launching frantic fund-raising drives to generate
money that they could then spend to buy food to give away.

Clark, bald, with a trimmed white beard and glasses, was sitting
in a tiny, file-filled office, behind the food room. Behind him, pasted
to the wall, was a piece of cardboard on which was typed a Martin
Luther King Jr. quote: "The ultimate tragedy is not the oppression
and cruelty by the bad people but the silence over that by the good
people." Clark had made it his mission in life to speak out.

> This is an area of the city that has probably seen the most poverty for
> the longest time. It's multigenerational poverty. It's an area where the
> housing stock goes back prior to World War II, most of it prior to
> World War I, and it has seen very little investment since that time.

The industry that existed historically has been leaving continuously. Families are generally unemployed. The population is predominantly seriously below the poverty line. The population that we serve, the unemployment is probably close to 95 percent.

North Philadelphia was an extreme case, but it was hardly alone in its desolation. Areas of New York City; Washington, D.C.; Newark; Detroit; Chicago; Los Angeles; New Orleans; and many other cities were equally apocalyptic.

In Detroit, for example, where hundreds of thousands of workers had once made good money working in auto manufacturing, so many people had departed the city in recent decades, and so many lots had been abandoned, that in large numbers of neighborhoods there were more vacant homes than occupied ones.

From the 1960s onward, plants started to shed jobs, as production processes increasingly became automated. In 1979, for example, General Motors was producing as many cars in Detroit as it had done twenty years earlier, but with half the number of workers. Finally, however, even those workers proved too costly, and companies shuttered their factories entirely, the jobs outsourced to nonunion sites in other states, or overseas. Once iconic factories, such as the enormous Packard complex that, at its mighty zenith, had employed 60,000 people, remained only as vast shells, the ground carpeted by broken glass, the entranceways to buildings that used to house state-of-the-art industrial machinery piled high with tires, bricks, and twisted metal piping. "Detroit had what appeared to be a curse," explained Shea Howell, a local university professor of communications and longtime community organizer, who had made something of a hobby of taking out-of-towners on tours of the Motor City's underside. "People left to follow a job. In the late '70s, there used to be a bumper sticker: 'Last one out of Michigan, turn out the lights.' It was so many people leaving so fast. They just walked out of the house, got in the car and left behind the house. You have magnificent one- and two-story brick homes built for the workers of the auto industry. And people walked out, couldn't afford them, couldn't afford the heat, couldn't pay the mortgages. It's overwhelming. Over 30 percent of the city is abandoned; over forty square miles. The abandoned land became a curse; it pulled the heart out of neighborhoods."

During the days, tourists, engaging in what locals termed "ruins porn" watching, would venture out to the Packard plant in their cars to take photographs of the ruins—as impressive in their own way as those of the pyramids of Egypt. At night, the ruins belonged to graffiti artists, the homeless, drug addicts, and scrap metal scavengers, who would load up stolen grocery store carts with their wares and cart them off to recycling plants. "Decay," one tagger had thoughtfully painted along one shattered interior wall, empty windows staring vacantly on either side. There was enough piping and other metal amidst the ruins to keep the scavengers occupied for decades.

From one neighborhood to the next, blight flourished, although the word itself didn't really do justice to the magnitude of the catastrophe. Jobs disappeared; factories ceased operations; supermarkets, banks and other basic business amenities closed up shop. And, in their hundreds of thousands, those residents who could left. Abandoned, their homes—once some of working-class America's loveliest housing—fell into disrepair, burned down, or crumbled to the ground. The lots became overgrown. At night, coyotes, possums, and other wildlife roamed free. For those who remained, two-thirds of them living at or near the poverty line, the poverty getting deeper and more entrenched by the year, converting the vacant lots to urban gardens became both a way to keep neighborhoods functioning and also a somewhat desperate pathway toward self-sufficiency in an environment increasingly hostile to the poor.

And thus the surreal sight, in the shadows of the Packard ruins barely a stone's throw from downtown, of small family farms dotting the landscape. Many of them were farmed by African American residents whose families had migrated from the rural Deep South decades earlier and who still retained knowledge of family farming methods from their youth. By 2012, there were perhaps as many as 2,600 such farms in the city, community organizers estimated. Some of them were just a few rows of vegetables; others, however, included rambling orchards, chicken runs, little plots on which resided sheep and goats; a few were even home to bulls and horses. One, run by a group of Capuchin friars, was experimenting with year-round growing techniques; others were using sophisticated organic methods to leach the myriad of pollutants from the topsoil. A minute or two's drive from the heart of what used to be one of America's largest and fastest cities, one could see locals, dressed in muddied jeans and shirts, straw hats atop their heads, pushing wheelbarrows filled with dirt down cracked sidewalks, and carefully hoeing their farms.

By necessity, said Howell, Detroit had become something of an incubator for a new kind of urban living, a kind of utopia carved out of despair and post-industrial desolation. "What will replace industrial society? How will people live? What creates work? How do we do that now? These are fundamental questions. Human beings are in a transition now that's as great as the transition from hunting and gathering to agriculture, or from agriculture to industry."

Things weren't quite as bad in New York City, financial capital of the world and home to many of the richest people on earth, but in many parts of the metropolis neither were they terribly good. By the end of 2009 close to 10 percent of the working population was unemployed. For African American men that number stood at 17.9 percent—of whom approximately four out of ten had been unemployed for more than a year; and, high though it was, even that figure masked the true extent of joblessness amongst the city's African American population. As of year's end 2009, fewer than half of all African American adults in New York were a part of the labor force, a number far lower than that of any other racial category in the city; hammered by years of high incarceration, by poor school graduation rates, by slightly higher than city-average disability rates,[3] and dramatically higher poverty rates for those who were disabled, hundreds of thousands had simply stopped looking for on-the-books employ-ment.[4] At the depth of the recession, only one-quarter of African Americans aged 16 to 24 were working in the city.

Smaller Rust Belt towns, too, such as Gary, Indiana; Flint, Michigan; and Camden, New Jersey, were shorthand for postindustrial mayhem. Defined by stunningly high levels of unemployment, rock-bottom wages for those who did have jobs, growing numbers of functionally illiterate residents, and staggering rates of violent crime, these communities were as broken as the more famous, and notorious, Detroit.

Take Gary: In 1970, its population was 170,000, and good work was to be found in the local steel mills. By 2012, its population had imploded—down to 80,000. Official unemployment even within this reduced populace stood at 9 percent, and the joblessness rate was considerably higher than 20 percent. One in five of its buildings were vacant. In 2011, its main public library was closed. In 2012, it laid off one-quarter of its teachers. And, according to an article by journalist Don Terry, in the *American Prospect* magazine, the town was so broke as a result of its collapsed tax base that it no longer even had a working street sweeper. "At one point," Terry wrote, "the mayor contemplated dispatching people doing community service into the streets with brooms."[5]

In 2010, after a few years' hiatus, Gary regained the unwanted title of "murder capital" of the United States for a city its size. The fifty-four violent deaths in the city that year made for a homicide rate of 0.51 per thousand residents. Out of all the cities, large and small, in America, only New Orleans, with a rate of 0.52, topped Gary.[6]

Many rural areas, too, remained mired in a poverty that would have been all too familiar to generations past. These were the landscapes traversed by Michael Harrington a half-century ago during his research for *The Other America*. In all likelihood, were Harrington still alive today, he would have little problem recognizing these areas of urban blight and rural dilapidation.

There are, explained economics professor Jim Ziliak, of the University of Kentucky in Lexington, five geographic hotspots of persistent poverty dotted around America, with "poverty rates in excess of 20 percent in each Decennial Census from 1970": central Appalachia; the Texas colonias; some Native reservations in the desert west; the Black Belt region of Alabama, Georgia, and South Carolina; and the Mississippi Delta. In these counties, poverty rates can be in the 30 percent range, and up to half of all kids in these areas live in poverty and survive on food stamps. One could add to Ziliak's list the Ozarks, too, in southwest Missouri, where the poverty is as stark as anything seen elsewhere in the country.

In the area that Ziliak studied, the central Appalachian region of Eastern Kentucky, "economic opportunities," the professor explained, "are few and far between. They tend to be either directly associated with resource extraction—either timber or coal—or affiliated industries. And those undergo a lot of boom and bust cycles. So incomes tend to be quite volatile for the people in these regions. From a year-to-year basis they're going to have a lot of uncertainty trying to make long-term plans. It makes it a lot more difficult to plan for the future. You have many, many people getting by on a hand-to-mouth existence. They have what's known as the heat-or-eat decision. Do they buy food and run out of money for heat? Or do they keep the heat on and run out of money for food?

In Eastern Kentucky, if you want to draw a caricature of poverty, you want to think of a person who's more likely than not to be white. They could be a child, they could be a senior; it spans the entire age spectrum. Their parents are likely to have been from here, and their grandparents. They're likely to be third, fourth, fifth generation, even more in the Appalachian region. They tend to love its beauty; but they have poor access to steady jobs, to healthcare, and deep challenges to access to fresh foodstuffs, especially vegetables. They have to travel extensively to get medical care, and often to find employment as well. They face a lifetime prospect of low wages, $10,000 to $15,000 in wages.

CARROTS, STICKS, AND PISS TESTS FOR THE POOR

Throughout history, philosophers and political figures have sought to distinguish between the deserving and the undeserving poor; or, to put it another way, between those whose poverty is caused by outside forces and thus merits society's sympathy and those whose poverty is the result of poor life decisions, or communal dysfunction, and thus merits our scorn.

Such a distinction is pervasive today in the United States, where politicians spend an inordinate amount of time trying to distinguish between those simply down on their luck and those trying to con the system. In doing so, we have set up a tremendous number of barriers to accessing anti-poverty programs. These barriers have, in all likelihood, stopped some ne'er-do-wells from gaining assistance they ought not to get; but such gains have frequently come at the cost of scaring away many others who do qualify but are deterred from applying by the cumbersome, frequently humiliating, nature of the application process.

Take Californians' relationship to food stamps, for example. While the Golden State doesn't have the highest rate of poverty or hunger in the country, simply by virtue of its size its raw hunger and food insecurity numbers are stunning. The state with the largest population in the country had, as of mid-2012, the highest number of food stamp enrollees, with more than 3.98 million residents on its Cal-Fresh program. Of these, close to one and a half million were children. Texas, with the country's second highest population, but one not much more than two-thirds California's size, had, according to USDA data, almost as many residents on food stamps—mainly reflecting stunningly high rates of poverty, especially child poverty, in the Lone Star State. New York and Florida, with considerably smaller populations, also had almost as many enrollees as did California.[7]

California would, however, have had far more food stamp recipients if it had done even a remotely decent job at reaching out to those poor enough to qualify for the federally funded program during the preceding years. As things stood, though, while some states successfully enrolled upward of 90 percent of food-insecure households, as of 2012 more than half of all Californians who should have been covered by food stamps remained outside of that part of the safety net. That translated to roughly four million hungry Californians going without basic food assistance from the government. To survive, these men, women, and children were reliant either on the largesse of local charities, churches, and food pantries, or they were simply missing meals to stretch their meager food dollars across as long a time as possible.

"California's about the bottom of the barrel," explained California Food Policy Advocate (CFPA) executive director Ken Hecht, of the low food stamp enrollment rate. Hecht's organization had published a report in 2010, titled *Lost Dollars, Empty Plates*, which concluded that approximately 3.6 million Californians who qualified for food stamps were nevertheless not enrolled—thus sacrificing federally funded benefits worth a total of more than $4.8 billion annually. Because food stamp expenditures circulate rapidly through the economy, the CFPA researchers calculated that the total cost to the California economy of these unclaimed benefits was a staggering $8.68 billion. Many who should have been on food stamps were deterred by the state's requirement that applicants be fingerprinted, as well as by the four-times-a-year means test that the state administered on recipients. It was partly as a result of this report that California's state legislators passed a series of reforms, in 2011, to kick in a couple years

later, that would streamline the food stamp application process, ending the fingerprinting, reducing the number of means tests per year,
and making the online application process easier. Whether this
would result in more Californians accessing the benefits remained to
be seen, however.

In the meantime, with enrollment rates still dismal, hunger advocates from around the state convened in Sacramento in 2011 to
highlight the urgency of the problem. Members of Hunger Action
Los Angeles showed up at the Capitol carrying cardboard cut-out
figures, on each of which was glued a paper plate on which was
printed out hunger data, generated by the California Health Interview Survey (CHIS), from individual counties.

In Los Angeles County, there were 1.138 million "food-insecure"
adults in 2009, the most recent year for which such CHIS data exists, most of them insecure because they were not enrolled in the
food stamp program. In Riverside County, the number was close to
a quarter of a million. In Alameda, there were 169,000 adults in this
category. Even in eminently middle-class counties, the numbers
were high: Sonoma came in with 51,000 food-insecure adults; Yolo
with 16,000.

Cumulatively, the survey found that statewide, even after the expansion in food stamp usage since the start of the recession, 3.7 million Californian adults were struggling to put food on the table in
2009, up from 2.8 million just two years previously.

———

California's ambiguous relationship to the food stamp program
was indicative of the country's complex relationship to poverty as a
whole. For those we deem the deserving poor, we provide carrots to
help get them back on their feet: tax breaks, perhaps; suspensions of
student loan repayments; mortgage loan modifications; in particularly harsh recessions extensions in the length of time people can receive unemployment insurance.

For those we see as the undeserving poor, we use sticks: tying welfare payments to job searches; barring felons from public housing; making addicts and those convicted of drug felonies ineligible for government-funded student loans and a raft of other benefits; requiring applicants for a host of government assistance programs to undergo regular drug checks and fingerprinting. Neighborhoods such as North Philadelphia, or Los Angeles's Compton, long crippled by extraordinary poverty rates and depressingly high crime rates, are exactly the kinds of communities most scorned by conservative social reformers. As a result, more and more of their residents find themselves cut off from government assistance, or simply unaware of its existence, and ever more reliant on the sorts of charity interventions provided by PhilAbundance.

In February 2012, building on laws enacted in the months prior by states such as South Carolina, Congress took one more step against the "undeserving poor"; in exchange for Republicans agreeing to extend a payroll tax cut for middle- and working-class Americans, Democrats agreed to a provision allowing states to mandate that men and women claiming unemployment insurance while applying for jobs that would require drug tests undergo these invasive tests simply to access their insurance benefits. Disproportionately this provision falls on blue-collar workers, because—with certain professions, such as airline pilots or police officers, being the exceptions—the higher up the pay scale one goes, the less likely it is that an employer will make you pee in a cup before being hired on. A related measure to withhold unemployment benefits from those who didn't have, or weren't trying to get, a high school equivalency diploma, was defeated by Democrats in the Senate.

Later that month, the *New York Times* reported that close to two dozen states were proposing similar laws, to make welfare recipients have to undergo regular drug tests. Mitt Romney, hard at work wooing conservatives on the GOP primaries campaign trail, was reported to have said he thought this an "excellent idea."[8] In April 2012, Georgia went a step further, passing a law stating that TANF applicants would have to take a drug test within forty-eight hours of applying for the assistance, *and* that they would have to pay $17 for the privilege.[9]

In the modern American context, all-too-often this discussion about whether or not impoverished residents are deserving of sympathy and of government aid takes place against a backdrop of racial and class animus. For while white conservatives use government assistance copiously—whether it be Social Security, or mortgage tax relief, low-interest federal college loans or Medicare—in their political discussions they tend to define their benefits as not being "welfare," in contrast to the somehow less noble assistance provided to their black and brown neighbors. The Cornell University political scientist Suzanne Mettler writes in her book *The Submerged State* that a self-identified conservative is 50 percent more likely than a liberal to claim never to have used a government program, despite the fact that 96 percent of Americans she surveyed *had*, in fact, utilized government assistance—from mortgage tax relief to federal farm subsidies, from Medicare to Social Security.[10] Certainly, no one has talked about drug-testing seniors before they can access Social Security, requiring people filing for mortgage tax relief to piss into a cup, or mandating that bankers seeking to access billions of dollars of bailout funds prove their cocaine-free bona fides before tapping TARP.

University of Pennsylvania historian of poverty Michael Katz had reached similar conclusions to those of Mettler. Most tax-based subsidies in America, he argued, go to the middle and upper classes. Less than 3 percent of these subsidies ended up going to the bottom 60 percent of the population.[11] Yet, listen to the political rhetoric around government assistance, and one could be excused for thinking that a nation of fiercely independent homesteaders was being undermined from within by a plot involving government bureaucrats, in league with the underclasses, working to redistribute hard-earned incomes ever further, and ever faster, down the income pyramid.

It's not a far leap from that to a more pernicious interpretation: that while the middle and upper classes live righteously and deserve whatever help is sent their way, the environs of those whom these government-assisted anti-government conservatives consider to be on welfare, the concentrated conditions of inner-city poverty of these other Americans, are, somehow, breeding grounds for social pathologies. Witness some of the comments on radio personality Sean Hannity's online discussion thread about the causes of poverty: "Giving away free and reduced breakfast and lunch sounds like a great policy to liberals," wrote Silkworm19. But, the commenter opined, "these parents are taking that money that should be spent on their kids and are using it for more drugs or more TVs or more luxuries that do not promote education." Another participant, using the screen name JKM, added: "Staying home with kids who clearly couldn't be afforded most likely from the beginning sets a bad example for the children." JKM worried that it was encouraging people to stay poorly educated and unmotivated, knowing they would end up with "free apartments, free medical care, free and reduced cost food to fall back on."

Hannity has not hosted similar diatribes against the huge subsidies doled out by the federal government at the other end of the food distribution process: to agribusiness, to corn producers, to the great combines that determine what we eat, how we eat it, and how much we pay for the privilege.

For conservatives, entrenched, dysfunctional poverty, bringing in its wake drug use, mental illness, breakdown in family structure, and underachievement educationally, is casually assumed to be a black or Latino problem, or also, in an expanded version of the analysis, a "white trash" problem. It's assumed to exist in concentrated, isolated, communities—be they inner-city racial ghettoes or exurb trailer parks—and to be largely immune to social interventions.

"Who are the poor?" conservative intellectual and onetime presidential hopeful Pat Buchanan asked in February 2012. "And in what squalor were America's poor forced to live?" Then, quoting a Heritage Foundation study, he proceeded to answer his own questions: "Well, 99 percent had a refrigerator and stove, two-thirds had a plasma TV, a

DVD player and access to cable or satellite, 43 percent were on the Internet, half had a video game system like PlayStation or Xbox. Three-fourths of the poor had a car or truck, nine in 10 a microwave, 80 percent had air conditioning." The sneering tone continued: It turned out, Buchanan wrote, that only in the "televised" version of poverty were masses of Americans homeless or hungry. In fact, Buchanan opined, in another example of a conservative quick to twist the language of Michael Harrington to his own ends, the crisis facing America was not one of poverty per se, but one triggered by a *culture* of poverty. That culture was epitomized by epidemic rates of illegitimacy, especially within Hispanic and Black communities; by high rates of drug use and school dropout rates among the poor; and by a propensity of the impoverished to get themselves incarcerated. "We have witnessed a headlong descent into social decomposition. The family, cinder block of society," he concluded, "is disintegrating, and along with it, society itself."[12]

Some of the assumptions around this form of poverty may indeed be true—stereotypes, after all, frequently have some minimal basis in reality from which they balloon to cartoonish proportions. But that largely misses the point. Whatever the prognostications of a conservative think tank or a right-wing commentator, poverty on an epic scale *is* a reality in today's America; and whether that poverty is caused by dysfunction, or the dysfunction is itself a product of the poverty, or, as is likely, the dysfunction and the poverty interact in ever more complex feedback loops, for the larger community to wash its hands of the problem represents an extraordinary failure of the moral imagination.

What should we do, for example, with someone like Emily, an elderly lady in Hawaii whose heritage consisted largely of violence, alcoholism, and abuse, and who had spent her life living in the shadow of these personal calamities?

> My father, my grandfather, and my mom and all them were alcoholics. My dad beat on my mom; my brother-in-law beat on my

grandfather—my grandfather died of a blood clot in the back of his neck because my brother-in-law karate chopped him. My dad beat my mom all the time; had sex with her in front of people in a party—he didn't care. And he beat me. I have cane knife scars; he beat me with a cane knife. My brothers beat me. One brother, a boxer, hang me up on a tree and beat me and left me there because I put a hole in his punching bag. He hung me in a tree and left me there. I got out. I was about eight years old; I washed myself up and looked at him and couldn't do anything because I was a little girl. When I was 21 and pregnant with my first son, he come back at me. I picked up a rock. He said, "What are you going to do with that?" I said, "You call me Tiny, and this is my equalizer. So that way you'll never, ever hit me again." And he never hit me again. And none of my brothers hit me since then. I had to show them I'm not a little child, I'm a woman.

When Emily was a young child, her mother ran away from her father. "I was the only girl. We walked miles with my Dad. Me and my younger brother, we had to go every place he went. We slept between graves because he wanted to go drink. If we said anything, he knocked us out."

Emily's grandmother died when she was 9 years old, and, said Emily, she ran away from home. She spent the next several years bouncing between the residences of distant family members, foster homes, and the street. When she was 13, she recounted, sitting in her small plywood home on the edge of the rainforest, deep within the impoverished backwoods of the Puna District, on Hawaii's Big Island, she was raped.

"I swore I would never raise my kids the way I was raised. I've never beat them. They've had spankings, yeah, when they got in trouble. But I never beat them. I had to change me. My foster mom told me, "To change you, you've got to be strong.' I'm strong. I'm not afraid of anyone but God. No one else can change me." Two of her children had steered clear of crime, and now had decent jobs.

But the other two—the oldest and the youngest—were frequently in trouble with the law.

Emily had worked many jobs over the years, including a half-decade stint working the guava fields of Hawaii, some time spent trimming cauliflowers in California, more time compounding and waxing cars on Maui, and a period collecting and recycling aluminum cans. At the same time, though, she never managed to save money; frequently spent what little she had on drugs, for kicks rather than out of any addictive craving, she said in explanation, perhaps somewhat optimistically; and for close to two decades had lived in a house the ceiling of which still had the holes that were poked in it by the mentally unstable previous occupant. Yes, by pretty much any measure Emily was somewhat dysfunctional, but do we as a society therefore wash our hands of her, denying her government assistance and pushing her ever further outside mainstream society's boundaries?

Maybe. But if we do so, we have to be aware of the consequences: that a woman in her mid-sixties, a great-grandmother, who in recent years had been working to stay clear of drugs and to care for several generations of her family, would be rendered destitute. That because of that decision she will go from chronic poverty, living on a few hundred dollars a month in Social Security and a few hundred dollars' worth of food stamps, to acute misery, from merely skimping on meals to actively missing them.

Or what should be done with Cruzanta Mercado and her long-time boyfriend Paul Abiley, also residents, far off the grid, of the dense tropical rainforest side of Hawaii's Big Island?

It's an extraordinarily beautiful part of the world, the lush green forest growing out of the highly fertile volcanic mud, except in the places where the lava flows have bubbled up out of the earth, creating miles-wide swaths of dead, black solidified lava fields. There, the rocks twist and turn, crack and knot like a mythical, hellish, austerely magnificent landscape—like an underworld such as that toured by Virgil or Dante. In one spot or other, in this part of the island, molten rock is always flowing.

Yet the beauty hides a fair dollop of despair. Along the unmarked, unpaved, rutted back roads, meth labs proliferate. Stolen cars are stashed in the bush. Houses are frequently robbed by addicts. In response, homeowners keep large, fierce dogs on chains to deter the would-be invaders.

It was in this hinterland that Cruzanta and Paul had, literally, made their home—building a tiny Heath Robinson–type plywood cabin, on stilts above the forest, from planks, boards, and nails. The living area had room for a propane stove, a tiny wooden table—the chairs for which were stacked atop it when it was not in use—some shelves, and a few toys for their son, Ikaika, 3 years old when I visited the family in early 2012. Separated off from this room by a hanging blanket was a tiny bedroom, really a closet with a bed. Like Emily's, theirs was a home without a toilet, without running water, without heating, without electricity. "We currently do not have any drywall in the house, no electric without our generator. You can see the framing—what's holding up the walls. When we run out of gas, we use candles for our lighting, or maybe some battery lanterns," Paul explained. "Other than that, we cook on our stove. When we run out of propane we make a grill outside, chop some wood. We take it like that, day by day. For the toilet, I have my uncle Ben, which is right across the street. Sometimes he's not home; I have a commode—like a toilet for an elderly person. I put a trash bag in it, I do my thing, I dispose of my thing inside the trash. I bag up my trash and take it to the dump; that's how I do my bathroom thing. I wash the dishes with rainwater."

Bare bones as this house was, though, it represented their dreams, a step up in life from what came before. Both Cruzanta and Paul went to juvenile hall as teenagers—Cruzanta explained that her transgression was assaulting a girl at another school; Paul said that he ended up being incarcerated for drugs and other offenses. In fact,

Paul, who claimed that his family had a multigenerational problem with narcotics, had been in and out of trouble with the law since early in his teenage years. Grand theft auto, assault, drugs, he'd done them all, explained the young man, as he sat in his home, head shaved, arms heavily tattooed.

For a long while, the teenage couple, playing out a desperado story, lived out of an old car—one that Paul had acquired, on the black market, for $300. Cruzanta graduated high school, they recalled, with a touch of nostalgia, while living in the vehicle.

"I tried every day to fight my demons—which was using drugs," Paul, who suffered from diabetes, acknowledged. "Because the pressure here is unreal, you know what I mean? When it's in your face, it's a different story from just saying you're not going to do it. I had some back falls. I took ten steps forward, yet another twenty back. My mistakes, I needed to learn from them, because I was making the same mistakes over and over."

Dysfunctional as their story sounded, however, the couple *were* committed parents to Ikaika, had worked hard—with help from the social workers at a Hawaii nonprofit named Neighborhood Place— to turn their lives around and to stay off of drugs, and had managed to eke out an existence for themselves, albeit one on the very margins of society. In the spring of 2012, both landed jobs at a local country club—he as a cart boy for the affluent golf crowd, she as a waitress. The work was part-time, paid just above minimum wage, and came with no benefits—but it was a start. "Right now, I don't look at my job as a retiring position, what I'm doing, you know," explained Paul. "But it does help, puts food on the table. I'm a cart boy; I wash carts, maintain the golf course, you know, take out the trash. I have a friend who gives me wisdom. He says, 'Think of it as blocks, you can only go higher and higher. From your tower falling down many times before, you're beyond that point; you know how to set your blocks—solid enough so that your foundation can rise.' And that's how I look at it."

Cruzanta and Paul's was, ultimately, a story that defied easy stereotyping. Neither were saints; and, on a bad day, both might be far, even, from averagely decent citizens. Yet both were trying to better their own lives and to create a home for their son. Not proffering help in such circumstances, based on the perceived moral flaws of the individuals concerned, is a striking example of cutting off one's nose to spite one's face, since head-in-the-sand policies also often end up costing us all more down the road. Helping Cruzanta and Paul, with assistance in getting onto the power grid, for example, or with childcare for when they are both working at the country club, with continued access to food stamps and Medicaid, or with heating subsidies in winter, might well defray a heap of additional, messier expenses down the road, be they criminal justice bills, welfare costs, healthcare bills, or the monies spent on providing interventions to help a child whose family lives in deep poverty.

And the same holds true in myriad situations across the country. Take the story of Katie, in the depressed town of Nampa in Caldwell County, Idaho. As a kid, she recalled, her overworked mother and drunken father fed her raw turnips for dinner. "They would cut 'em up, sometimes cook 'em, sometimes they were raw. We didn't have anything with them. And then we moved up to potatoes." She laughed wryly at the memory. By the time she was 15 Katie had gotten pregnant, moved in with her meth-addicted, violent boyfriend, and dropped out of school. By the time she was in her twenties, she had herself developed a meth habit, had four children—three of whom ended up living with her own mother—and, while she had managed to leave her abusive boyfriend, in most other areas of her life she was a complete mess.

It would be easy to say that Katie had brought her poverty upon herself—although, clearly, the depressed, abusive environment in which she was raised had also helped push her down several wrong paths. It might even be easy, from a distance, to categorize the young woman as part of the "undeserving poor," and to wash society's hands of responsibility for her well-being and for that of her children, to declare her ineligible for food stamps, to deny her children access to state-funded healthcare. But, as with Paul and Cruzanta, Katie, 28 when I met her, was struggling mightily to get her house in order. Three years earlier, she had gone into drug rehab; she had managed to kick her addiction and was now working as a staffer at a local community-organizing center—she liked the work, but all too often, when the center ran low on funds, she was temporarily laid off. She had remarried, this time to a man who had a job—stacking pallets at a local company—didn't beat her, and never pushed drugs on her. They were trying to make a go of it; but the financial odds were against them. Neither one's employment came with benefits. Neither had credit—which meant when they bought a secondhand car they ended up paying an exorbitant 29 percent interest rate. And if they weren't renting a home owned by his grandfather, their repeated late payments on their rent would surely by now have landed them out on the streets.

Katie's dreams were modest, yet like so many others in her position even these looked outlandish at times. "Ten, fifteen years from now I'm hoping to own our own home. Which would be nice," she said, a short woman with an endearing, self-deprecating, smile, her mouse-brown hair falling down her shoulders. "And own a couple of vehicles. Having a full-time position. The American Dream, to me, it means to have a home and be happy; to not be living on the streets. Sober. To me it's not having a bunch of money. I don't think so. Being able to live and have food, and be happy. That would qualify to me."

Withholding aid from the "undeserving poor" is often penny-wise but extremely pound-foolish. In 1965, Philip Stern reported that the existence of pockets of blight around America ended up costing taxpayers huge sums of money: in New York City, he wrote, "blighted areas contain 27 percent of the city's population, yet account for 45 percent of the city's infant deaths, 71 percent of the venereal disease, 51 percent of the juvenile delinquency, 73 percent of the dependent-children-on-welfare." In Los Angeles, for every dollar the government spent on more affluent communities, it ended up having to spend $1.87 to police poorer neighborhoods, $1.67 to provide fire services, and $2.25 to cater to healthcare needs unmet in impoverished communities by private insurers.[13]

Take another, more recent example. In New York City a variety of rent-subsidy programs exist for ex-homeless people who have gotten jobs and started to sort out their lives. They cost, on balance, about $800 per month per recipient, not a huge sum in a metropolis where the average rent for a one-bedroom apartment in 2012, even before Hurricane Sandy left tens of thousands homeless and added further pressure to an already overheated rental market, was a staggering $2,568 per month.[14] But the city worries that if it makes the application process too easy, people who don't genuinely need the aid will sneak onto the rolls. And so it makes applications deliberately difficult. The result? More people end up going to shelters. But here's where things get really crazy: since the city has a policy in place saying that it cannot turn anyone away from shelters, it ends up with higher bills. Instead of paying $800 per person in rent subsidies, it runs an emergency shelter system that can cost up to $25,000 per year per resident.[15]

Or take the fact that during the post-2008 crash, many states either removed dental treatment from amongst the services offered to Medicaid recipients or reduced the amounts they paid practitioners so much that most stopped serving Medicaid clients. The result, according to a report by the Pew Center for the States: huge increases in the number of emergency room visits for untreated dental problems. Teeth that could have been filled easily in a dentist's office are left to rot until they abscess; minor traumas become major infections. In 2009, the authors estimated, emergency rooms were used more than 830,000 times for preventable dental conditions. That year, more than half of all kids on Medicaid did not receive even a routine dental exam. In Florida, in 2010, Pew estimated, these dental-related ER visits cost $88 million.[16]

Or the decline in services provided to the destitute mentally ill in
the community. From 2008 to 2011, visits to psychiatric emergency
rooms around the country increased by upwards of 20 percent. Why
did that happen? Probably because, according to the National Association of State Mental Health Program Directors, in the years following the financial collapse state funding for mental health services
declined by $3.4 billion even as the number of people requesting
mental health interventions grew by several hundred thousand.[17] In
the 2011–12 budget cycle alone, according to the National Alliance
on Mental Illness, California cut $177 million from its mental
health services budget and New York State cut $95 million.[18] With
nowhere but the hospitals to turn to, the mentally ill flooded emergency rooms from one state to the next.

THE MISSISSIPPI EFFECT

It is easy to be an armchair critic of those who rely on government assistance; to denounce them as crazy, manipulative, lazy, or dysfunctional; to declare them their own worst enemies; to urge them to
stand on their feet and pull themselves up by their bootstraps. Get beyond the tired, clichéd, sound bites, however, and one enters a world
of frequent humiliation, of desperate poverty, of shrunken horizons.

Witness the life stories of many of the students who populated
principal James Kuzman's Rancho High School, in the desperately
poor region of North Las Vegas—an area scarred by precarious tent
cities under freeway overpasses, with halfway houses and drug treatment facilities, with overcrowded rental units and the omnipresence
of gangs and violence. About half of the students were enrolled in a
well-regarded magnet school on the site; these kids commuted in
from all over the metropolis. The other half were locals, most of
whom attended Rancho's non-magnet classes. The school, Las Vegas's second largest, which in 2011 had close to 200 homeless students out of a total of around 3,000 enrollees, was barely three miles

from the northern end of the fabled Strip, home to some of the world's most famous hotels and entertainment centers. Yet Kuzman had found that a large proportion of the local teens had never ventured outside of their own few square blocks. The Strip, for them, might as well be on the moon.

Many of our students are coming from families of generational poverty; parents have come from another country and are struggling to make ends meet, working one or two jobs. We have difficulty getting many of our neighborhood, zoned students, to participate in activities at school. The children are often asked to go home to babysit, to provide care to younger siblings; or they're asked to work, too, to meet the needs of their families. It prohibits them from fully taking part in activities at our school. Anything from helping their fathers in a landscaping business to trying to sell things. Go up and down our streets at night, you'll find all sorts of vendors selling food products. For our homeless students we provide backpacks they can take home. They need toilet paper, shampoo, soap, deodorant. The things we take for granted when we open up our medicine cabinet, they don't have, especially if they're moving from house to house. This year, we did a door-to-door campaign to look for seniors who didn't show up on the first day of school. We came up with a list of 229, out of a group of seniors of 700.

Some of the students were playing truant. Many, however, had had to move to other schools, either in Las Vegas or elsewhere, after their families had been forced to move following evictions, foreclosures, or job losses.

A few years ago, when I was still at Von Tobel middle school, we had a straight-A recognition ceremony for some kids. So we took about twenty kids to Ricardo's Mexican restaurant, and a place called Mountasia, where they have miniature golf and bumper cars and whatnot. I was talking to the kids; they'd lived here their whole life and they'd never seen the Strip, never been out of this area. Here's these people that live in this town that people are coming from all over the world to visit, because of the pomp and the grandiose buildings and the light, and here's people living here who've never even seen it. At school there's only so much kids can learn. What you learn from most are your experiences. Their experiences are so limited; they don't have a lot to relate to. If you're teaching a student a geography lesson and you make a reference to Washington, D.C., if you've been to the Smithsonian or to the Capitol, it's easier to relate to than if you don't even know where it is.

Despite the myth of a welfare-addicted population, for the overwhelming majority of poor families in today's America, the central part of the welfare system, Temporary Aid to Needy Families, is not an option. When Harvard sociologist Kathryn Edin spent years interviewing impoverished residents of Philadelphia and Camden in the years surrounding the onset of the Great Recession, she found that almost none of the young people used TANF, or believed that they *could* use it. Moreover, for most of those few who do manage to qualify, the amount of cash assistance available amounts to only a fraction of that needed simply to raise a family up to the federal poverty line.

In California, for example, as of 2012, 22 percent of kids lived in poverty, but only 3 percent of kids were members of families on welfare. The maximum amount those families could receive was $643 per month, but only one in five welfare recipients got this level of assistance. For the childless indigent, aid options were even sparser. Only about half of the states still provided cash assistance to this group, and even in those states that did the amounts were tiny. For "unemployable" individuals, New Hampshire led the pack, providing

$688 per month, followed by Hawaii at $418. Washington and Massachusetts each gave a little more than $300 per month. Other states ranged downward, all the way to Delaware's $95. For the twelve states that still provided some general assistance to the "employable"—or able-bodied—and childless poor, down from twenty-five states in 1989, recipients received a few hundred dollars a month but could only access the aid a few months out of each year.[19]

However one crunched the numbers, even in a state traditionally as generous as was California, welfare, at this point, really was only for the poorest of the poor: people at or below half of the federal poverty line, with no assets to speak of, and no ability to generate income. In California, as elsewhere in the country, as the political leadership sought to deal with its deficit problems, increasingly it was this most vulnerable part of the population that was being asked to shoulder a disproportionate share of the burden.

In many ways, the Golden State, for all its liberal promise, was now taking a lead from ultraconservative states such as Mississippi, its safety net imploding under the weight of a relentless anti-tax ideology embraced by voters in a series of initiatives dating from the late 1970s onward and by the modern-day Republican Party—a minority in the statehouse but, until the 2012 elections delivered a supermajority to California's Democrats in both state houses, a large enough minority to block tax increases.

And that didn't bode well for California's millions of impoverished residents, or, by extension, for the country. After all, historically, perhaps nowhere in the country have the anti-welfare mentality and a general contempt for the lives and needs of the poor held more sway than in Mississippi. The Magnolia State has, throughout much of American history, ranked at the bottom of all the states in terms of150its poverty data. Choose your measure, and Mississippi underperforms. In 2008–09, at the start of the recession, Mississippi's average household income was roughly $35,000, barely half that of New Hampshire, the state with the best average. Its public school math and reading scores, as well as graduation rates, were worst out of all fifty states. Its life expectancy was the lowest in the nation. And its infant mortality rate was the highest.[20]

Mississippi Delta attorney Bill Luckett ran for the Democratic Party's nominee for governor in 2011. His platform was an anti-poverty platform, with a particular focus on increasing educational opportunities for low-income residents. Luckett came a strong second in the primary election; but even if he'd won, it wouldn't have made a hill's bean of difference; these days, Mississippi is a lock for the Republicans.

A large man with a shock of white hair, exuberant, charismatic, Luckett has a finger in many pies. He's a lawyer, a real-estate developer, a co-owner, with actor Morgan Freeman, of the best blues club in Clarksdale—home of the birthplace of that musical genre; a politician, an anti-poverty activist, an advocate for more investment in education.

> We have the lowest paying jobs, the lowest educational attainment levels. Poverty means an inability to sustain oneself. Mississippi has the highest federal poverty rate, somewhere around 22 percent year in, year out. We have another 15 percent of our population here who cannot sustain themselves. So, almost four out of ten people here in the Mississippi Delta cannot make it from paycheck to check. We have the highest rate of infant mortality in the country—and it's more pronounced here in the Delta. It cuts across race lines. But if a comparison were done, you'd have a higher percentage of blacks poor than of whites; but it's not exclusive. We've never enjoyed true prosperity compared to the rest of the country; so we don't suffer a recession or depression as much as the rest of the country do. We have chronic high unemployment; we have chronic seasonal workers. Two or three months with no work at all—looking for a part-time fill-in and trying to draw unemployment benefits.

Yet despite—or maybe because of—the large numbers of its residents who, even in the good times, struggle merely to subsist, the state's conservative political culture makes the life of the poor as unpleasant as possible. Accessing welfare in the state is an exercise in humiliation, both in terms of the obstacles placed in the way of applicants and in terms of the value of the aid made available. "Welfare is short-lived, hard to get, and not much of it. The average welfare check to a person who qualifies is $66 a month," averred Luckett. "There's a two-year lifespan on it unless there's an extreme circumstance. They live looking for day work, and a lot of people turn to crime. We, along with Louisiana, have the highest rate of incarceration of any jurisdiction in the world. I said that correctly. In. The. World."

Accessing expanded unemployment benefits, funded by the federal government, post-2008 was made difficult by the state's refusal to modernize its unemployment insurance system. And despite the fact that close to four out of every five Medicaid dollars spent in the state are provided by the federal government—since poorer states get more of their Medicaid expenditures reimbursed by D.C.—for able-bodied adults it's harder to qualify for Medicaid in Mississippi than in most other states in the union. Childless adults have no access to the program; out-of-work parents only qualify if their total income is less than a quarter of the federal poverty line.[21]

This is a poverty that cloys to entire communities. Said Nekedra Blockett, a social worker at the St. Gabriel Mercy Community Center in the desperately poor Delta town of Mount Bayou, in Bolivar County,

> A lot of the clients that come into our center have various different reasons of their poverty. Some have been laid off from their jobs, some have disability, some have applied for disability and they can't even receive that assistance. Quite a few of them don't have income at all. A lot of them survive through federal assistance, maybe food stamps. A lot of the women with younger children may receive TANF—they may have to take a class or do volunteer work, twenty to twenty-five hours per week. That's how a lot of them survive around here. You know, looking at it in their way, sometimes it

hurts. It's a chain, a cycle. Some people may come from a poor family; as they grow up they take on the same cycle. This community had a lot of farmers who owned land. You don't have too many people in this area who farm now. A few of them actually make it out, they might leave here and find a better living for them and their family.

Blockett's colleague, Sister Donald Mary Lynch, talked of clients who came to their center just to use toilets and bathrooms, because they had no running water in their homes. "It does happen on a regular basis. Many of these families are single-parent homes. Many of the young men end up in prison, so they're not in the homes. Many of the young girls get pregnant in high school, so they don't finish high school. Their education limits their job opportunities. And without jobs they don't have money. That's how the cycle continues. They live in government-subsidized housing, there's a lot of it here in Mount Bayou itself, and also in the county."

Blockett continued: "Today, I had a client that came in; her only income is her disability, which is $674 a month. She came to us today because she had to take her daughter in, with her two grandchildren, into her home. She comes to me for food today, and she needs assistance with the light bill. She only had $26. She needed some medicine; she was in pain. Right now, she's having to make the choice of food, shelter, medication, different things like this. Many of them [Blockett's clients] are illiterate; a few have a high school education, and it's rare they have a college."

The lucky ones might snag a job at Parchman Prison, a huge penal complex in the nearby countryside that housed 3,000 inmates; or they might drive further afield, to the casinos one and a half hours north of town—where locals worked nonunionized jobs, with few benefits, at near-minimum wage. Most, however, stayed closer to home. And, said Blockett, they either remained jobless, or they ended up with dead-end work at fast food chains and big box stores. "[They work at] McDonald's and Wendy's and Walmart and Kroger. Some Dollar Generals. Different things like that."

HURRICANES, TORNADOES, AND SOME AWFULLY BIG BILLS

Were he to return to life, Michael Harrington wouldn't be pleased that modern-day poverty in a place like Mississippi, or in the Appalachian towns studied by Jim Ziliak, or in the urban community of North Philadelphia, still survived; but, nevertheless, as a student of the history of poverty he would understand it. What he wouldn't fathom is why other, more affluent regions were adopting Mississippian attitudes to the poor. Nor, I suspect, would he easily come to terms with a host of other triggers for economic collapse in twenty-first-century America. In particular, as someone who came of age during the heyday of can-do American liberal governance, he would be bemused by the country's paralyzed political processes, and as a result of this paralysis, by its inability to get on top of both natural and manmade disasters; he would be both surprised and horrified at how profoundly tragedies doled out by nature and by corporations can quickly morph into scandal.

How, for example, would a post-war American optimist—even one with as keen an eye for the underbelly of America as Harrington—have interpreted Hurricane Katrina, and the destruction both of the physical infrastructure of much of New Orleans and also of a huge number of lives? How would he have reacted to the orgy of impotent finger-pointing that was indulged in by local, state, and federal officials both during the flooding itself, and then in the months and years following—as swaths of land were left to decay and the rotten wooden hulls of thousands of homes were simply left to pockmark the devastated city?

There's a loneliness to this landscape, a Mad Max edge. It looks like a world abandoned to its own devices, with street after street of destroyed, gutted houses, and acres of overgrown lots where once stood stores and homes, churches and schools. It is an utterly apocalyptic landscape; yet it is also a strangely invisible one—off the beaten path, away from the decadent, jazzy splendors of Bourbon Street, a place of national shame that, for those fortunate enough not to have lived in the area, is all too easy to forget exists.

It is, explained Darren McKinney, a middle-aged resident on disability and food stamps who had spent the years since the hurricane hit working with a nonprofit group to salvage some of the wooden homes of the Lower Ninth, "like a ghost town at nighttime."

Taking a break from working on one graffiti-covered skeleton of a building, on Caffin Avenue, in the last weeks of 2011, McKinney sat on a concrete slab that used to be the base of a house, and looked around. "That was a barber shop, that was a grocery store. That slab right there, it used to be a doctor's office. That place used to be an after-school place for kids. This here used to be a church right behind us," said Darren, pointing to the rear of the empty lot. "I stood, watched the water come up fifteen feet, fifteen to twenty feet in this area. St. Claude and Delaware, I watched it. I watched the little birds and fishes in the water, people yelling at nighttime for help. I lost my step-mamma, a couple of my best friends in the storm." Surveying the damage, half a decade on from the storm, Darren struggled to put a positive spin on things. "Up in this area, you might have 30 percent of the people back. It's getting better—'cause every day I see a new person moving into the neighborhood, someone moving back in. The neighborhood coming back; but it's going to be another five to six years to get some action back into the neighborhood again. You just gotta think positive."

Of course, much of New Orleans's troubles, much of the texture of its poverty, predates Hurricane Katrina not just by decades but by centuries. It is a city long plagued by violence, by racial and economic divides as stark as any in America—fully half of the residents of Orleans Parish were low-income even prior to the hurricane—and by endemic levels of corruption. Yet all of these were worsened by the calamitous events of the late summer of 2005. Disproportionately, it was African Americans who were left behind in the city as those with cars evacuated. Disproportionately, it was African American neighborhoods like the Lower Ninth Ward that suffered the most physical damage and then were least likely to be speedily rebuilt after the disaster. By contrast, more affluent areas, like the fabled French Quarter, which had grown up on high land over the years, suffered less damage during the flood and returned to relative normality within months of the waters draining out of the city. For tourists, in town to splurge on *les bons temps*—booze, food, and extraordinary music—the city presented a near-intact public visage within a remarkably short stretch of time. But, barely a couple of miles from Bourbon Street, entire city blocks were still obliterated years later, concrete foundation slabs resting at odd angles amidst overgrown grass, graffiti-covered house shells still waiting to be torn down.

And, while the number of African Americans who died in the flood was roughly proportionate to the percentage of the New Orleans population who were African American, disproportionately it was the poor, and elderly, of all races who were the ones to die in the flood itself and its chaotic aftermath. In a city where the public health system had already suffered epic cutbacks—losing a majority of its public-sector hospital beds and in-patient mental health facilities in the years preceding Katrina—the disaster simply overwhelmed the first-responder system. It was one's economic status in New Orleans that was the best predictor of whether one would survive or succumb to the flood; and, after the flood, for the survivors it was one's economic status that generally determined one's access to housing, to healthcare, to all of the basics of life in a shattered community.[22] Fully a quarter of local residents had no health insurance, and for African Americans that number was higher.[23] As for work, a year before the disaster, the unemployment rate stood at 12 percent, roughly double the national average.[24] Despite the construction boom generated by the hurricane, in the years immediately following Katrina, unemployment remained stubbornly high: More than one in ten workers in the shrunken city were unemployed in the first few years.

And, later, during the post-2008 recession, when the city's unemployment numbers actually dipped below the national average, demographers believed that at least in part this number was an illusion; it was based on the fact that so many former residents who lost everything during the flood—a large number of whom counted amongst the city's poorest and least employed residents—had yet to return to the city.[25] Yes, the Big Easy's unemployment rate *had* gone down, but the total number of abandoned homes still hovered in the tens of thousands. In 2010, the *Los Angeles Times* reported that the advocacy organization UNITY estimated that the homeless population had doubled in the years following Katrina, and that 6,000 New Orleanians were living in these abandoned buildings.[26]

As for child poverty—one of the key measures of societal health—in pre-Katrina New Orleans, U.S. Census Bureau data showed that about 40 percent of African American children under the age of 5 were living in poverty. That number was terrifyingly high—but not as high as the estimates six years later. Post-Katrina, the Census Bureau found that more than 65 percent of black children under the age of 5 in New Orleans, many of them still living in the blitzed landscape of the Lower Ninth and other devastated neighborhoods, were living at or below the poverty line.

———

Hurricane Katrina is where old poverty meets new, where the intergenerational poverty of the inner city becomes magnified by natural disaster and political ineptitude. It is where the plight of the poor is most clearly exposed—as an ongoing experience in vulnerability, as people thought of as being somehow disposable. It is where people without cars were left to die by a city that hadn't worked out how to effectively evacuate its poor residents using mass transit vehicles, and where residents in low-lying, impoverished flood zones were left peculiarly at risk of disaster by underinvestment in a crumbling, publicly owned and operated, levee system.

Five years after Hurricane Katrina, the Gulf Coast communities were hit by a second disaster, this time entirely man-made. On April 20, 2010, the Deepwater Horizon oil well, owned by BP, exploded, and huge quantities of oil began spilling into the sea. For local fisher- and oystermen, the impact was immediate and devastating.

Down in Pointe á la Hache, a small, ramshackle, oceanfront community reachable by an ancient ferry from the mainland south of New Orleans, oysterman Byron Encelade had only recently managed to rebuild his small fleet of boats—hurled inland to the highway, over the first set of levees, by the force of Katrina's waves and winds back in 2005. Prior to the hurricane, he'd had five boats; now he was down to two. But the oysters caught from those two vessels, combined with money he'd made transporting catches to markets around the region, had been enough to give him a fairly secure income. "I was able to recover," said Encelade, his voice soft, slightly hoarse, his hands expressive in their movements, standing on his boat, sandwiched between a small stove and a built-in bed, in the docks. "I took my trucks, made myself a little more diverse, focused on the transportation part of my business, and was able to keep myself going till I could get my fishing boats back. This boat here we're sitting on, I invested over $100,000 in it. It was sitting out there in the woods—and FEMA did not help me. I took my eighteen-wheeler out to the highway to move my boat because no-one would help us."

Then the oil spill hit, and the oyster industry all but died. All along the Gulf Coast, the already-battered economy took another beating.

"We have no little oysters, we have nuttin' to look forward to," the oysterman, 57 years old when we met in late 2011, explained glumly.

We're looking at years to recover, and there's nothing really we can do about it. We don't have the funds to rebuild ourselves again.

Katrina, we borrowed money, we scraped, we did what we had to do to recover from the hurricane. Now five years, six years later, we have to recover again, from a disaster which to us was worse than Katrina. We're sitting here with a situation, another disaster, we don't have no way to go to work. The oysters are dead. This community is an oyster community. Without the oysters, this community cannot survive. We're making ten-twelve sacks a day, as a company there's no profit to it. But these are my family. They have to pay their light bills. By the time you pay fuel, boat, groceries, there's nothing left. No way I can catch more than fifteen sacks a day. Right now, they're wondering what's going to happen at Christmas. Most of them have to go home and face their families. So do I. I have to buy my grandkids presents, can't do that this year. I just had to have that conversation with my kids. Most of them just barely scraping up enough money to pay their light bill, if that. This season that started a few weeks back, it's over. It was over when it started. There're no oysters. They're dead. There are no little 'uns to leave there. How am I gonna retire? With what? What am I gonna leave my kids? Bills? Most of the fishermen in this business are in their forties, fifties. Then this. What are you gonna leave your kids? A boat with a bill? You get depressed, because there are people sitting up here selling a bad bill of goods. I've been to London; heard the lies; and they're still going. You've destroyed these people's way of life.

For Byron's younger cousin, Elton, aged 54, standing on the docks in blue jeans tucked into rubber boots, his galoshes crunching against a carpet of discarded shells accumulated over the decades, times were as bleak as he had ever known them. "The only people doing this are people who come from a family of generations doing this. Some like it, some didn't. I love it. It was good for me." Elton started making his living with oysters when he was 17, back in the mid-1970s. "We were wiped out [in Katrina], but since then you get a little hustle here, a little hustle there. We took it day by day, took a little assistance, lived as best you can."

Then, with the oil spill, "we stopped for a year or so, maybe more. Here comes this year's season, we were able to think we could make enough money to get back up—at least $800, $900 per week. [But] you can't make $150 to $200 right now. It take us two days to make twenty sack of oysters. I ain't making no money. I sleep on the boat, because I can't travel back and forth when I'm not working. It's something I have to go through, till it get a little better, you know. It ain't cuttin' the cake, you know what I'm saying? I eat, but I don't know about other needs, keeping insurance on my truck, running back and forth. I don't see it getting any better no time soon. I see it getting worse. That's the way it goes, man, I don't know. Just bad times ahead."

In 2005, insurers paid out $61.9 billion to cover natural disasters in the United States. Hurricane Katrina, of course, America's costliest-ever natural disaster, figured most prominently amidst the catastrophes.[27] Five years later, the oil spill that followed the explosion of BP's Deepwater Horizon rig, in the Gulf of Mexico, resulted in more than $40 billion in damages and cleanup costs,[28] with the livelihoods of thousands of Gulf Coast fishers destroyed. In 2011, a year of epic tornadoes throughout the mid-rift of the country, tens of billions of dollars in damage was done to homes and businesses—insurers paid out $35.9 billion in what the industry terms "catastrophe losses"—and thousands of jobs disappeared as large swaths of towns such as Joplin, Missouri, were literally obliterated. In late 2012, super storm Sandy devastated much of coastal New York, New Jersey, and states further north along the eastern seaboard, resulting in several tens of billions of dollars' worth of damage. Seven of the ten most costly natural disasters in American history have occurred since the year 2000, a product of overbuilding in vulnerable areas; climate change; and a cavalier failure to both upgrade man-made levees and other protections, such as flood control mechanisms for the New York City subway system, against nature, and also to protect nature's own defense systems—mangrove swamps, wetlands, and the like.

With the exception of the Northeast, for which Sandy came as a shocking example of the impacts of climate change on everyday lives, these are parts of the country long used to the forces of nature intruding on, and often ending, lives. Hurricanes, floods, tornadoes, all occur with enough regularity that their presence has been somehow factored in to the daily calculus of life. Yet, as wetlands have been destroyed to make way for tract housing, as the number of fragile trailer parks in tornado zones has grown, as the quantities of marginal people living in marginally served neighborhoods has increased, so the vulnerability of these regions to nature's dark side has grown too.

When they're hit by hurricanes and tornadoes, these communities rely on the Federal Emergency Management Agency (FEMA) for rescue efforts, the provision of emergency shelter, potable water, and myriad other daily needs. Where insurance companies fall short, as they do especially in poor, underinsured neighborhoods, FEMA's responses are frequently all that stand between devastated communities and mass destitution. Hence the horror felt when FEMA trailers provided to the newly homeless in post-Katrina New Orleans were frequently uninhabitable, with stories of units being left unconnected to sewage lines, water pipes and the electricity grid, and with many of them showing signs of formaldehyde contamination.

That FEMA performed abysmally in the days and months surrounding Hurricane Katrina is beyond dispute. That the solution to this is to starve the agency of resources is, however, less obvious. Yet, in 2010, FEMA's budget was cut by more than $700 million. And in mid-2011, Congressional Republicans attempted to cut FEMA's budget again, this time by a whopping 55 percent.[29] They failed. A few months later, however, Congress *did* cut nearly $1 billion from a variety of disaster relief programs, including FEMA, run by the Department of Homeland Security.[30]

The message of these cuts, layered one atop the other, is none too subtle. To be poor in America is increasingly to be vulnerable: to economic collapse for, say, residents of cities such as Flint or Detroit; to natural disaster for, say, residents of New Orleans's Lower Ninth Ward, or Staten Islanders left to scare off looters in blacked-out streets for days and weeks after Sandy devastated their community, and told by FEMA representatives to call 911 when they expressed concern that their unheated residences were unsafe to live in as the New York winter approached. For both groups, to have to rely on government assistance is, increasingly, an exercise in frustration and futility.

CHAPTER SIX

STUCK IN REVERSE

Air force veteran Mark Williams and wife, Theresa, at Oasis Motel, Phoenix, where they live in one room with their three children.

Septuagenerian farm worker Fidencio Fabela in the Sin Frontera Community Center in El Paso.

Subprime mortgages might not, on the surface, have a whole lot in common with hurricanes and oil spills. And yet, time after time, commentators—many of whom had made careers out of boosterish rhetoric around property values—described the housing market's collapse from 2006 on in as utterly unforeseeable, as something akin to an act of God. They were, in this sense, simply following in the footsteps of a slew of theorists who had worked to undermine the social insurance systems built up from the New Deal years onward, and who believed in the inherent, *and desirable*, instability of economic life. While the New Deal had created what Yale University political scientist Jacob Hacker, author of *The Great Risk Shift*, describes as a "security and opportunity society," in which risk was pooled and social benefits widely accessed, from the 1970s onward risk was recalibrated to fall more heavily on individuals. It was, he argued, the modern American economy's defining feature.

"Economic risk is a lot like a hurricane," Hacker wrote a year after Katrina slammed into Louisiana. "Hurricanes strike powerfully and suddenly. They rip apart what they touch: property, landscape, and lives. They are common enough to affect many, yet rare enough still to shock." Pushing the analogy between natural disaster and individual economic calamity in an era in which the safety net was being shredded, he wrote, "What happens in an instant may change a life forever."[1]

And so, ignoring multiple warning signs and past history suggesting the run-up in property values was but the latest in a series of delusional investment bubbles, politicians and economic decision-makers sat out the onset of the crisis. From the sidelines, they issued words of reassurance that turned out to be as hollow, as inept, as did the assurances of politicians in Louisiana in the run-up to the catastrophe that they had the situation under control.

"At present, my baseline outlook involves a period of sluggish growth, followed by a somewhat stronger pace of growth starting later this year as the effects of monetary policy and fiscal stimulus begin to be felt," Federal Reserve chair Ben Bernanke told the Senate Banking Committee in February 2008.[2] Also testifying that same day, Treasury Secretary Henry Paulson declared that the economy was "fundamentally strong, diverse and resilient."[3] Subsequently, as one major part of the financial system after another collapsed in the months following, government statisticians concluded the economy was already in recession when Bernanke and Paulson made their Pollyannaish comments.

Two months later, President George Bush told an audience in New Orleans that the country was experiencing a "slowdown," not a recession.[4] Instead of intervening to cool the overheated market, almost until the day the entire housing market edifice crumbled, the country's top economic opinion-shapers were encouraging more people to take out ultimately unaffordable loans. Instead of regulating banks to ensure that the mortgages they were "bundling" were actually safe investments with which to flood global financial markets, they sat back and watched as "toxic" assets accumulated in the investment portfolios of pension funds, banks, hedge funds, and the like.

As a result of the inaction, what could possibly have been a controllable, localized problem was allowed to fester. When the bubble finally burst, it brought misery not just to individuals, but to entire communities—with people stuck holding properties they could no longer afford, and with basic public functions, such as adequately funding schools, stressed to breaking point by the lost revenues that followed from declining real estate values combined with rising unemployment.

And yet, even then, with the wreckage in plain view, a startling number of senior figures were attempting to minimize the scale of the disaster. In mid-September 2008, with the stock market in free-fall, with oil prices careening up toward $150 a barrel, with major investment banks collapsing, with the credit markets frozen, and with Congress pondering emergency intervention to keep the banking system afloat, Republican presidential candidate John McCain announced to a Florida audience that "the fundamentals of our economy are strong."[5] Barely a week later, a humbled President Bush was forced to address the nation, informing a shell-shocked public that the country's "economy is in danger," and urging Congress to pass extraordinary measures to shore up the global financial system. The country, its leaders were now telling the public, was closer to a complete collapse of its economy than at any time since the Great Depression.[6]

For an increasing number of Americans, what the political leadership was just cottoning on to was something that they had been living in the shadow of for years. For homeowners in California cities such as Stockton or Modesto, or in Arizona or Nevada suburbs, for unemployed construction workers, or social workers in hard-hit deindustrialized regions, poverty was just a part of the landscape by 2008. Omnipresent. Ugly. Too often soul-destroying.

In April 2010, a group of educators and organizers from around California walked hundreds of miles up the Central Valley, from Bakersfield to the state capital of Sacramento, protesting education cuts and holding rallies and meetings with residents along the way. One of them was a middle-aged English teacher named Jim Miller, a tall man with a ponytail, who taught at a community college in downtown San Diego.

The marchers walked along dusty back roads, through communities that had been hammered economically over the previous several years. New poverty layered atop old. Broadly, they followed the route taken by farm workers' organizer Cesar Chavez in his fabled march for economic justice decades earlier, passing shanty towns, tent cities, campgrounds now lived in by foreclosed-on ex-homeowners. Sometimes trade unions gathered their members to join them for stretches of the walk, other times students came out to walk with them. Evenings, they slept in campgrounds, in union halls, in churches.

"It wasn't just educators on the march. There were also people who were working in homecare services, people working as nurses, in other kinds of public safety areas. We wanted the march to say it's not just about our interests as teachers, but everybody—about California's future as a whole," Jim explained.

> You can read in the paper that a quarter of the people who live in the Central Valley live in poverty and one-third of the people in the Central Valley are on some form of public aid. But when you're walking through communities you really see this in a visceral way. So we would be camping somewhere near Delano with farm workers, and you'd have a man whose daughter was just laid off from working in a cafeteria in a public school, drive out and knock on the door of the motor home where we were staying and say "thank you." Simple things.
>
> After a while, it became quite overwhelming, day after day after day of taking in the stories people told you along the way. When you think about the landscape you're going through, you viscerally saw the foreclosure crisis; you'd walk through streets in small towns on the edge, where you'd have blocks of boarded-up houses. We'd stay in trailer parks. Some of them were kind of small towns constructed by people who'd lost their houses and didn't have anywhere to stay but their trailer. All the way up the Valley we found this. You're in the bathroom in the morning shaving, getting ready to march, and you see someone putting on their clothes, getting ready to go to work, because that's where they live now. You're near Fresno and you see something exactly like a Hooverville from the 1930s. It was quite moving, and something you can only get your head around if you're not whizzing past those communities at eighty miles an hour on the I-5.

The walkers wound their way through communities such as Stockton, blighted by vast, impersonal, economic forces. Areas where construction projects had suddenly ground to a halt, leaving half-built ghost towns, and where city services like policing and street lighting had been massively cut back as tax revenues plummeted.

They encountered stories similar to that told by Matthew Joseph, the sheet-metal worker with the devalued Stockton home, whom we first encountered in this book's prologue. "I work in an industry that has been hit hard. I'm a steelworker. What happens is, one day all of us get called into a room. There's a hundred of us; two hundred of us. All of a sudden they say, "In two weeks you're losing your job." How am I going to survive? How am I going to go home and tell my wife?" Joseph wanted to know. "Something's happening to my stature. How am I going to make my house payment? How am I going to support my children?"

For Joseph, his community had become a tapestry woven out of heartache.

In the last few years all you see is people losing their houses. There is no jobs. When you start seeing people even having to turn off their water, and their lawns are getting brown, all of a sudden you see houses falling apart; you could see on the outside what was the hurting part on the inside of each and every one of my neighbors. I have never ever in my life seen more neighbors during the day than I was seeing. Never. I'd go to the mailbox; I noticed there was a ton of people out. I'd never seen so many garage doors open. There was no work. I'd look around and I'd say, "What happened to you?" My neighbor across the street lost his job at the Numi plant where they was building cars. The neighbor next door to me was in the computer business; he lost his job. The neighbors down the street had to move out and move in with their parents and rent their house. I've never seen so many neighbors in my life. When you were younger, you saw your dad go to work, you saw your dad come home. I thought, "How is it I can go out and all my neighbors are out?" None of us are working. You'd see garage sales—things being sold that they didn't want to sell, their most valued possessions. Almost every three houses there was a garage sale, all days of the week. They were selling things just to be able to make ends meet. We had more and more people going through our garbage cans looking for recycles. You have scrappers coming in large trucks looking for metal. They'd go into houses and strip out the wire, pull it out through the ceilings. They take every last single thing you could think of. Leaving the houses with holes, basically nothing inside there. Every last thing down to the light bulbs. We're talking toilets, every fixture you can think of, the lamps, the microwaves.

In Tucson, Arizona, the housing crisis was taking down owners and renters alike. Homeowners unable to pay the monthly bills were losing their homes; renters in foreclosed homes were being evicted. And others, not in foreclosed homes, were losing their jobs, falling behind on their monthly payments and also ending up without roofs over their heads.

Air force veteran Mark Williams, his wife Theresa, and their three young kids were one of these families falling behind. When Mark lost his job, the family could not keep up with the rent; they were evicted, and ended up bouncing from one shelter to the next, looking for a home that felt safe. In one shelter, there were twenty-eight people living in a small house. Several of the residents were on hard drugs. The Williams's daughters got into their first-ever fistfight. In another, they worried that one of the residents was a child molester.

When I met them, the Williams family was crammed into one small room in an emergency shelter run out of the Oasis Motel, a small inn on the edge of town. There were palm trees in the parking lot, and a rather weathered neon sign rising up into the desert-blue sky from atop the office. It was the sort of temporary stopping point one sees all across the country—anonymous, bare-bones, the kind of place one beds down in for a few hours, showers, and then leaves behind. Except for the Williamses it was now their home, the place from which the kids left for school each morning, the place they returned to each night to do their homework. The family's life's possessions were stacked on the floor and in the closet, toys were strewn on the few square feet of floor space, there were recyclables kept in bags in the bathroom, ready to be exchanged for cash later on. For food, they relied on food stamps—Theresa heated the food in a small microwave; for medical care, the kids were on Medicaid and Mark received care through the VA. "We're getting by," said Mark, "but it's hard the way it is right now. I used to get hired anytime I asked for a job. Now, it's not happening. I worry about it a lot. I try my best, try to worry about what I can do and not what I can't. It's day-to-day living. I see light at the end of the tunnel, but I don't know where the light's coming from. I see glimmers of hope, but it's hard to see where it's coming from." Theresa added, "It makes me feel crumpled living here. There's days, I sit and cry on the bed. Hopefully one day we'll have a place to call our own apartment. Not a motel."

BUBBLES AND BUSTS

For 56-year-old Gail Sacco, a onetime restaurateur and longtime volunteer with Las Vegas's growing homeless population, the web of stories that the people whom she worked with brought to the table were endlessly fascinating: returning veterans who couldn't navigate civilian life; addicts and the mentally ill who bounced from one overstrapped agency to the next; families down on their luck and living off of Sin City's scraps. Partly, the stories were deeply personal; partly, they intersected with broader economic trends.

Sacco and her husband frequently drove to Las Vegas's skid row, in Alphabet City, a grid of lettered streets north of the Strip. They ministered to the residents of some of the meanest, rattiest-looking shantytowns anywhere in America, cardboard-and-metal improvised shelters under freeway on-ramps, places where violence was rife and communicable diseases such as tuberculosis incubated.

> There's a lot of issues surrounding homelessness: Some are homeless because of a loss of a job; or because of an illness—medical bills;

foreclosures. Sometimes alcohol and drugs have a lot to do with it. Sometimes people get out of prison and they can't get a job. You can't get food stamps or government help without a state ID. To be able to get a state ID you need a birth certificate. And before you can get a birth certificate you need a state ID. So there's a lot of issues that make it very difficult for the homeless to get off the streets. Some people become homeless and they're not dysfunctional; and once you're on the street two or three months it's enough to make anyone dysfunctional. We have so many veterans coming home from Iraq and Afghanistan. Nevada is the biggest foreclosure state in the country. We have homeless families. We have homeless children.

I have a second house I bought specifically to put troubled homeless in. We bought the house in 2007. We've helped a lot of homeless people, in and out of the house. We've helped the homeless get in touch with family they hadn't seen in ten, fifteen years. We've had a couple people die of cancer at the house.

When I talked with Sacco, the home, worth less than half what it was when she and her husband purchased it, was teetering on the edge of foreclosure.

———————

These were stories familiar also to Artensia Barry, the onetime food pantry worker and anti-poverty activist in California's Bay Area who had taken sick and moved to Las Vegas to live with, and be cared for by, some close friends—a woman, whom she considered to be like her sister, who was a medical assistant; and the woman's husband, who worked at Denny's.

Barry had seen poverty from the perspective of a volunteer—talking with hungry children, providing food to the homeless and so on. Now, living on a few hundred dollars a month in disability payments, she was experiencing it firsthand. Her friends' home, a spacious house with a small pool out back, in a cozy-looking suburb a few miles outside the metropolitan center, was being foreclosed on, after the higher mortgage interest rates that followed the low initial teaser rate kicked in and left the occupants unable to pay their housing bills, and Barry herself was sinking ever deeper into hardship.

> We've been squatting for some time. It hurts. I've had it hard before, but this is the hardest I've ever had it. In August I had to leave, because our air conditioner broke down, and it was going to cost $8,000 to get it replaced. There was no way we could do that. This winter we'll just have to bundle up, because we don't have no heat. We just barely have enough money with the tips he gets from his job at Denny's, we just barely have enough money to eat on. This is what's going on all over Vegas. We're not an exception to the rule. On this block alone, a majority of these homes are being rented; they've been foreclosed on. My neighbor across the street, he's squatting too. He's got a child. Sometimes I sit here and I cry. I know there's a need out there, but there's no way I can help myself let alone help anyone else. And it just breaks my heart.

———

While the housing bust spilled into almost all regions of the country, disproportionately it hit African American and Latino households. In July 2011, the Pew Research Center released an analysis of government data that concluded the median wealth of white households was a staggering eighteen times that of Hispanic homes and twenty times that of African American households. Fueled by disproportionate home foreclosures and underwater mortgages amongst African Americans and Latinos, this data indicated a reversal of decades-long trends toward reducing such inequalities. "From 2005 to 2009, inflation-adjusted median wealth fell by 66 percent among Hispanic households and 53 percent among black households," the authors wrote, "compared with just 16 percent among white households."[7]

In working-class African American neighborhoods of Boston, for example, predatory lenders targeted residents for years, encouraging them both to take out variable rate mortgages and also to borrow heavily against the paper value of their homes. When the market collapsed, many of these homeowners were left with no way to pay off their debts, leading to an epidemic of foreclosures.

Take the case of the Boston cop who had bought his three-story home from his parents in 1985, intending to rent it out for extra cash. During the housing boom, its value had skyrocketed and he had refinanced and then refinanced again, taking on one dubious, adjustable-rate, subprime loan after another. At its peak, the home was worth $560,000 and he owed $470,000 on it, with monthly payments of $2,800.

But, it turned out that was just the teaser rate. After three years, the variable rate kicked in and his mortgage payments jumped to $4,000; and at the same time, the value of the property collapsed down to about $280,000, making it impossible for him to refinance. Despite his policeman's salary, he fell behind on payments, and at the beginning of January 2010 he stopped paying entirely and the bank began foreclosure proceedings against him.

Then there is the story of Sophia Marks, 39 years old in late 2010, when she had to show up at Housing Court to plead to be able to stay in her home. Marks, who worked as a secretary, took a variable-rate mortgage out for $330,000 in 2005 and then watched in horror as her monthly payment rose from $2,000 to $2,600 just when her house's value collapsed to $150,000 and her husband got laid off from his job with the city's transit authority. Despite wiring thousands of dollars to the company that held her mortgage to try to avoid going into foreclosure, Sophia's home was eventually sold out from under her for $165,000.

GORDIAN KNOTS

If we had been paying more attention, as a society, to our economic problems, we would have noticed a spreading series of poverty-lesions around America in the early 2000s. We didn't pay enough attention, however; and thus it came as a huge shock when the housing market collapse, the financial crisis, and the cascading unemployment that followed in its wake, demonstrated just how hollowed out much of the economy had become.

The housing market crisis, Timothy Geithner—at the time a senior figure in the Federal Reserve, subsequently to be President Obama's Treasury Secretary—confidently declared in late 2006, as evidence built that house prices were in for a period of steep decline, wouldn't grow into a full-blown financial crisis. There were, said Geithner, ways to produce a soft landing that wouldn't create "collateral damage."[8] Of course, the housing market *did* end up crashing, at least in part because debt-ridden homeowners couldn't weather the blows when their houses ceased to be worth what they once were, or when their home equity lines of credit dried up, or when the variable rates on their subprime mortgages kicked in. And when it crashed, the collateral damage was catastrophic. Had more opinion-makers been paying attention to just how financially vulnerable America's working poor had become, this would not have been a surprise.

Nor would they have been surprised when the financial crisis, once unleashed, triggered a soaring increase in poverty. After all, financial collapses invariably bring devastation to the job market. And when people don't have rainy-day funds to fall back on, even short spells out of work can cause them economic mayhem.

All of which brings us back to the Gordian knot, tying in place a massive level of poverty in the heart of the world's most powerful economy. In communities long defined by their affluence, residents find themselves awash in debt through a toxic combination of job losses and the collapse of the housing bubble. Suburbs depleted of their tax base have seen infrastructure corrode, public services and schools decay, and quality of life for residents decline. Individuals who have long considered themselves solidly, safely middle-class find themselves sliding down the economic ladder. It is, argued Yale University political scientist Hacker,

> an erosion of the sources of economic security. People are much less likely to have health insurance through work than they were a generation ago, unlikely to have a defined benefit retirement plan; we've seen workplace insecurity rise. It used to be that corporations would internalize a lot of the risk for their workers. Corporations value those risk protections less than they once did; they don't want to carry the cost. They've off-loaded them onto individual workers and their families. The corporations that are off-loading these risks are also in many cases writing the rules and the laws, or pushing back against efforts to try to deal with the resulting fallout from their actions.

This has huge impacts on people's daily lives. "It means that people are much less secure financially," Hacker explained.

> Debt levels have dramatically risen. Bankruptcy is much more common than it used to be. In the early 1980s, we are talking about a few hundred thousand Americans filing for consumer bankruptcy. By the mid-2000s, there were about 2 million households filing for bankruptcy. That's a huge change. In recent years, poverty has risen to the highest levels we've seen in twenty years or more. Many Americans are struggling to get good benefits and good pay. What's really striking are those falls down the ladder, those big drops in income have become much more frequent over the last generation. In recent years, about 20 percent of individuals in the United States have been seeing household income drops of 25 percent or greater

in any given year from one year to the next. For the last three years, every year we've been seeing more than one in five individuals seeing those kinds of drops.

For "Lisa," (not her real name) a well-qualified, college-educated, middle-aged divorcée in Salt Lake City, the choices became increasingly stark after she lost her job as a retail analyst in early 2008, at the start of the recession, ran through her unemployment insurance, and depleted her savings. Unable to keep up the house that she had emerged from her marriage with as a part of the divorce settlement, and behind on her car payments, Lisa finally packed up her bags and moved to Colorado, hoping to start life afresh in a state in which she had many friends. It didn't happen. Still unemployed, and with her money supplies further dwindling, Lisa returned to her home town with $69 to her name, began couch-surfing at friends' houses, and started posting adverts on Craig's List asking if anybody would temporarily house her for free. Nobody said "yes," but, she recalled, several people sent her back lascivious emails, suggesting that she turn to prostitution to make ends meet. It wasn't a savory choice, but, with her options pretty much exhausted, Lisa, who was then 46 years old and a new grandmother, decided it was worth a try. And so, she stated, trying too hard to sound matter-of-fact, she started "sleeping with men for money. It was terrible. [But], I was married to a man I didn't have love for for the last seven years of my marriage. I stayed with him for the security. I thought this [the prostitution] is no different from marriage. I just shut it out."

Eventually, Lisa found a new, more legitimate job and tried to forget about what she had done. But, she realized, she had become far more aware of life's fragilities. "In a week it can change drastically. I'm older now, have absolutely no safety net for my retirement. I had no health insurance. I needed things done. I didn't. My shoulder's frozen now. It's taken its toll on my health." The tough face suddenly crumbled, and all at once Lisa started to cry. She wiped

her tears away, smiled, put on a face of bonhomie. "As my grandmother used to say, my bladder's between my eyes."

The tears welled up again. Once more, she batted them away.

WHEN WORK DOESN'T PAY THE BILLS

That so many people were seeing huge drops in income, with the resulting, and all-too-predictable, impacts on their ability to pay their
mortgages, rents, and other basic bills, wasn't just to do with unemployment. It was also to do with a political push to dismantle prevailing wage structures, and to keep the minimum wage extraordinarily
low in many states. In fact, in the years prior to the onset of the Great
Recession, much of the worst poverty data came out of states with
lower-than-average unemployment. In places like Idaho and Texas,
the jobs were there; they just were no longer paying enough to live on.
In 2011, researchers with the Economic Policy Institute estimated
that if the government entirely absented itself from the business of tax
subsidies and assistance to the poor, the poverty rate in America
would immediately jump up to 23.7 percent. The reason? As was the
case in Victorian-era England, millions of twenty-first-century Americans, living in a period during which trade unions were on the wane
and the power of employers on the rise, were having to work jobs that
didn't even get them up to subsistence-level living.[9]

While some liberal states created their own higher-than-the-
federal minimum wage, and a handful of cities, from Santa Fe to
San Francisco, adopted what they called "living wage ordinances,"
other states moved in the opposite direction during the latter years
of the twentieth and early years of the twenty-first centuries. By
2012, twenty-three states had adopted so-called "right to work"
laws, which made it harder to organize workers into trade unions.
The "right" they codified was, in reality, a right to work for lower
wages than was the case in states where unions retained more power.
A majority of these states were in the South; but, increasingly, as

conservative groups such as the American Legislative Exchange Council and the U.S. Chamber of Commerce championed the legislation, this was a movement with national legs. States such as Utah and North Dakota adopted these laws in the 1950s; Idaho, which had once had a proudly militant union culture, in 1985; Indiana, in 2012. In states with these laws, union membership plummeted, and, predictably, wages fell.[10] As a result, even before the Great Recession hit, real incomes for working-class Americans were lower in the early 2000s than they had been a generation earlier. To remind readers of the salient numbers here: The median wage peaked in 1973 at $33,000 in 2010 dollars. By 2005, during the roaring decade that preceded the financial collapse, that median wage was down to $29,000; and in the years following, as the broader pillars of the economy tottered, it fell still further, toward the $26,000 mark.[11] Millions of people were working full time yet being inexorably swept backward economically.

That was why Pastor Royce Wright started running a food pantry for residents of low-income communities outside of Boise a few years before the Great Recession kicked in. And that's why, even after the recession technically ended, his Oasis Food Center—operating out of a complex across Simplot Avenue from the railway lines and potato processing plants, about half a mile from a large and particularly down-at-the-heels trailer park—still gave out boxes of free food twice a week. On Wednesdays, the doors opened early, and catered mainly to the out-of-work; on Thursdays, the pantry gave out food from four to six in the afternoon, with a clientele, said Royce, mainly consisting of low-wage and part-time workers from the nearby towns, people working but still being buffeted by the economic storm. An hour before the doors opened, hundreds of men and women, along with a fair number of children, would line up outside, given a number that would entitle them to leave the facility with some bread, milk, a bag of cheese, if they were lucky some frozen hot dogs, and on a good day a handful of vegetables.

It was also why Texas Governor Rick Perry could enter the presidential primary contest in 2011 claiming that he'd presided over a period of extraordinary job growth in the Lone Star State, while his opponents could decry the fact that 17.9 percent of Texans lived in poverty, and 7.4 percent in extreme poverty; that 6.3 million Texans had no health benefits, which meant that a larger percentage of the population in Texas had no access to medical coverage than in any other state in America; and that a higher percentage of the state's residents were "food insecure" than in all but one other state.

Both sets of claims were true: Texas *was* seeing more jobs being created—between January 2006 and January 2011 it added over half a million positions, while other states were hemorrhaging employment. But they were low-paying, non-benefited, and frequently dead-end in character. The state wasn't educating workers well enough to help them move up the economic ladder; it wasn't investing adequately in job training programs; it wasn't putting resources into monitoring workplace conditions. For employers, Perry's Texas was a low-wage, low-regulation paradise. For employees, too often it was a place of crushing drudgery.[12]

Unfortunately, where Texas goes, so goes much of the nation, an argument developed by *New York Times* columnist Gail Collins, in her 2012 book *As Texas Goes*. Increasingly, at the state level, conservative GOP legislators and governors, at the urging of groups such as the U.S. Chamber of Commerce and the American Legislative Exchange Council, have moved against public sector unions, welfare recipients, against services offered by federally funded programs like Medicaid, and even against the unemployed—in Florida and elsewhere, legislators have pushed for unemployment insurance applicants to have to be fingerprinted and drug-tested, essentially putting in place practices that send out the none-too-subtle signal that the unemployed are to be viewed and treated as criminals. Georgia and a handful of other states, have pushed similar measures on welfare applicants.

In Wisconsin, Tea Party–backed governor Scott Walker spent the first several months of his gubernatorial tenure attempting to break public sector unions in the state. His counterparts in Ohio and Indiana launched similar campaigns, as did Paul LePage, in Maine.

The unions, Walker announced, were "special interests," stubbornly unwilling to negotiate away unreasonably generous benefits to help a hard-pressed state balance its books. His message, however manipulative, resonated with a significant percentage of the workforce. When the trade union movement generated enough petition signatures to force a recall election against Walker, outside groups such as the U.S. Chamber of Commerce spent tens of millions of dollars on a campaign defending the governor. On Election Day, in June 2012, Walker handily won re-election.

DOING BUSINESS TEXAS-STYLE

If the private sector experience with rampant anti-unionizing efforts, and the emergence of a workforce lacking decent benefits and having almost no clout in negotiations with management, is anything to go by, Wisconsin's public sector workers, as well as those in the other states contemplating changes to their collective bargaining rules, have plenty to fear.

Let's return to Texas again, this time to hear from 67-year-old Mary Vasquez, whose Social Security check was $600 and whose rent was $500. A little woman, her health broken by cancer, heart attacks, diabetes, high blood pressure, and a multitude of other ailments, her crinkled face a map of pain and heartache, Vasquez, to make ends meet, worked as a phone operator at a Walmart on the outskirts of Dallas. When we met in December 2011, she showed me her pay stubs to date for the year. In the first eleven months of 2011, she had earned slightly under $23,800. After taxes, exorbitant health insurance premiums, and automatic deductions to buy Walmart stock—a faux-savings option that the mega-company strongly encourages its employees to make, despite the fact that most such workers remain too poor to ever be able to retire on these savings—in those eleven months she netted $15,887, a large part of which went to pay for medical expenses covered neither by Medicare nor her Walmart healthcare plan; much of the remainder of it went to pay down usurious payday loan debts that she'd accumulated in recent years as her health declined.

Sitting in a union hall in the suburb of Grapevine—Vasquez was one of a handful of local Walmart employees pushing to unionize her workplace—the elderly lady, who hobbled around using a walker, explained how she skipped "mostly breakfast and sometimes lunch." Diabetic, she was supposed to eat fresh produce; instead, she said, for dinners "a lot of times I buy a TV dinner; we have them on sale for 88 cents. A lot of times, food I can't pay for." Vasquez's plight was all too common in the Lone Star state. Recall, again, that according to the Center for Public Policy Priorities, three years into the Great Recession, despite boasting relatively strong job growth, Texas had the second worst rate of food insecurity in the country.[13] Yet, at the same time, compared to much of the country, it had a low unemployment rate: as of the summer of 2012 it stood at 7.2 percent, far below California's 10.7 percent, or New York's 9.1 percent, and significantly below the national rate of 8.3 percent.[14] Texas governor Rick Perry had run his ill-fated campaign to become the Republican presidential nominee in large part by touting his state's low unemployment numbers.

So why the skyrocketing food insecurity in Texas? In large part because more and more of the working poor, in a state with only the federal minimum wage, were earning rock-bottom wages. In 2010, the U.S. Bureau of Labor Statistics estimated that Texas and Mississippi were tied for having highest percentage of their workforces earning only at or below the federal minimum wage of $7.25 per hour. Fully 550,000 Texans were stuck at this wage level—about half of them actually earning *less* than the legal minimum—with millions more earning not much more.[15]

For companies such as Walmart, all of this was, quite simply, great for business. Taking advantage of the anti-union, anti-labor environment, the world's biggest retailer opened up dozens of stores in the 1990s and 2000s in the Lone Star state. In the Dallas region alone, by 2012 it had more than twenty outlets.[16] Texas's low-wage environment apparently meshed perfectly with Walmart's employment philosophy. According to the online wage-monitoring site Glassdoor, as of mid-2012 the average pay for a Walmart sales associate was $8.88 an hour; for a "guest service team member" it was $8.42; for a cashier $8.62.[17]

When meat-cutters in its Jacksonville, Texas, store tried to unionize in 2000 to better their working conditions, the company responded by eliminating the butcher's section from its store, limiting itself to prepackaged meats instead so as to avoid having to negotiate with a labor union.[18] It's a tactic the company has perfected all over the country—rousing the wrath of organizations such as Human Rights Watch but proving remarkably good for business.[19] In 2011, Walmart posted profits of more than $15 billion.[20] After all, keeping workers nonunion allows the company to pay wages so low that the children of many employees end up on Medicaid, the workers themselves on food stamps.

In October 2012 several Walmart workers in the Los Angeles area launched a strike against the company; and a month later, on Black Friday, the biggest shopping day of the year, Walmart workers in several stores around the country, including some in Dallas, walked off the job, in a rolling attempt to force the company to recognize the UFCW and other unions. Walmart's response? A spokesperson denounced the action as a "union-funded publicity stunt."[21]

But for the employees, this wasn't a stunt; it was about basic dignity. Mary Vasquez routinely borrowed from payday loan companies to tide her over; she scrounged food from friends and relatives; she had so little money set aside for retirement that she believed she would have to work until she died. Several of her co-workers, she confided, were in their seventies; one, in her eighties, worked until she finally couldn't do so anymore and then, lacking the money to stay in her own home, had to go to live with one of her children. "Makes me feel cheated," Vasquez declared. "Just the way I feel; don't know why I feel like that. You don't know what it [poverty] is unless you've experienced it, unless you've been down that road."

Trapped by circumstance, Vasquez had no way out. She had the misfortune to be an elderly, low-wage American worker during a time of growing insecurity and—when it came to poverty—national myopia.

"If America was a corporation, it would today be the equivalent of IBM in the early 1990s—an industry giant that's failing to keep up with the times," wrote the statistician and United Nations health economist Howard Friedman, in his 2012 book *The Measure of a Nation*. "Once a world leader, it is now facing bankruptcy, lagging behind in major market segments like health, safety, education, democracy and even equality."[22]

INEQUALITY'S A GOOD THING . . .
UNLESS YOU'RE POOR

The low-wage-low-benefit vortex generally affects not just individuals but whole communities. Bereft of opportunity, such locales prove unattractive to those with options—with education, with valued skills, with drive. These men and women tend to leave, to bigger cities, to other states. Left behind in small towns with only low-wage employment, the rest of the population face daunting prospects.

Drive into a speck on the map such as Caldwell, in Canyon County, Idaho, and one is instantly hit by a sense of futility. The storefronts are beaten up; the homes ramshackle, paint flecked, walls akimbo. On the afternoons that the local food pantry is giving out boxes of food, about half a mile from a sprawling, mean-looking trailer park nestled off to the side of a freeway on-ramp, the lines are quite simply immense.

Many of the pantry clients are out-of-work loggers. Others are farmers who can no longer make ends meet. Some are on disability. Several are on unemployment or welfare. There's a *Grapes of Wrath* quality to their appearance, something weathered, stoic, patient. They stand in line by the score, still, quiet, under the large pantry logo of two palm trees rising up on the edge of a gorgeous blue sea, waiting for bags of old lettuces and onions, soggy cucumbers, frozen hot dogs and bologna, and lots of bread.

Not surprisingly, given this diet, most of the clients are chronically overweight. Others, like 60-year-old Robert Burke, a disabled ex-logger, trucker, and general jack-of-all-trades, in battered jeans, a faded green T-shirt, and a thick red-and-black parka, are skinnier, harder looking. "When you can't afford it, you can't afford it," he said in simple explanation for why he was on line for free food, his sandy eyebrows raised slightly, his face deeply lined. "You've got to find it someplace. I've done ranch work, logged, trucked, worked on most everything I can work on. And now I can't. I don't feel right doing it [visiting the pantry]. But they give you canned goods, frozen food, meat, bread, potatoes, onions, carrots." Two-thirds of his meals, he estimated, came from pantry donations. "I'm taking care of three grandkids, and they eat before I do. It's hard. You go without what you can go without. Sometimes you go without fuel; sometimes you go without gas, propane—for cooking. I cook on open fire. Ever since the job situation has been going down, a lot of people been needing." One-third of Burke's friends were out of work. "Truck drivers, ranchers, some of them just been common laborers. A lot are on unemployment. People need it [food], got to get it. It hurts a lot of people."

———

For many conservative politicians, however, that squalor isn't all bad. In fact, an increasingly vocal line of reasoning, harking back to the Social Darwinism, survival-of-the-fittest rhetoric of the late nineteenth century, has it that it represents something quintessentially hopeful. The flip side of inequality, they argue, is opportunity. Anyone can, in America, strike it rich. All one needs for success is a little bit of gumption and a willingness to take risks. That was, in many ways, the key argument that GOP presidential hopeful Rick Santorum laid out in a major speech before the Detroit Economic Club on February 16, 2012. "I'm about equality of opportunity. I'm not about equality of result when it comes to income inequality. There is income inequality in America. There always has been, and hopefully, and I do say that, there always will be," Santorum told his audience, in a city in which two-thirds of children were currently living below the poverty line. "Why? Because people rise to different levels of success based on what they contribute to society and to the marketplace. And that's as it should be. And we shouldn't have a society that has a president who envies or creates class warfare or envy between one group of people and another. We should celebrate like we do in the small towns all across America—as you do here in Detroit."[23]

How were Detroiters celebrating America's economic buoyancy in 2012? By increasingly resorting to small-scale urban farms to avoid hunger. By arguing over Mayor David Bing's desperate proposal to declare largely abandoned swaths of the city beyond municipal limits and thus to withdraw basic services such as street lighting and police protection from those areas, as well as close to half of the public schools within its district. Maybe by scratching their heads and painstakingly attempting to interpret the Detroit Regional Workforce Fund report from a year earlier that had found 47 percent of the city's residents to be functionally illiterate.[24]

Utterly wedded to a rigid market ideology—to a belief system that holds that whatever outcomes the market, left to its own devices, generates must be right—the Social Darwinists of modern politics simply cannot fathom why a society would need to intervene to break cycles of poverty that, again by definition, are caused by personal failings. Once upon a time, the absolute social mobility that they believed produced fair economic outcomes *might* have been the case for certain groups in society. Not for enslaved African Americans, clearly; not for Native Americans kicked off their land; not for women; almost certainly not for poor white sharecroppers. . . . But possibly for other non-share-cropping white males. Yet, even by the logic of that truncated definition of "society," today clearly America is not a land that produces equal opportunities for all to excel. In fact, a slew of recent studies have found that Americans born into poverty move up the income ladder less frequently than their peers do in areas of the world such as Germany, the Scandinavian countries, Canada, France, and many other advanced industrial democracies; and that the incomes of children born into poverty end up more closely resembling their parents' income than is the case elsewhere. The reports come not just from liberal academics and think tanks, but also from establishment institutions such as the Boston branch of the Federal Reserve, and government data-collecting agencies such as the Bureau of Labor Statistics. On measure after measure, social mobility in the United States has fallen off from where it was in previous eras; and, as worrying, a host of other countries that used to trail America in terms of the opportunities they afforded the impoverished amongst their citizenry now stand out as providing increased levels of opportunity.[25]

For a country built on notions of self-improvement, home to millions of immigrants and their descendants—who came, and come, to a country they believe gives them opportunities to succeed that they would have nowhere else on earth—that curtailment of opportunity at the bottom of the economy is peculiarly devastating.

Today, the scale of inequality, and the concentrated nature of poverty, ossify rather than free up society. They lock huge numbers of people into place. And condemn cities such as Detroit, towns such as Caldwell, and numerous villages and informal settlements around the country to near-certain decline and economic depression.

LIVING LIKE KINGS

These days, many of the poorest workers are undocumented migrants, the tier of the population most despised by the broader community and most exploited by employers but, ironically, the part of the population one can argue has the most in common with the Horatio Alger types so celebrated by Santorum and others. After all, these are the men and women who decided economic conditions in their home countries were too desperate, and who made the decision to better themselves, albeit without legal documentation backing them up, by crossing over into America to look for work and prosperity. They come seeking pavements plated with gold; frequently, instead, they find base metal.

They are women such as Maria, who, as recounted earlier in the book, fled Mexico after one of her daughters was shot dead, and who ended up homeless in Albuquerque, going from house to house with her youngest surviving daughter, begging for food. Eventually, a local church took pity on them, and found them a family who would give them shelter in exchange for them looking after an elderly man who lived in the house. They gave her food, and, sometimes, a few dollars. But what they didn't give—and she couldn't ask for—was a salary. Years later, she was still working as a live-in home help, for another family. In theory she *was* now paid a salary, $8 an hour for thirty-three hours per week. In practice, however, she was on call twenty-four hours per day, seven days a week, putting her far below the hourly minimum wage.

Fifty-one years old, Maria had no savings, no bank account, no pension, no home of her own, nothing to call hers but a few outfits of clothing that she had picked up cheap from yard sales, or that employers had given to her once they had decided to no longer wear them.

Or they have stories similar to another woman named Maria, and her husband, a couple who had lived in Phoenix, Arizona, for years, but who moved out of the state in 2010 following passage of the state's SB 1070, one of the country's harshest anti-illegal-immigrant laws. Fearing that they would be either harassed or deported, Maria's husband, who had worked as an equipment operator on building sites before losing his job during the recession, packed their furniture into an old truck, and drove his family's possessions to a small apartment in a run-down barrio in south Albuquerque. There the couple now lived with their two daughters. In a good month, he might make $800 painting houses and doing other casual work. Five hundred went straight away to pay the rent. They received $366 in food stamps for their daughters, who were born in the United States, and the children were on Medicaid. But for the adults, there was no aid, no medical care, no relief except for the charity food that Maria picked up on Thursdays from a local church.

As mentioned earlier in the book, the presence of millions of such workers in America has made discussions of anti-poverty programs more complicated than was the case during the 1960s, when far fewer undocumented immigrants beat the path to America. Absent a pathway to legality, absent a comprehensive immigration reform being implemented, these workers will continue to exist in the shadows. And, in those shadows, they will continue to be horrendously maltreated.

Half a mile south of El Paso's old, brick-and-stone downtown, Ninth Avenue runs along the railway tracks that abut the Rio Grande. South of the river is Juarez, Mexico. The two international bridges that daily disgorge thousands of visitors, migrant workers, and would-be immigrants, do so onto Ninth Avenue. All along that street, in plain view of the barbed-wire-surrounded Department of Homeland Security compound, migrants sleep, their meager possessions hung in plastic bags from the low-hanging branches of trees planted into the sidewalk; and, come midnight, they wake up to seek out the street's ubiquitous labor contractors. If they're lucky, they get hired for the day, are put onto trucks at 3 A.M., and then are driven to fields throughout south Texas and southern New Mexico. By daybreak, they are hard at work.

And so, it makes sense that it is on Ninth Avenue that Carlos Marentes, a onetime political cartoonist who migrated to the United States in the mid-1970s, runs a community center for impoverished farm laborers, some of them legal, many others in the country without documentation. There, they can get a free meal, a place to sleep, some hand-me-down clothes, and a bathroom. Evenings, before the midnight stampede, dozens of men, women, and children doze back-to-back in its halls and offices. Some of the migrants have lived out of the center for years.

"We provide services here," said Marentes in a soft, gentle voice. "All kinds of services. From access to education, problems associated with becoming unemployed, and that the family has nothing to eat or they're facing eviction. Referrals to other agencies and other services."

For Marentes, the ongoing border wars, the brutality of the language surrounding the immigration debate, largely missed the point: His clients were doing work that others didn't want to do, for wages others wouldn't accept, and not only did they face ongoing hostility simply for being in the country, but, increasingly, they also found their wages bid down because so many agricultural jobs were now done by machines. "You have an oversupply of labor," Marentes explained. "That is a condition the employers take advantage of. The result is the farm workers are the poorest of all the workers."

Seasonal agricultural workers in the El Paso region, estimated Marentes, earned on average a mere $6,000 per year, putting them so deeply into poverty that merely reaching the federal poverty line was an all-but-impossible dream.

Septuagenarian Fidencio Fabela, who lived in Marentes's community center for years, sleeping on whatever few square feet of floor space was available, before moving into a small apartment, and who still routinely got up in the middle of the night to hire himself out to contractors, explained it this way: "I work in anything from the chili harvest to preparing the lettuce harvest, and in the cotton fields cleaning the rows of leaves." A wizened, toothless, short-of-stature man, with the wrinkled face of someone who has spent decades working under the hot sun, speaking in Spanish he added that, "at this age, I don't have steady work. I just get temporary jobs. I get $8 per hour. The work starts around six, and goes to two or three in the afternoon." Onion harvests, he declared, were the hardest. "You're bent over. People in that harvest don't last. It gets so bad that after a little while you can't sit down. There's no remedy. Within a short time you experience a lot of back pain."

Laurentino Loera, a large man in his late fifties, with a hangdog mustache and kindly, sympathetic eyes, had a similar story. A seasonal worker who grew up as a *campesino* in Mexico, he spent his evenings sleeping at the center—he had lived there on and off since it had first opened—and his days looking for work.

Autumn opportunities for Laurentino were few and far between. Some days before I met him, he had had to pawn his only possession, a small, portable, black-and-white television, in order to get money for food. And, when he did find work, picking chilis, Laurentino would bring in only about $30.

> I lived in Juarez for a while. Then I lived in San Antonio. I've been here [at Sin Frontera] on and off since it's been in existence, since 1994. We just sleep in the common areas—brothers. We all sleep there. I keep my possessions in the top room. Before, I used to have some things. At this point I don't have any things. It's been two years since I've been separated from my wife. I just exist. As far as clothes, I have a few, maybe six or eight changes of clothes. I have no savings. I'll look for some work; I'll find some work at some point. We try to figure out how to survive. Before, I used to travel north to look for work during this period of slowdown. I've gone through different states in between the harvests. Where I used to work, they're not hiring Mexicans anymore—they mainly hire people from the U.S. now.

At this point, I'm waiting for the end of the year, for the next opportunity to work. I'm looking forward to work. In the meantime, I'll make do.

How will you live if you survive long enough to reach retirement age? I asked him tentatively. He laughed, a deep, full-throated laugh. "Like a king," Laurentino answered, and chuckled again at the naïveté of my question.

CONCLUSION

In early twenty-first-century America, increasingly the visual boundaries of poverty have blurred. A middle-class African American community might have beautiful homes but have been devastated by predatory lending. A suburb of Las Vegas might look like a commercial for a sunny tomorrow, but in fact be home to a calamitous concentration of downward mobility. An upper-middle-class widow, bankrupted by her dying husband's healthcare bills, might be on food stamps. A church deacon, recently made unemployed, might be skipping meals as he tries to keep his home.

No longer constrained by boundaries of geographic region, ethnicity, urban neighborhood, or history, poverty—given free rein in large part by the housing collapse, by cascading unemployment and underemployment, and by the exorbitant cost of healthcare—is showing up around the country.

The older, more ingrained hardship described so vividly by Michael Harrington in 1962 is also still alive and well, in devastated urban centers and isolated rural communities, in the shabbily constructed, often illegal, colonias lived in by large numbers of undocumented migrants and in manufacturing regions left to sink in an era of outsourced jobs.

Taken as a whole, poverty now afflicts tens of millions of Americans. Too often their stories have been ignored. In the preceding pages, I have sought to present their voices, to bring out of the silent shadows the experiences of these millions of men, women, and children. In the pages to come, I shall detail a set of policies intended to reverse the country's shocking slide toward mass economic insecurity.

That a new societal assault on poverty, a War on Poverty Mark II, if you will, is needed has, I trust, been established by the stories in the first part of this book, as has the necessity of a concentrated effort against the political and economic conditions that generate chronic, mass insecurity. That such an undertaking can succeed will, I hope, now be shown.

PART TWO

Building a New and Better House

WHY NOW?

Lower Ninth Ward landscape. Darren McKinney was working on the shell of a building to the left of the photo when the author interviewed him.

Shortly after the 2008 presidential election, longtime anti-poverty organizer Jim Wallis, head of the nationally renowned group Sojourners, which had campaigned on social justice themes since the early 1970s, asked Barack Obama if he would commit to a goal of cutting poverty in half in ten years. It was a goal that had recently been articulated by a coalition of progressive organizations under the catchy title Half in Ten. Obama, according to Wallis, replied that he would.

But in the years following that conversation, the momentum toward a new War on Poverty stalled. Preoccupied with preventing further economic collapse following the cascading crises of 2008, the Obama administration focused on damage control rather than a proactive anti-poverty program. "No one's even talking about that now," Wallis noted sadly. "All we're talking about is a circle of protection," a *cordon sanitaire* around existing programs, thus sealing them off from the most aggressive cuts being bandied about in D.C. "No one has an anti-poverty agenda." Here is one indication of how far out of the political spotlight poverty had fallen: as of mid-2012, of the approximately 5,000 registered lobbyists in Washington, D.C., only one firm, Advocates for the Other America, marketed itself as focusing exclusively on legislation relating to poverty and to low-income Americans. Advocates for the Other America had a staff of one registered lobbyist, Brad Penney, and one ex-legislator from West Virginia, Arley Johnson, who hoped to soon become a lobbyist. "Every time you turn around, low-income discretionary programs are being cut. And one reason is they don't have that lobbying voice on the Hill," argued Johnson, who had grown up in a ten-child family in a hardscrabble mining community deep in Appalachia. "Members [of Congress] don't feel there's a price to pay, because the poor don't have political clout, don't participate civically, don't vote in the same numbers as some of the larger voting blocs."

Yet, behind the scenes, for many years now a slew of academics, policy wonks, community organizers, and economists *have* been developing ideas about what a new war on poverty, and more broadly a renewed relationship between government and populace, would look like. "We've got our critique of the current economic moment down pat," noted George Goehl, executive director of the National People's Action organization. "We've been talking about how do we pivot to the aspirational, the economy as it *could* be. The direness of the moment has created a new openness to new questions. The appetite for rethinking things is much different from anything I've experienced."

———————

My hope is that the stories in the first part of this book will serve to stimulate both our national imagination and our empathy, opening the door to a more general conversation about how best to tackle cascading poverty. My intent is that the second part of the book will present a roadmap to change, a blueprint for a new War on Poverty, as the country starts to pay long overdue attention to this crisis.

In this second part, I shall touch on many vital reforms—and will point the reader toward experts in specific areas whose work goes into more detail on individual changes than I will be able to do in the space of these pages.

My purpose is not to suggest that we enforce absolute equality on a population of 300 million people. Despite the fearmongering raised by conservatives whenever conversations about equity take center stage, absolute equality is neither possible nor remotely desirable; it is, in fact, a straw man. Rather, I hope to suggest ways of limiting the extreme levels of inequality that have, increasingly, come to derail the American civic project in recent decades, as well as developing quality uses for hard-earned tax dollars so that large numbers of Americans are willing, once more, to fund the sorts of ambitious societal investments that allowed for the creation of Social Security, Medicare, and unemployment insurance. Nor is my goal to undermine important moral and philosophical notions about the importance of personal responsibility; rather, it is to suggest ways of giving everybody an opportunity to maximize their own potential.

Last, my intent is certainly not to propose a set of policies that inexorably increase the national debt; nor is it to suggest that the country's political leaders somehow spin money out of nothing. The size of America's economy, as of this writing, is in the region of $16 trillion per year. That's large, but it's not limitless. In an era of anxieties about ballooning budget deficits, I want to show how, in redistributing a few hundred billion dollars per year of that $16 trillion economy, through changes to the tax structure and changes in how we prioritize federal and state spending—or, to put it another way, in reprioritizing who receives and who spends about 2 to 3 percent of the vast national pot of wealth that is America, while leaving undisturbed the remaining 97 to 98 percent—we can create a set of vital anti-poverty initiatives that have the potential to dramatically improve the lives of tens of millions of Americans. And I want to show how, if done smartly, these initiatives can serve as a down payment for a decades-long push that has the potential not just to ameliorate poverty once it arises but to make its presence a rarity rather than a commonplace in mid-twenty-first-century American life.

My design, in these chapters, is to sketch the general outlines of a truly national anti-poverty campaign, a new War on Poverty that tackles both short-term hardship and long-term destitution, that deals with difficulties faced by individuals and by communities, and that seeks to set in place a series of support beams within the economy and the body politic to minimize people's vulnerability to the exigencies of the market.

Readers should come away from *The American Way of Poverty* with an understanding of the interconnectedness of these issues, of the complexity both of the world of poverty and also of anti-poverty strategies, and with a sense of the changes—both in political attitude and practical administration—that need to be embarked upon in order to reverse the increasing economic polarization that, more so by the day, is coming to define twenty-first-century America.

Any systemic push to first significantly reduce poverty, and then to prevent its rapid recurrence, will, of course, have to include many moving parts: local, state, and federal government involvement, including changes in how we raise taxes and how we spend revenues. Attention must be paid to the kinds of debt that we as a society encourage people to accrue, and the sorts of institutions we allow to issue that debt. Additionally, we must consider immigration reform, new energy policies, and changes in the way we use the criminal justice system. Overuse of incarceration is both expensive, and thus a huge drain on limited public resources, and also inimical to the public policy goal of eliminating entrenched poverty. We must look to public-private partnerships as well as nonprofit and philanthropic engagement in arenas such as education, services for the mentally ill, programs available to foster youth as they age out of the foster care system, and the building of affordable housing units. We need aid tailored to meet the needs of geographically distressed regions—and so on.

Poverty is, after all, a web of problems enormous in their complexity. It bubbles up because of systemic failures in how the economy and the political process functions and at the same time, it also emerges because of individual choices and behaviors. Any simple solutions, any one-size-fits-all promises of reform, are doomed to failure, and anyone who claims to have found a magic bullet to once and for all banish poverty from America's shores is either a scam artist or a Pollyanna.

If we can't drive a great stake through poverty in all its manifestations, however, we can certainly do a whole lot better than we are doing currently. We can make a bigger effort, both at the local level and nationally, to eliminate its symptoms and to knock out its causes. And we can prioritize investments and institutional reforms that minimize the scope, the intergenerational transmission, and the geographic concentration of poverty when it does emerge.

Obama might not have talked about the specifics of these issues in his re-election campaign, but he certainly had them on his mind after he got re-elected. The day following that election, a shirt-sleeved Obama spoke to campaign workers at his headquarters in Chicago. In an emotional, teary-eyed address, the president talked about how he had come to Chicago as a young man, "knowing that somehow I wanted to make sure that my life attached itself to helping kids get a great education, or helping people living in poverty to get decent jobs, and be able to work and have dignity; to make sure that people didn't have to go to the emergency room to get healthcare. I ended up being a community organizer on the South Side of Chicago. The work that I did in those communities changed me much more than it did those communities. It taught me the hope, and the aspirations, and the grit of ordinary people." And, the president continued, as he talked of Bobby Kennedy's "ripples of hope" idea, "I grew up, I became a man during that process."

Above all, as Obama is all too aware, we have to get the government out of the business of selling lemons to taxpayers and into the business of selling the service equivalents of Cadillacs. It used to be able to do so—witness the durability of Social Security and the ongoing public support for keeping the program viable. Design modern-day government-backed Cadillac programs, and broad swaths of the public could come to feel, as they did in the heyday of the New Deal, that they have a stake in a revitalized social compact, that their tax dollars are being put to use in ways that manifestly benefit them and their children.

We could, for example, create two more dedicated trust funds to complement those for Social Security and Medicare. Adding a half-percent payroll tax, divided equally between employees and employers, would allow for the creation of a massive Educational Opportunity Fund (EOF) capable of giving out roughly $20 billion per year—*or $5,000 to every child born in the United States*—the money to be invested into education accounts so that those children could, eighteen years later, attend college without saddling themselves or their families with catastrophic debts. Employees win because suddenly college becomes a whole lot more affordable. Employers win because they end up with better-trained and -educated workers.

With the money left over, for the next couple decades the government could give out grants to those born before the launch of this fund so that they, too, benefited from the program. For those children who don't attend college, their portion of the fund could be converted into additional Social Security payments once they retire. That way, everyone has a vested interest in the program. It's a relatively painless way to share the costs, and benefits, of higher education.

Adding a 1 percent payroll tax, again divided between employers and employees, would allow for the creation of a huge public works trust fund that could be tapped during periods of prolonged recession so as to effectively put large numbers of unemployed workers back to work quickly, and on projects that benefit the public good. Again, if the money were dedicated to this particular program, one that would clearly help millions of workers during years such as the ones that followed 2008, it ought to be possible to craft political coalitions, similar to those that have kept unemployment insurance and workers' compensation on the books for generations, to support such a tax. It would be the ultimate social insurance buy-in. After all, as the recent collapse has shown, almost nobody's job security can be taken for granted when the financial system wobbles.

In addition to adding these two large pillars to the social contract, a host of other important measures also stand out. Major parts of such a redesigned compact would include reforming federal and state tax codes that too often protect the assets of the affluent while socking it to the poor; raising federal revenues for anti-poverty investments by creating a financial transaction tax and energy profit taxes; and investing in an ambitious community infrastructure to support low-income children in high-poverty schools.

It would also involve using networks of state banks and microlending institutions to make credit more affordable to the poor and to bolster vital environmental and other infrastructure projects. These could form the backbone for a series of investments in a national industrial policy that, as with those in Germany and Japan, would stimulate well-paid blue-collar employment.

The renewed social compact would protect already-negotiated pensions from being reneged on and shore up other retirement systems that, for a generation, have shifted the risks onto retirees. It would change how and when we use the criminal justice system, what services we provide drug addicts, and how we fund treatment centers for the mentally ill. And it would require passage of a number of state and federal laws aimed at boosting minimum wages and ensuring that large-scale employers don't abuse systems like the Earned Income Tax Credit (EITC) by underpaying workers.

It would involve promoting worker-owned companies as an alternative to bankruptcy and mass layoffs, increasing access to affordable healthcare and housing, and providing energy subsidies for the working poor when gas prices spike.

In addition, Washington should create regional development funds modeled on the New Deal's Tennessee Valley Authority or the Great Society's Appalachian Regional Development Act. One good candidate for such a fund might be the Sun Belt states peculiarly hard-hit by the mortgage foreclosure crisis. Recognizing that this crisis threatens to sink the residents of large areas of the country in decades-long debt, the federal government could create a housing development agency with the mandate to channel targeted relief to individual homeowners. In addition, the federal government could target relief to the local governments reliant on their property taxes in areas within the Sun Belt such as California's Central Valley; Phoenix, Arizona; and Las Vegas, Nevada. Another candidate for targeted relief might be the Rust Belt, and in particular the cities left destitute by the loss of millions of American manufacturing jobs in recent decades. Partly, the relief might take the form of localized boosts to welfare programs. Partly it could involve additional tax credits, job training money, and direct subsidies to cash-strapped city and county governments. Partly, in areas where entire industries have vanished, it ought to take the form of public works. Partly, it could take the form of region-specific mortgage mitigation packages for areas with critical masses of underwater homeowners. In some cases, the money would be distributed in block grants to states. In other cases it would be more regionally specific.

The latter, said the University of Kentucky's Jim Ziliak, was a necessary approach in states such as his, where there were huge economic disparities between wealthy urban hubs and desperately poor rural counties—especially in the Appalachian east of the state. If extra resources only became available when the entire state's unemployment or poverty rate exceeded national averages, a whole lot of poor people ended up missing out on benefits, even though they lived in counties that even in the good times experienced levels of poverty and unemployment far higher than average.

In the Appalachian region, the professor noted, "it's pretty common the poverty rate is 25 percent in any given year. We have a large population who are poor; economic opportunities are few and far between. On a year-to-year basis they're going to have a lot of uncertainty trying to make long-term plans. Employment in Eastern Kentucky for men 25 to 60: about 65 percent are employed; nationally it's about 85."

MARKETS RUN AMOK, SHIVERING IN THE RAINFOREST, AND THE END OF HISTORY

Regional development alone, however, won't be enough. After all, some problems, such as the massive growth in unemployment seen in the post-2008 years, have national implications. To tackle them, we need to marshal energies at a federal level. There will have to be an expansion in the resources available to meet the needs of the long-term unemployed and jobless, as well as resources to keep the short-term unemployed out of poverty and to preserve the assets of

the working and middle classes during particularly acute economic
downturns.

On one level, an anti-poverty program suited to meet the needs
of America in the twenty-first century has to be about a better-built
welfare system and a more finely woven safety net. But on another
level it is about creating more flexible systems to respond both to
downturns and to regional discrepancies in wealth, education, poverty, and unemployment. More generally, it must be about tackling
conditions of inequality that lead to poverty not only for those without jobs but also for an increasing number of people who *have* employment but work for unlivable wages.

Ziliak believed that to effectively grapple with poverty we first
had to understand its true scale. "I would change the way we measure poverty in the country," he argued.

> Let's get a better count of who is poor and who isn't. That's really im-
> portant. We've been measuring poverty the same way for about fifty
> years. It's a useful measure. But most people agree that it's not really
> capturing what's going on in America today amongst the poor popu-
> lation. For one thing, the poverty line is based on food spending pat-
> terns in the mid-1950s. And in the mid-1950s a typical American
> spent one-third of their budget on food. The way we draw the line,
> we design a food budget for a given family size and then multiply
> that dollar amount by three. Today, though, the typical family
> spends [only] one-eighth of their budget on food; so technically the
> line should be two and a half times higher than what it is; if you took
> that standard measure and adjusted for the fact we only spend one
> eighth on food, the poverty line for a family of four should be closer
> to $50,000 than $22,000.

The proposal put forward by Ziliak might sound outlandish—
after all, it would have the effect of dramatically raising the number
of Americans who qualify as poor simply by changing the definition
of poverty; but it has influential proponents. In 1995, the National

Academy of Sciences proposed a new poverty measure, similar in its design to that used by most European countries, based on consumption patterns of food, clothing, shelter, and utilities. Ziliak would add transportation to the list, but otherwise he thinks it's pretty realistic. It would factor into income measures the government cash aid and food benefits received by people and would subtract out taxes and work-related expenses.

Simulations of this more sophisticated poverty measure, along with others like it, usually find that the American poverty rate would go up slightly overall, but fairly dramatically amongst older Americans once their out-of-pocket medical expenses are deducted from their income. Because older people tend to spend much more on medications, such a change is far from being superficial.

And then, concluded Ziliak, once we had a more accurate measure of what the real scale of poverty in America is, and which parts of the population are most impacted, we would be better able to tailor our responses accordingly. We could, for example, quickly expand the Earned Income Tax Credit and food stamp eligibility to meet the new poverty measures; we could redesign TANF so that enrollment expands during times of recession.

———

That we have been slow in calibrating the true extent of poverty and remiss in crafting ambitious, big-picture solutions to that poverty is, I believe, manifested in three main ways.

First, existing programs, both for the unemployed or jobless, and also for the working poor, have withered, either through benign neglect or through active political opposition—an assault on the Keynesian project, launched by think tanks such as the Heritage Foundation, policy-crafting entities such as the American Legislative Exchange Council, and business organizations such as the U.S. Chamber of Commerce. In 1996, 45.7 percent of poor kids were getting some form of cash assistance from the government. Thirteen years later, only

18.7 percent received such aid. "The Great Recession," Randy Albelda wrote in a report for *Dollars and Sense*, "pushed 800,000 additional families into poverty between 2007 and 2009, yet the TANF rolls rose by only 110,000 over this period."[1] And, she might have added, most of those receiving TANF benefits were getting far smaller monthly checks than they had been a few years earlier. The value of TANF in Mississippi stood at 11 percent of the poverty line, and while Mississippi was the bottom of the barrel, several other states all clustered below 15 percent of that line. Even in California, historically among the most generous of states, TANF alone did not bring a family to even half of the poverty line.

Second, new programs, needed to meet the new demands of a twenty-first-century populace and a twenty-first-century workforce, haven't been developed with nearly enough rapidity or ambition. Or when they have been developed, we have sidled into them while ignoring the looming presence of poverty in the background. Hence the fact that we have, for example, invested a huge amount of effort, money, and talent into school reforms in recent decades, while largely ignoring the fact that most underperforming schools are being daily undermined by the conditions of poverty in which so many of their students live.

"In seeking to close the achievement gap for low-income and minority students," wrote the economist Richard Rothstein in his 2004 book *Class and Schools*, "policy makers focus inordinate attention on the improvement of instruction, because they apparently believe that social class differences are immutable, and that only schools can improve the destinies of lower-class children."[2] But, he continued, in all likelihood "establishing an optometric clinic in a school to improve the vision of low-income children would probably have a bigger impact on their test scores than spending the same money on instructional improvement."

Raising the minimum wage so that the parents of these children were earning enough money to adequately feed, clothe, and house these same kids would work even bigger wonders. In fact, argued Rothstein, increasing the minimum wage or boosting the EITC "should be considered education policies as well as economic ones, for they would likely result in higher academic performance from children whose families are more secure."[3]

Rothstein calculated the cost of a series of big-picture reforms that would use schools as epicenters in a broader communal effort against poverty and its consequences. How much would it cost to create a set of conditions that would allow kids from impoverished backgrounds to approximate the experiences, both educational and life, of more affluent children? His answer: $156 billion per year.

Now that's a huge sum of money and one that clearly isn't going to be freed up by federal and state governments anytime soon. But, as Rothstein points out, it's about equal to the amount of money redistributed back to the super-wealthy as a result of the tax cuts enacted during the early years of George W. Bush's presidency. That's not a nebulous comparison: In a world of finite resources, tax cuts have consequences. One of them is that less money is available for government to promote what we might call "the commons," a set of public goods that benefit everyone and that can be used as tools to tamp down broader societal inequities. Yes, in the current political moment any politician who proposes raising taxes to fund a $156 billion per year increase in education spending would be printing themselves a one-way ticket to political oblivion. But, in another moment, defined by a different set of priorities, a country as wealthy and dynamic as is America could, clearly, fund some extremely ambitious anti-poverty, and pro-education, measures.

Rothstein's yardstick is, though not politically realistic, at the very least a wakeup call. Even if massive *infusions* of funds are off the table, surely states oughtn't to be *slashing* ever more money from already-stressed schools. For when they do, when states such as California remove billions of dollars from being spent on K-12 classrooms, year upon year upon year, and reduce the length of the school year to further trim costs, inevitably the poor get hurt the most. And, as inevitably, when that happens, inequality increases, and the long-term life prospects for large groups of Americans deteriorate.

———————

In failing to adequately account for how poverty creates its own specific set of challenges across the board—from small ones such as shortsighted kids coming to school without glasses, to larger ones such as public health emergencies created by a paucity of community medical clinics and a failure to provide any social protections to the undocumented—we routinely end up with policy solutions that fall far short of what is necessary. Or, worse, we fail to even begin to discuss reforms that would be easy and affordable to implement if we only had a better understanding of the needs of poor Americans, and a better sense of empathy for the plight they too often find themselves in.

For example: Over the past decade, we have regularly had oil price spikes that have been nothing more than a nuisance to the affluent, but have been cataclysmic to the poor—especially to retirees on fixed incomes and to the working poor in rural areas, who tend to work minimum-wage jobs and to drive long distances for those jobs, or who are more likely to heat their homes using old-fashioned oil-based heating systems.

Witness, for example, the damage caused the precarious finances of John and Stephanie France, grandparents living off the grid on the edge of the rainforest on Hawaii's Big Island, when gas prices in the state veered near $5 a gallon in the winter and early spring of 2012. John, a disabled air force veteran, and his wife lived on small Social Security checks and a couple hundred dollars a month in food stamps. "We have a generator, and I have to buy gas for the generator. But it's $4.69 a gallon for gasoline," John explained. "It's not easy; that's what I have to do every day. I try to make it [money] stretch to the end of the month. But by the end of the third or fourth week we're out of money, out of everything. There's us, my daughter, her husband, and their four kids. Her husband goes fishing, but he doesn't have a job. We help with the children."

When they ran out of food, "we go to the church. We go to the food bank," said Stephanie. "I make sure we stretch our food stamps out. We don't have no icebox, so we also have to get ice. Every other day we have to get ice; that's about $2. We don't have electricity, so that's why we have to have the cooler. If we had an icebox, we'd have to have the generator on all the time. Then we'd have to fill it up with gas."

John added, "We leave the generator on four hours a day; at the end of the month, two hours a day. We turn it on about four or five o'clock. We go to bed about seven o'clock, because it's dark, and you can't see. When we turn the generator on, that's the only time we can use the bathroom, because we don't have running water otherwise."

Stephanie had a hacking cough when we met, one probably not helped any by the omnipresent damp weather and the fact that her home was never heated properly. The Frances wore multiple layers of clothes when it got cold and rainy, and prayed, on a daily basis, for something most Americans have taken for granted for more than half a century. "I'd like to have electricity, but electricity cost too much. The last time I had electricity it was four hundred and something dollars, and I couldn't afford that. If we had electricity, it'd be a lot better," John announced softly.

Like the Caros in southern New Mexico, hoping against hope for the day that they owned a flush toilet while living in their windowless storage unit, this was both an insanely modest expectation and also one that they were unlikely to realize anytime soon. For years now, the Frances had been going in reverse, their incomes and their options constricting, their chances of enjoying the amenities of modern life fading away by the day, their finances held hostage to energy economics and the vagaries of oil politics.

While America clearly needs a national energy strategy that works to stabilize long-term energy prices, in the short term the country also needs financial assistance programs that can be speedily directed to the poor during price spikes. In the same way that some states are now experimenting with methods of automatically enrolling people in certain income brackets in food stamps when they apply for other programs—SSI and Social Security, in particular— so it ought to be possible to send out gas stamps, worth, say, five gallons per week, to recipients of food stamps and other means-tested benefits once gas hits a certain predetermined price. Flexible, short-term, and not particularly expensive to the government, they could, in fact, easily be paid for by raising taxes on oil producers' profits during price spikes; after all, in the first six months of 2012 alone, the five biggest oil companies made windfall profits of more than $62 billion.[4] The assistance provided by gas stamps could prevent spiking prices from pushing the rural poor into hunger, into having to skip medicines and all the other unpalatable choices that the poor routinely make when one part of their financial calculus changes.

In the contemporary anti-tax environment, such a proposal might seem farfetched. It isn't. In fact, a very similar law, the Crude Oil Windfall Profit Tax Act was passed by Congress in 1980, and remained on the books until it was repealed, at the urging of President Reagan, eight years later.

The act imposed windfall profit taxes on producers that ranged from 30 percent up to 70 percent, and was designed to generate approximately $227 billion during a ten-year period. The money raised was to be ploughed back into tax reductions for the working poor, low-income assistance, and investments in energy and transportation programs.[5]

If, with today's high oil prices, a similar profit tax were enacted, bringing in revenues in the $30 billion per year range, fifteen million households (roughly the number of households receiving food stamps) could each be given $20 per week in gas vouchers, and that would still leave the federal government with an additional $15 billion per year to use either for other assistance to the poor, or for reducing the national deficit. Why hasn't such a tax been enacted? Not because it's impractical; not because it would bankrupt oil companies—but because those companies pump a huge amount of money into lobbying against such measures, and because today in America the political process is far more finely tuned to meeting the needs of the affluent than those of the poor.

———

This leads to the third and last problem: until the Occupy movement grabbed the political spotlight, for decades America's poor had come to think of themselves as ever more disempowered, ever more passive in the face of their poverty. And to a large extent, the assumption of powerlessness became self-fulfilling. Unable to influence the body politic, more and more people simply opted out: not voting in elections, not joining trade unions, and not informing themselves about the great issues of the day. And, in opting out, they all but ensured their continued marginalization.

In 1974, the English political philosopher Steven Lukes published his book *Power: A Radical View*. In it, he argued that there were three core ways in which power could be exercised, each more pervasive than the next. The first was raw coercion: one person, group of people, or institution had power and through force compelled others to bow down before it. The second was slightly more subtle, but even more effective: The groups with power managed to convince their underlings to legitimate that power, both by shaping people's preferences and, as effectively, by determining what they *didn't* want in their lives. In such a society, those without power voluntarily acquiesced in their own situation. The third, and most dominant of all, occurred when powerful individuals and institutions managed to so control the psychology of those without power that populations no longer even realized they were being manipulated. They acquiesced in their powerlessness and no longer could even envision alternatives.

In such a scenario, power relationships were so utterly omnipresent that they had become invisible; they were simply the background to every experience, to every choice made in society. And, in a world so governed, the manipulation of the many for the benefit of the few became normal, the currency of political business.

That, unfortunately, is indeed how too many transactions are conducted in American politics today. That's how people who live just inside the margins are convinced to blame those just outside the margins for their poverty; it's how people whose wages have shrunk, whose benefits have been eviscerated, and whose access to government assistance has waned are convinced to vote for anti-tax, anti-regulatory, anti–safety net politicians who will further batter their pocketbooks and throw them into insecurity. It's how people without pensions are convinced to blame public sector workers who still have pensions for the country's economic plight, rather than asking why more workers in the world's wealthiest country don't have secure retirements in the first place.

Looking back at a half-century of economic justice organizing work that he had been involved in, Harvard's Marshall Ganz believed that many of the anti-poverty movements in the 1960s, had a broader political agenda. "They were movements for dignity, fairness, economic rights, justice," he stated. Then, increasingly, poverty came to be thought of as a sickness rather than a consequence of unjust social systems and relationships.

> The War on Poverty has gotten a terribly bad rap, given it did a hell of a lot of good; part of the Great Society dealing with health, beautification. There was a whole package of reform of which it was a part. By naming it an anti-poverty program, it became more vulnerable politically. I don't know, there's this odd dissonance there, something clinical about "poverty." Describing that condition of life as "poverty." It misses the critical moral, social resources that people draw on to survive and transform their conditions of life. It's

injustice. It's people having to live in conditions of deprivation that are unjust. It takes a justice issue and turns it into a social engineering problem or a charity problem.

Arguably, that's one reason why the original War on Poverty failed: Moral arguments, such as those detailed by Harrington, brought poverty center stage, but, once there, technocrats took control, essentially reducing a massive moral conundrum—poverty amidst plenty—into a set of scientific and statistical data. And once that occurred, the energy was sucked out of the process. Thus, even while a "poverty industry" grew up that developed ever more specialized knowledge about *how* to tackle particular manifestations of economic hardship, the political language about *why* we should do so dissipated.

Without a re-energized political process, without more people participating politically, without a more informed electorate and a renascent grassroots movement, twenty-first-century poverty will *never* receive the attention that it so urgently deserves. This is not, primarily, a book about grassroots politics. But, that said, readers should continually have an awareness of the political conditions in mind as they read this second section of *The American Way of Poverty*. The solutions that I advocate, taken as a whole, would go a long way toward ending poverty in this most affluent of nations. But the initial catalyst for pushing such systemic reform will only occur once more people participate more proactively in the politics and the movements that, like it or not, define all of our worlds. In both 2008 and 2012, Obama's campaign team activated more voters and more organizers than their opponents thought possible. After 2008, much of that energy was left to dissipate. After 2012, if a progressive set of policies is to be nurtured, it has to be sustained, to provide an ongoing citizen-led impetus for reform, to push the political process, from the ground up, to enact a new economic fairness agenda.

CHAPTER ONE

SHORING UP THE SAFETY NET

Food pantry client and cancer patient Vicenta Delgado in line for food in North Philadelphia.

That poverty increased so dramatically not only during the George W. Bush presidency but also once Barack Obama assumed power in January 2009 is one of the great political tragedies of the age. After all, Obama had spent years working as a South Side Chicago community organizer; he understood poverty, and cared about both its causes and its consequences. Prior to assuming office, he had a solid track record on the issue. And in getting elected, a core part of his appeal had been that he would represent the ordinary men and women of America and not its elites. The festivities surrounding his inauguration in January 2009 had been marbled with grandiose historical references to renewal; to a reinvigorated social compact; to the unsung, working-class heroes who had helped to build the country.

So why, despite all of that, did Obama's administration find it so difficult to stem poverty's floodwater?

In part, the failure to get a true handle on surging poverty represented a lack of willingness on the part of Obama's inner circle, many of whom were avowed moderates who had cut their teeth during the Clinton years, to expend precious political capital on a group of people with almost no political clout that could be tapped in return to replenish the well. In part, because poverty has, however wrongly, long been seen by many primarily as an affliction of the African American community, Obama's advisers likely feared that the country's first African American president would come to be seen by whites as having a "black" agenda if he made poverty as much a priority as had Lyndon Johnson. In part, however, even when their impulses were good, they were hamstrung by reforms signed off on by the president's Democratic predecessor, Bill Clinton, twelve years before Obama was elected.

From the 1930s through the mid-1990s, the central cash component of America's welfare system had been the federal aid distributed through the Aid to Families with Dependent Children (AFDC) program. Then, in 1996, under pressure from a conservative Congress to slash welfare, President Clinton pushed for welfare reform. AFDC was replaced with a block grant to the states, and women's ability to access welfare was limited; from now on, Temporary Aid to Needy Families (TANF) would be the norm—aid would be tied to the search for work, it would be strictly time-limited, and how it was distributed would be largely at the discretion of states. The result? Plummeting welfare enrollment.

Out of the gates, this was touted as a grand success: A booming economy meant that rolls could fall, and at the same time, the nation's poverty rate could also decline. But from the start, critics such as the Urban Institute's Harry Holzer were concerned that in a prolonged downturn the poor would be hit hardest, as states raided TANF funds and as soaring need levels and increasingly scarce work opportunities both pushed more families into poverty and made it that much harder for those at the bottom of the economy to find work. In urging the federal government to make more TANF money available to states and to develop an emergency contingency fund that would be "uncapped" and would increase in size to meet growing need, in April 2001 Holzer wrote, "If a recession occurs, job availability for those seeking employment will decline." While unemployment would increase amongst all demographics, Holzer worried that it would be particularly pronounced vis-à-vis "those with limited skills or labor market experience."

He was, it turned out, right to be concerned. In many ways, TANF is now an irrelevance when it comes to counter-cyclical anti-poverty strategies. When the Harvard sociologist Kathryn Edin did immersion-based investigations into the life of the poor in Philadelphia and Camden, New Jersey, in the early years of the century, she found that few young people even viewed TANF as an option.

WHEN THE GOING GETS TOUGH . . .
THE TOUGH TAKE IT OUT ON THE VULNERABLE

"Welfare reform has worked very well, then, if receiving welfare is a bad thing," wrote University of Massachusetts at Boston economics professor Randy Albelda, in the 2012 *Dollars and Sense* report "Different Anti-Poverty Programs, Same Single-Mother Poverty."[1] "Indeed, advocates of the new regime tout the rapid and steep decline in welfare use as their main indicator of its success." But, Albelda cautioned, "fewer families using anti-poverty programs does not mean less poverty, more personal responsibility, or greater self-sufficiency."

"AFDC used to be counter-cyclical," said Jim Ziliak. "And it's no longer so at all. There's no automatic stabilizer component to TANF." Immediately after the recession hit, there *was* a $2 billion federal contingency fund that states with unemployment 2 percent or more above the national average could access; but they didn't have to, and so many didn't. Moreover, by December 2009 that fund was used up. Congress added $5 billion to the fund as a part of the American Recovery and Reinvestment Act, but by mid-2011 that was gone too. In June 2011, the Center on Budget and Policy Priorities (CBPP) reported that "*no* additional resources are available from the federal government for the first time since TANF's creation in 1996, despite today's hard economic times." To counter this, the CBPP proposed that states receive additional TANF funds as soon as they reach an unemployment rate of 6.5 percent or more, and that they have to spend those extra dollars on helping more people rather than simply replenishing their existing funds.

"Here we are, worst recession of our lives, and we didn't suspend the lifetime limit, or exempt households who've met the lifetime limit," Jessica Bartholow said, in amazement. Worse, many states had actually *decreased* the number of months a woman could access welfare: California, for example, took it from sixty months to forty-eight, and during budget negotiations in late 2011 Governor Jerry Brown tried (though failed) to reduce it still further, to a mere twenty-four months.

Bartholow recalled a 40-year-old woman she had recently encountered who had been laid off from her job of nine years, who lacked any financial assets and had just had a new baby. But because of the fact that she'd been on welfare for a few years more than a decade earlier, when her first son was a child, she had run up against the lifetime limits and couldn't qualify for aid. She and her baby became homeless, and her elder son ended up having to drop out of college to try to find work and support his mother and half-sibling.

How could TANF be made more responsive to downturns? By bulking up federal aid to the states, by replacing the block grant system with a nationally mandated baseline eligibility system akin to Medicaid enrollment, and by automatically suspending lifetime limits during economic downturns that last beyond a certain number of months. How much would it cost to boost TANF rolls by 50 percent? Elizabeth Lower-Basch, a senior policy analyst at the D.C.-based Center for Law and Social Policy (CLASP), estimated that it would be somewhere in the region of $7 billion, a not-insignificant amount of money, but, to put it in perspective, less than 1 percent of the cost of bailing out the financial industry following the 2008 meltdown. Or what America was spending every week or two in Iraq during the height of that war.[2] In fact, in 2008 *New York Times* columnist Nicholas Kristof calculated that the United States was spending $5,000 *per second* in Iraq.[3]

Could these expansions of the welfare system be enforced? Yes, but probably not without restructuring the federal-state responsibilities for the delivery of assistance to the poor. Currently, the federal government mandates that states provide certain benefits and services, but doesn't mandate *how* the states fund these requirements. As a result, in many more conservative states legislators simply adopted deeply regressive tax systems—such as imposing sales taxes on food to fund social services or, in the case of Alabama, calculating higher state tax liabilities for the poor if the poor have been given a federal subsidy such as the EITC—to cover their increased obligations. These are pure examples of robbing Peter to feed Paul, and they are particularly ironic given how vocally anti-tax most of the political leaders in states such as Alabama are. Any rational anti-poverty strategy would immediately alter such tax codes so as to make them more responsive to the needs of the poorest of taxpayers.

Failure to do so would only stoke the suspicion that when conservative southern politicians proclaim their hostility to taxes, what they really mean is a hostility to the sorts of taxes paid by the sorts of affluent voters who tend to make up their electoral bases and a reluctance to fund the sorts of programs generally used by people who aren't part of that base.

Because so many states have proven themselves so unenthusiastic about funding federally required safety net programs with progressive taxes, Katherine Newman and coauthor Rourke O'Brien conclude in their book *Taxing the Poor* that many of these programs ought to be federalized, funded by increasing federal taxes on affluent individuals and on big business, and bypassing the states entirely.

———

Absent such a fundamental reform of TANF, the central countercyclical institution propping up the welfare system these days is, and will likely continue to be, SNAP (colloquially known as food stamps), which, as of 2012, was helping to feed about 46 million Americans. These men, women, and children received on average $133.80 per person, and $283.65 per family, per month in food assistance.

Since SNAP is available to anybody below a certain income threshold, it ends up being used in recessions—as well as in periods of collapsing wages for the working poor—by far more people than can use TANF or general cash assistance programs. To gauge the true scale of the discrepancy, witness the following numbers: Between 2000 and 2012, the number of Americans on food stamps increased from 17.2 million to 46 million; meanwhile, the number of Americans on welfare stood at only a little over 4 million.[4] Food stamps are available to people with a gross income of 134 percent (and in some states 200 percent) of the poverty level, but to access them, one's net income, after high housing and healthcare costs have been deducted, cannot exceed 100 percent of the poverty line. And even then, the benefits available are fairly meager. To qualify for a "high" level of benefits you have to be at about 50 percent of the poverty line. In other words, tens of millions of families qualify for some food assistance, but dig below the headlines, and one finds that for many of these families the assistance is small indeed.

We last encountered Vicenta Delgado waiting on a food line in North Philadelphia, on a chilly late fall morning in 2011.

Vicenta's husband received a little more than $1,000 a month from Social Security; she qualified, she said, for $27 a month in SSI, and the couple received an additional $34 in food stamps. With copays for her medications eating up her limited income, and with the food stamps covering almost none of her and her husband's nutritional needs, she ended up on a food pantry line each Saturday morning, waiting for charity food that would keep her from going hungry.

Raising the food stamp aid thresholds, and letting benefits kick in for the working poor as well as the deep poor, would instantly make the plan more counter-cyclical, better compensating for lost earnings as hours worked and hourly wages decline. And making it more available would also stimulate local economies, thus boosting tax revenues and allowing the expanded government program to at least partly fund itself.

Additionally, there are glaring holes that need to be fixed in SNAP—holes that wouldn't be so important except for the fact that the program has now become *the* central component of America's welfare system. During normal economic times, able-bodied adults can only access food stamps if they can prove that they are actively looking for work. This provision can be suspended regionally when local unemployment rises a certain amount above the national average. And in 2009, recognizing the severity of the need, and the unavailability of jobs at the depth of the recession, the authors of the American Recovery and Reinvestment Act (ARRA) suspended this requirement for most recipients of SNAP nationwide. Yet two groups weren't exempted from the work requirement: the first was students. Thus a working-class student trying to better him- or herself by enrolling in college after being laid off would still have to work twenty hours a week to get food stamps. If that person couldn't find work, he or she would lose the benefits. But if he dropped out of college, he'd qualify even without finding work. It's a catch-22 poverty trap.

The second group was made up of those on TANF whose food stamps were tied to their welfare checks, which in turn were only available to those in a welfare-to-work program. Waivers could be granted at a county level, at the discretion first of the state and then of the county, but when there's a low unemployment county such as Alameda, California, with a high unemployment urban core like Oakland, there's precious little guarantee that the big-city residents won't get shortchanged.

In the country's largest city, New York, welfare recipients, even at the height of the recession, were having to work for their welfare *and* food stamps, even while others were able to access SNAP simply by proving their newfound poverty. In an October 2011 *City Limits* article titled "Workfare for Food Stamps?" journalist Neil DiMause wrote that New York City's Human Resources Administration was ratcheting up its enforcement efforts of these workfare requirements. DiMause reported that, "Late in 2010, according to the low-income membership group Community Voices Heard, people receiving food stamps began receiving letters reminding them that they could be asked to work for their benefits. Ken Stephens of the Legal Aid Society says that in the following months, he started hearing from clients receiving food stamps who had lost their benefits for as small a violation as missing one job-search appointment."[5]

Sondra Youdelman, executive director of Community Voices Heard, recalled a client who had gone from TANF onto disability and then applied for food stamps for herself and her two sons, aged 17 and 19. *Sorry*, she was told, *your family can only access the assistance if the two boys, one in college, one still in high school, work for the benefits.*

"If you don't comply you are sanctioned. You can appeal, but 80 percent of people who are sanctioned don't," Jennifer Hadlock, a colleague of Youdelman's, stated. "They screw up all the time, and cut people off who are actually complying. Ten thousand at any one time are sanctioned, out of 180,000 on cash assistance." Community Voices Heard had documented stories of welfare recipients either doing make-work or literally having to sit hours a day doing nothing in a jobs center that is such in name only, just so that the Big Apple's welfare bureaucracies could say that work requirements were being met. It was a façade worthy of the fabled Potemkin village creators.

Similar situations abound around the country. In 2012, in California alone, according to Jessica Bartholow, 72,000 adults were being sanctioned with a loss of food stamps because they couldn't find jobs.

All of this makes for a double-whammy on the poorest and most difficult to employ section of the population. In the middle of this extraordinary recession, noted Youdelman with deliberate understatement, ramping up punitive enforcement efforts when the poorest of the poor attempted to gain food assistance "seemed odd and counter-intuitive to us."

While the Obama administration waived most work requirements for food stamp recipients during the recession, it never found its way to lifting this burden on the bottom part of the economy. The result? While food stamps served to limit the slide into poverty for the newly unemployed working poor, the program did little to halt the slide into ever-deeper poverty for those who had no jobs to lose in the first place.

A related program to food stamps, school meals, *is* also counter-cyclical, but in a peculiarly delayed way. It works best when students enroll at the start of the school year. But if a recession kicks in mid-year, as, inconveniently, most do, with rapid job and income losses, the school lunch enrollment systems operated by states struggle to keep up. Usually there's a gap of weeks to months between when a family falls into poverty and when the kids start receiving free meals. Making matters worse, at the same time school years are being cut by cash-strapped states and school districts, meaning more days when children go hungry, and partially canceling out the benefits accrued kids by access to the breakfasts and lunches.

To make this nutritional program more fully counter-cyclical, so-called "feeding programs" have to be properly funded for the periods when school's out. The federal government already has pilot programs, in Kansas City and other locales—the programs Rush Limbaugh so colorfully denounced for creating dependent little serfs—doing this. In the coming years, expanding such funded programs would better integrate this nutritional assistance into the overall welfare system.

BURIAL PLOTS, BROKEN GLASSES, AND OTHER PROBLEMS WITH MEDICAID

One other core part of the safety net is also largely counter-cyclical, designed to kick in with greater assistance when the need increases. And that is Medicaid, which grants families with kids access to healthcare once they reach a certain threshold level of poverty.

But while Medicaid is a whole lot better than nothing, it has, historically, been severely restricted in a number of ways. In fact, until all the major Affordable Care Act provisions kick in, in 2014, most states won't extend Medicaid to childless adults. At the same time, a minority of states, again mainly southern ones, will continue to place huge restrictions on adults of *any* status, even those with young children at home, gaining access.

The problem, however, goes beyond one of gate-keeping. Even in states that have relatively liberal eligibility requirements for their programs, there are strict asset tests in place that have the effect of forcing the temporarily out of work and/or cash poor to strip themselves of almost all their worldly possessions (homes, car, retirement accounts, savings) simply to gain healthcare—even if this ends up condemning them to long-term poverty by depriving them of the possessions and financial cushions that people need before they can even start working their way up the economic ladder again.

How, for example, can an unemployed person in an area without public transport get a job, and travel to that job, if he has had to sell his vehicle so as to get medical coverage? Or how can a person afford to retire if she has had to liquidate her small nest egg for that healthcare access? What should the middle-aged businessman in California who had lost his business during the recession and who needed knee surgery before he could take on new work do when he was told that he couldn't get medical assistance, and thus couldn't get his surgery, until he had stripped himself down to a maximum of $2,000 of assets? It is, truly, a Faustian bargain into which large numbers of Americans have been pushed.

In some instances, the asset tests are particularly macabre. Linda Pratt was a mother of four, and a guardian to three more, and a woman who had spent her entire adult life in near-minimum-wage jobs—most recently working with mentally disabled children for $8 or $9 per hour. Pratt's husband, Lloyd, several years her junior, was a construction worker. Neither had insurance through their work, and both earned so little that, as a family, despite the two incomes they were below the poverty line. When Linda's husband had a stroke, in his late forties, and ended up hospitalized, the couple were bankrupted by their medical bills. Their home had already gone underwater because of the collapse in the housing market; now their van was repossessed. But when they applied for Medicaid, they were denied. The reason they were given: they had too many assets. And the assets they had? Each of them had bought a burial plot, so that when they eventually died they wouldn't be confined to a pauper's cemetery.

"There is no kind of medical coverage for either me or Lloyd; and we go to work every single day," Pratt said quietly, sitting in a little wooden church, built on a small back road in Flint, in which she went to pray. "My husband still does not have any feeling from his knees down—they're permanently damaged from the stroke. But he still goes every single day. Lately he's been having chest pains and didn't want to tell me because he would have to go to the hospital."

In other words, while Medicaid *does* enroll more people during recessions, it does so in a way that, at times, might actually have the effect of tamping down economic recovery down the road by locking recipients into a deeper poverty than they were in when first they lost their income. In deep recessions, in particular, modifying, or eliminating, asset tests for Medicaid would go a long way toward keeping people both healthy and out of long-term poverty. Yet that hasn't happened. The political will simply isn't there.

Finally, state after state is limiting the services covered by Medicaid, meaning more people still end up paying out of pocket, or doing without, when it comes to such vital services as eye-care, dental work, and mental health clinics. Recall Patty Poole's experience in New York when she needed a compression stocking to manage her lymphedema. Or put yourself in the shoes of Albuquerque resident Jamie McBride, a mother of two young children and wife to a recovering alcoholic and drug addict who, when I met her in December 2011, had spent over a year making do without needed eyeglasses because she had broken her previous pair and Medicaid no longer covered replacement glasses more often than once every three years. McBride's husband had run a handyman's company until the economic recession put a stop to that. Now, their income came from Jamie looking after her sister's children, for which she received about $100 a week; when that didn't cover their bills, the couple borrowed from other family members. They no longer had any credit cards— and no credit with which to open a card. Once they borrowed from a payday loan company they had seen advertised on television for gas and car repairs—using their car as collateral—and ended up paying, within a month and a half, 100 percent interest on their loan. They had not enough of value to be able to pawn anything for cash. Paying out of pocket for new glasses was, quite simply, out of the question. Penny-wise and pound-foolish, such cost-saving decisions, likely to grow in number if Republican attempts to convert Medicaid into a block grant program to the states come to fruition, both stack up a host of medical issues down the road and also undermine the public's confidence in the quality of services provided by Medicaid.

DIAL 211

Let me repeat what I wrote earlier. We know what to do to fix these problems. There's no mystery, for example, about how to improve Lisa's situation: When she was hard up, she ought to have been eligible for Medicaid; now that she's less hard up, she oughtn't to be hobbled by paying off loans for tens of thousands of dollars in medical expenses.

Around the country, we know how to craft big-picture federal reforms. We know how to let states tailor their own supplementary safety nets best suited to meet local conditions—witness, for example, the extraordinarily innovative thinking behind the network of coordinated care organizations in Oregon, championed by Governor John Kitzhaber, which are intended to rein in medical costs by encouraging more preventive and primary care, and low-cost interventions such as the provision of air-conditioning units, free of charge, to poor elderly residents, and those with congestive heart failure, during heat waves. And we know how to stimulate local programs, through combinations of federal aid and private sector and nonprofit grants, to improve the lives of millions of Americans.

We know what to do regarding unaffordable healthcare bills. So we also know how creative a role the federal government could play in generating jobs during times when millions are out of work. What we need is not more information, but more *political will* to do what is right by America's residents.

Were that will to reform in place, we could, for example, take up the suggestion by Harvard's Richard Parker that the federal government should expand what he terms "public works-lite," especially for the millions of marginally disabled Americans currently enrolled on

SSI because they are "refugees" from other parts of the shrinking welfare system. Such a public works program, he said, ought to kick in automatically during either regional or national downturns, with money targeted to high unemployment zones within states.

A regional allocation of resources of this kind could be expanded to cover other welfare benefits as well, thus allowing deprived areas to access additional funding even if the state as a whole didn't qualify. This would have the added benefit of bypassing often highly dysfunctional state agencies that operate in increasingly partisan state political environments, and it would give localities an incentive to link their most impoverished residents up with federally funded entitlement programs, rather than with state systems operating under limited block grants. In other words, it would replace disincentives for enrolling people with strong fiscal incentives, thus producing a safety net resilient in the face of stress instead of one that, increasingly, fails to catch those who fall during downturns. We could, for example, channel funding for childcare programs for low-income families directly to localities—instead of leaving such funding up to states that, all too often, cut access to programs once the economy heads south. We could do the same with drug treatment programs, mental health services, and shelters for the homeless.

And because of sophisticated database technologies, this could mostly be implemented at speed. If high numbers of people from one region start enrolling in programs available only to people below certain income thresholds, why not use those enrollments to trigger automatic membership in other programs? Low-income Social Security applicants, who have traditionally enrolled in nutritional assistance programs at only very low rates, could be automatically enrolled in food stamps—as will soon be the case in California and some other states.

In California, Assembly Bill 69 mandated an exchange of information between the Social Security Administration and the state's Department of Social Services, allowing what Ken Hecht, executive director of California Food Policy Advocates, calls a "pre-population of the food stamp application" when a Social Security application is filled in. Translation: Fill in one form, and the computer system will communicate that information to another government department with the intent of enrolling you in all the programs you are eligible for.

Similarly, food stamp enrollment for families could automatically trigger children's Medicaid or S-CHIP enrollment. A version of this is already being done in Louisiana, where 40,000 low-income kids were given "express lane eligibility" into S-CHIP—a somewhat surprising accomplishment, noted CLASP's Elizabeth Lower-Basch, given how abysmally Louisiana performs on most other poverty measurements. And a person released from prison without income and without up-to-date identification could be enrolled in, say, food stamps or Medicaid at the same time that his driver's license is processed.

To a degree, such coordinated efforts already exist. In 1997, Atlanta began a 211 phone service. Twenty-four hours a day, seven days a week, residents could call the hotline and ask how to get connected to various different agencies and nonprofits to help them with an array of needs—be they energy assistance or drug treatment. Many other regions followed suit. In California, for example, large numbers of cities and counties now have their own 211 systems in operation. Taking these efforts a step further, through the coordination of benefits described above, would be neither difficult nor expensive. In an information-and-technology era such as ours, one-stop shopping for benefits makes sense both for individuals seeking help and for government agencies with the mandate to supply that assistance.

SOMETHING MUCH BIGGER IS AT STAKE

Individually, none of these strategies would come close to tackling the scale of hardship in twenty-first-century America. But, taken as a whole, they would move the country a whole lot closer to a coherent, ambitious, new War on Poverty. They would provide a strong foundation upon which an innovative set of reforms could be erected.

Georgetown University's Peter Edelman, who had cut his teeth as a youngster by working for Senator Bobby Kennedy while he toured the country familiarizing himself with poverty, talked about the need for a range of new policies. He saw a need to shore up dilapidated mental health systems; using the law to ensure that workers received livable wages, as well as to make it easier for workers to organize into trade unions; and to make it the responsibility of states to subsidize childcare for the working poor. A lifetime of work on these issues had taught him how interconnected they were. But they wouldn't come about, he believed, until people were willing to engage in a more sensible discourse.

> People who feel insecure themselves feel threatened by the idea that somebody who's demonstrably worse off than they are is going to get help and they're not. They have an instinctive feeling these people are not deserving. There's been a divide and conquer thing coming from people and interests higher up the income level. We've had an unremitting attack on welfare that started in the late '60s. An unremitting drumbeat saying people who are in need are actually just not trying hard enough, they're lazy, have become dependent on welfare and it's ruined their character, and all the rest of it.

Pastor Ed Bacon of the All Saints Church, in the southern California suburb of Pasadena, agreed with Edelman's urging of a holistic approach to poverty. For the past several years he had been working to build an understanding of these connections amongst his congregation. His team had focused on nine key economic justice themes— from the role of money in politics, through to "the need for taxation in a civilization"; from the influence of the military-industrial complex, through to the disproportionate economic hardship borne by minorities during the post-2007 recessionary years. "We see," he explained, "the reflection of economic disparity in each of these issues, which means we also see a power disparity. They all contribute to structural violence—where you get things like the school-to-prison pipeline."

As the economy worsened, more and more of Pastor Bacon's congregants had hit the skids. They felt, said one of his colleagues, ashamed; they wanted to hide their hardships. Instead, Bacon decided to bring them out into the open. His church began holding what he called "Life and Livelihood" meetings to talk about these problems; they began linking up destitute church members with families who were better off, who could afford to dole out some aid to the needy; they began encouraging the unemployed to network for jobs within the church community. After a while, the church even began acting as an informal healthcare exchange, linking up the newly uninsured with doctors who would be willing to treat them at a discounted rate.

For Bacon, the economic cataclysm unleashed on so many of his congregants couldn't be reduced to party politics or to sound bites about which side cared more, or less, for the plight of the poor. "It really must transcend partisan identity," he argued. "Something much bigger's at stake. For me, it's the well-being of the human family." In his theology, when one person was hurt, all suffered. His hope was that an increasing number of anti-poverty programs would be crafted so as to minimize the population's overall economic misery rather than, simply, to pinch pennies. Clearly, with programs like TANF that was no longer the case. With other parts of the safety net, however, there was still some room for optimism.

———

Let's now return to our central observation here: Welfare systems work best when they expand automatically during economic downturns—in the technical jargon, they act as "automatic stabilizers"—rather than relying on acts of Congress or state legislatures to do the right thing by the nation's poor.

That's how SNAP works—and has worked for forty years, as the country has moved from county-by-county buy-ins to food stamps to a nationally mandated system. It's been remarkably successful. In addition to keeping people fed, it has also improved the long-term health of recipients. University of California at Davis economist Hilary Hoynes had studied health outcomes in counties that adopted food stamps in the early days compared to those that came into the program later. The earlier food assistance was offered, she found, the better the health indicators for those ultimately provided food stamps. Early adoption resulted in adults decades later having fewer sicknesses such as diabetes and heart disease. Delayed adoption, and the resulting malnourishment or reliance on cheap and unhealthy foods, stacked up health problems for residents down the road.[6]

That's also how the original Aid to Families with Dependent Children program was designed. The formulas by which the program allocated money to the states meant that as unemployment and poverty rose, so too did the number of AFDC clients. As we've seen, at the height of this program's reach, more than three-quarters of impoverished families with children received assistance. But when federal programs are redesigned as block grants to the states—with a set amount of money allocated per state, and with the states given tremendous leeway to raid these funds for alternative uses—the poor generally end up shortchanged. That's what happened with welfare; it's what will happen with Medicaid too if the healthcare program is turned over to the states. It's an effective way to ensure frugality; it's an appalling way to ensure that poor people's needs are met.

America's political leaders are not about to resurrect AFDC; nor should they. What's past is, after all, past. But new programs, building on what was good about the old system, the better aspects of the newer system that replaced it, as well as entirely fresh innovations for a new era, could, and should, be created.

States could, for example, take a leaf out of the Earned Income Tax Credit book when it comes to crafting welfare policies, temporarily *increasing* welfare checks when a person gets a job, instead of immediately cutting them back. EITC is credited with moving tremendous numbers of people out of poverty precisely because it gives ongoing incentives to people not just to work but to seek higher-paying jobs without immediately risking their cash subsidy. Modern-day welfare programs have done the opposite, looking to move people off the rolls as quickly as possible with far too little thought given as to whether the ex-aid recipients end up with sufficient cash to survive.

Using U.S. Census Bureau tabulations from 1996 to 2005, Randy Albelda calculated that, ten years after welfare reform had kicked in, the poorest 20 percent of single-mother families had seen their total available cash fall. The next-poorest 20 percent were earning more, but almost all of that additional income was being canceled out by declining welfare payments.[7] That's simply a bizarre way to tackle poverty.

Instead of the current punishment-based approach to welfare— find a job at all costs, or you'll be cut off from welfare—Americans would benefit from, and the country's best impulses would be showcased by, an incentive-based solution that rewards those who find work with extra help. This help should range from an expanded Earned Income Tax Credit to ongoing childcare assistance, from transportation subsidies perhaps on up to top-up welfare checks from the state for a specified period of time while those who have spent months or years on public assistance navigate the tough early days in a new job. Such a strategy would go far further toward raising low-income families out of poverty—to eliminating the poverty trap traditionally associated with welfare—than a great bundle of sticks each used to whack poor Americans harder than the one before.

———

None of these fixes would be cure-alls. After all, as Marshall Ganz had said, poverty is merely the "miners' canary," alerting the broader polity to the presence of systemic problems: growing inequality, declining access to quality education, increasingly insecure labor conditions, and a political process too paralyzed to tackle these crises.

But, while repairing and strengthening the welfare system doesn't provide a larger political-cultural fix, it *would* at least represent a starting point both for getting beyond the era of mindless austerity, especially at the state level; and also for having a discussion about equity, one that can frame poverty as a national problem rather than simply a malaise for the individuals mired in it. It is, in other words, a precondition for a more just economy, but in and of itself is nowhere near sufficient for attaining such an end goal.

We have the knowledge and the technological wherewithal to create flexible, fast-responding, non-punitive, counter-cyclical welfare programs. Such programs would be an amalgam of traditional assistance models, public health and nutritional aid systems, and progressive taxation policies. We have decades of institution-building from the middle third of the twentieth century to look to for guidance, and we have a number of innovative, cost-effective programs being developed locally in recent years to help us on our way as well.

Ultimately, if we cannot work out a language with which to highlight poverty's corrosive reach, and posit solutions to the problems facing those at the bottom of the economic ladder, our democratic institutions will themselves suffer. In the long run, the cost of inaction will far surpass the price of intervention. Far better to get it right now than to deal with decades of collateral damage from our inaction today.

CHAPTER TWO

BREAKING THE CYCLE OF POVERTY

Ruins of the Packard auto factory in Detroit.

Improving a dysfunctional welfare system might, however, be the easiest part of the anti-poverty equation, being both relatively affordable and also building mainly on existing institutions and programs. Far harder is how to break cycles of poverty so that eventually fewer people need to fall back on long-term state aid in the first place. Doing so involves thinking holistically about such big-ticket items as housing, healthcare, education, criminal justice systems, drug treatment, mental health programs, banking, and labor markets.

Hugh Espey, the wiry executive director of Iowa Citizens for Community Improvement, talked of broader popular involvement in key economic decisions. "Much less income inequality. A democracy truly by, of, and for the people, where more people are sharing in the wealth we are creating."

In Chicago, a few hours' drive east along the I-80 from Espey's office, George Goehl of National People's Action (NPA) had come to pretty much the same conclusions. He'd grown up in a working-class town in southern Indiana, and had ended up in the Windy City after years as an organizer in his home state. "The appetite for rethinking things is much different from anything I've experienced," he said, speaking of the post-2008 environment.

Despite the fact that he was thin as a rake, Goehl's voice was a baritone; when he talked—a small man in a checked shirt, with short, mussed brown hair—he sounded far larger than he was. His gray eyes locked in on his audience as he spoke. "The themes that keep coming up: be more explicit about race and racial justice; more community control of money." In a series of meetings NPA had convened in church basements, houses, community centers, and the like, he and his colleagues had held what they called Big Ideas conversations, probing ever deeper on issues such as race relations, corporate power, and the role of government in society. Change, he believed, would "happen at the local level first; we have to figure out how to disband really bad structures, and then build new institutions." In these conversations, Goehl and the other participants discussed such ideas as worker cooperatives, communally owned homes, and shops in which low-income people could use government-issued Electronic Benefit Transfer (EBT) cards not just to buy food but to purchase a host of other consumer items.

BIG, HAIRY, AUDACIOUS GOALS

There was no shortage of suggestions, and no shortage of issues vying for attention in any national campaign against ingrained poverty.

For JoAnne Page, executive director of the Fortune Society, in New York City, breaking the cycle of poverty involved finding ways to help people with their addictions, their mental illnesses, with diseases such as HIV/AIDS, and with the host of dysfunctions that pushed ever more people toward spells in jail and prison.

Page, the child of Holocaust survivors and a graduate of Yale Law School, had worked with impoverished clients for decades, building up a reputation as one of New York City's foremost advocates for the poor, the addicted, and the incarcerated. She had set up several large transitional housing centers for men and women returning to the community from prison—and those centers had proven themselves remarkably successful in turning people around, keeping them off of drugs, securing them jobs, and ultimately helping them move into their own apartments. Clients and coworkers described with awe her dedication to their well-being, and her willingness to work with them despite their failings. A short woman, with frizzy hair and an irrepressible smile, Page never failed to stop and talk with her clients, to shake their hands, to hug them—even if the hands she was shaking and the torsos she was hugging belonged to people with a veritable host of contagious diseases. As a result, her clients trusted her; they talked with her and shared their fears with her. Knowing her clients' stories as she did, Page had come to believe they really weren't that different from anyone else—except they were poorer. And that, she knew, ended up making all the difference in the world.

"Poverty is when the money that you need isn't there, and you have to make choices that compromise your health or your future or your ability to care for your family," she said, sitting in her ground-floor office at the multimillion-dollar Castle transitional housing center that her organization had built for ex-prisoners, many of them with a history of drug addiction, on a street in northern Manhattan where the Harlem and Washington Heights neighborhoods merge. "Where you don't eat fresh vegetables, go to the emergency room instead of a doctor, cut your medications in half, make choices between heat and eating, and your kids weigh less during the winter. That's poverty."

Given all of this, Page prided herself on thinking outside the box. She supported reducing the staggering amounts of money that twenty-first-century American cities, states, and the federal government spent on locking people up and using the savings to fund an array of other programs: ones that allowed members of economically vulnerable groups to pay lower security deposits and brokers' fees when renting apartments. That expanded access to public housing—after all, a study in Boston in the early 2000s had found that children in families on waiting lists for public housing lost weight in winter as compared to children who lived in public housing, because parents of the former were having to pay for their heating instead of for food.[1] That provided structured living arrangements, complete with counseling, drug testing, and job training, for addicts who had run afoul of the criminal justice system, and for the mentally ill who couldn't make it on their own. "If we hadn't done what we do here," she proudly asserted, "they'd be sleeping in a shelter, or prison, or [be] dead. I see somebody whose life my work has made a difference to. I get hugged by lots of people. I work in a warm and caring environment. I work in a place I wish the world would be like. There's an acronym: BHAG. It means 'big, hairy, audacious goal.' I get an enormous kick out of making things happen."

It was that sense of possibility, that innate belief that most everyone deserves a second chance, that no matter how many times an addict returns to his dope he's still capable of change, that had saved Bronx resident Francisco Ortega when he arrived at the Castle in his late forties. Addicted to heroin for more than thirty years, in and out of prison, the little man—five feet four in his shoes, skinny, with a sparse, graying goatee and tattooed arms—finally decided enough was enough. "I used to sell the drug to support my habit. Steal. The more I had, the more I'm using. That monkey on my back, telling me to keep using; it took everything of mine. Family. I just didn't care. I lost a lot of good jobs. Lost a job as a porter—I was in a union. One day I woke up and was tired of being tired. I decided to start from the bottom. I went to a shelter at Bellevue, and then I went to parole and told parole I was dirty and I needed help. He put me in a methadone program. They took care of me."

A lady friend of Ortega's suggested he approach the Fortune Society to see if they would house him. "They accepted me, gave me a room, took me in. I started giving clean urine. Fortune got me here, to the Castle. Everything been working ever since. I work for Fortune, in the kitchen, as a cook. I always volunteer, because I owe Fortune. If it wasn't for Fortune, I'd be on the street, in jail, perhaps dead somewhere. It *feels* good. I've been clean two and a half years."

Ortega was living in a small studio on the eleventh floor of the Castle. He was touchingly house-proud, nervously wiping down his tabletop with a cloth, making sure the surface of his toaster oven was spotless, pointing out his flat-screen Hitachi TV, quite possibly the first honestly acquired item of worth in his life. "This is the first time I ever had my own apartment," he explained, his tone one of wonderment. "When I have money, I buy things for the bathroom, curtains. It feels good. Every day you see it. I used to spend it on drugs. Everything's falling into place right now."

———

For David Onek, a whole bunch of good could come out of expanding the network of specialized treatment courts that had emerged in various parts of the country over the previous few years. People charged with low-end crimes were being shifted into specific kinds of courts. If they had an addiction, they went to drug courts so that case-workers could link them up with treatment services. If they were living on the streets and needed help getting a roof over their heads, accessing medical treatment, getting a photo ID so that they could apply for work, and so on, they were sent to homeless courts. Some courts met the needs of military veterans who might have committed crimes while suffering from posttraumatic stress disorder. Still other courts were peopled with staff trained specifically to deal with mental illness.

Onek was in his early forties, charismatic, self-confident, and quick to break into a smile during an animated conversation. The scion of a political family, he had worked in the San Francisco mayor's office of criminal justice, gone on to found the Berkeley Center for Criminal Justice and had then run as a reform-minded candidate for San Francisco District Attorney. He hadn't won, but his ideas were, increasingly, sought out by people interested both in criminal justice reforms and in anti-poverty initiatives.

"It's fascinating that we're doing things that clearly do not make us safer, and are bankrupting our state and states around the country. We need to reduce recidivism, be smarter on crime. We need to do something differently. We're at a pivotal moment right now. Let's come up with a criminal justice system that's rational, that's fair, that keeps us safer."

Onek talked about the importance of stopping people from going to prison in the first place, through more investments in anti-truancy programs so as to help troubled teens stay in school, drug treatment services and the like; and of working with them, if they still did go to prison, to help them navigate their way in the free world once they were released. He urged what reformers were calling "justice reinvestments," taking money saved by locking fewer people up, and investing it in programs that would lower crime rates through tackling poverty, addiction, mental illness, and other massive societal problems.

Use the criminal justice system to deal merely with the criminal symptoms of a person's underlying problems, and you solve nothing, Onek understood. Instead, you just spend a ton of money locking people up—money that ends up being diverted from other parts of county and state budgets. And you effectively brand a large pool of people with a modern-day scarlet letter, one they will carry with them when they leave jail or prison, and that will have the effect both of limiting the kinds of work they can do subsequently, and also reducing the amount of money they will earn over the rest of their lives. In 2012, the Department of Justice reported that a spell behind bars can reduce a person's future earnings by 40 percent.[2]

Imprisonment is, quite simply, all too often a response to poverty, and overwhelmingly it serves as a one-way ticket to lifelong penury. It is, for this and many other reasons, a powerful weapon to use against someone, and as such it should be used sparingly.

Of course, when people are dangerous, when they are predatory, when their crimes seriously harm others, and when there is no way to keep society safe from their actions other than by locking them up, then incarceration is entirely appropriate. But when, as is all too often the case in a country that has more than quintupled its incarcerated population since the early 1970s, and that now houses far more nonviolent inmates than any other country on earth, a jail or prison sentence serves mainly to allow society to blow off steam at misfits and miscreants, then, surely, it is better to look for alternatives. After all, to reiterate a point previously stated, in many parts of the country locking someone up costs more, per year, than sending a person to an Ivy League college. And, in the same way as the parents of a Harvard student expect bang for their bucks, so, too, taxpayers have a right to expect criminal justice expenditures to make society safer and reduce the likelihood that people will return to crime once their sentences are completed.

"We've embarked on the biggest prison-building binge in history, and we're paying the price for it now," Onek explained of California, a year before the state began, finally, scaling back the size of its prison population. "We have an absolute fiscal crisis. The number-one driver of that crisis is the cost of prisons. Meanwhile, teachers are getting pink-slipped, police are being laid off, social services are being cut. Certainly there are people who need to be locked up for long periods of time. Unfortunately, we have lots of people being locked up who don't meet that description." Onek talked of a three-strikes inmate serving life for breaking into a soup kitchen, another serving life for stealing a pair of socks. And he spoke angrily of how it would cost California nearly $5 billion during the following twenty years to keep incarcerated its population of *nonviolent* three strikers. "Obviously, life in prison, any reasonable person would say, is completely exorbitant punishment for the minor crimes they have committed. It is foolish; it is literally bankrupting our state. And we can't afford it." Several months after I spoke with Onek, voters in California came to the same conclusion: By a nearly two-to-one margin, they passed Proposition 36, an initiative intended to restrict three strikes for use only against people whose third offenses were serious and violent, and one that allowed for thousands of three-strikes inmates to be resentenced—and released on time served—based on the narrower parameters of the new law.

———

For Martha Sanchez, a well-known environmental and education activist in Los Angeles, her issue of choice was schooling—specifically how to ensure that low-income kids, such as her own children, could attend schools not dangerously polluted by industrial byproducts, could get the same educational opportunities as their more affluent peers, and could have their needs taken as seriously by political leaders as were those of other families.

Sanchez, who had migrated to the U.S. from Mexico as a young woman, had made a name for herself campaigning to expose the serious environmental pollution that a local metal-plating company in her industrial, East Los Angeles neighborhood had inflicted on her children's school grounds. She had called out the company, the school district, and local political officials in a series of public meetings—at first in pidgin English; later, as she devoted more time to her studies, in better English; finally, after she began studying law, in English laced with legal references. She had organized residents and teachers to fight back against the presence of sickness-inducing heavy metals in the soil on which the school was built and in the air that her children daily breathed. And after years of campaigning, she had succeeded in getting the school cleaned up, the company to stop operating in the vicinity, and had secured for her community grant money to convert the onetime factory into an ambitious affordable housing complex.

For Sanchez, it wasn't just about cosmetic improvements. Rather, the more she had put her heart and soul into the issue, the more she realized that this was a profound question of justice: kids being educated in overcrowded, polluted schools, who routinely came home vomiting, with rashes and nosebleeds, finding it hard to breathe, weren't just losing classroom time; compared to more well-to-do children, living and attending schools in better neighborhoods, they were losing their opportunities in life.

"You have to tell them that that is not right," Sanchez realized, talking of her early interactions with the school district. "Certain chemicals are known to cause cancer, and this particular community had been exposed to these chemicals."

It became the cause of her life.

The last six years we were always, twice or three times per month, doing a community action—writing letters, demonstrations, trying to find the laws that weren't protecting us, trying to redirect resources, trying to bring experts to do tests on people. The air quality department agreed to place an air monitor in one of the classrooms. The school district changed its policy about building new schools. They started to implement rules. They visited the school to check how the kids were doing. We won mobile cleaning of the play-ground. They came every month to offer free treatment for the kids who were suffering from asthma or allergies. They were there for three years. They were also following the company, and they did surprise visits. They forced the company to place filters in the building, to change some tanks and the way they were operating. The company stopped using spray paint. One day in 2005 the air quality person organized a big press conference to tell the people he had charged the company $65,000 for illegal disposal, and he announced the company had to face criminal charges because of that. It was a huge event.

ROBIN HOOD AND THE INCREDIBLE HULK

Whatever one's additions to a national anti-poverty wish list, whatever one's choice of big, hairy, audacious goals posited during conversations such as those coordinated by George Goehl, or put forward during legislative hearings, none of them come free. Injecting widespread opportunity into long-downtrodden communities; developing newer, better approaches to crime and punishment, addiction, mental illness, pollution; and revitalizing long-neglected public infrastructure, from antiquated school buildings in heavily polluted urban centers to transport systems connecting poor communities to employment hubs—all of these require new revenue sources.

Building on a model proposed by community organizers such as Goehl; progressive think tanks such as the D.C.-based Center for Economic and Policy Research (CEPR); leading economists such as the University of Massachusetts's Bob Pollin and CEPR's Dean Baker; and billionaire investor Warren Buffett, I would suggest the centerpiece here be a new financial transaction tax of the kind debated in many European capitals since 2008 but in America shelved largely because of opposition from the financial sector. It could be titled, simply, the economic justice, or fair play, tax. Some proponents have labeled it the Robin Hood tax.

The concept isn't new. For the better part of three centuries, the United Kingdom has leveled a small stamp tax on stock trades. Japan had a wide array of financial transaction taxes on the books into the late 1980s. And even in the United States, where the financial industry has long been hostile to such levies, from the early years of the 1900s through to 1964, stock trades were subject to a small tax. Indeed, during the New Deal years the tax was expanded enough to generate significant amounts of revenue: a 0.04 percent tax on the trade in stock, combined with a 0.12 percent tax on new stock issues. Such amounts, practically invisible on a daily basis to individual investors, would, said Baker, if they were still on the books today, be generating approximately $25 billion per year in revenue for the federal government.

Reintroduce this tax and expand it (at varying levels, depending on the kind of transaction) to include *all* forms of financial trades, from stocks to bonds, from currency trades to credit default initiatives, and the government could, Baker argued, easily bring in $150 billion per year without slowing down the workings of the broader economy.

In December 2009, scores of economists from around the country signed an open letter circulated by CEPR, urging the adoption of just such a tax. "The cost of trading financial assets has plummeted over the last three decades as a result of computerization. This has led to an enormous explosion in trading volume, with most trades having little economic or social value and redistributing disproportionate resources to the financial sector. A set of modest financial transactions taxes, which would just raise trading costs back to the level of two or three decades ago, would have very limited impact on trades that have real economic value," the economists wrote. "Such taxes could both reduce the volume of speculation in financial markets and provide substantial revenue for either important public purposes and/or deficit reduction. Financial transactions taxes could be an important part of a reform package that seeks to remake the financial sector so that it better serves the larger economy."[3]

Critics argue that in the globalized financial environment of the twenty-first century, no single country can implement such a tax; that it's good in theory, but would somehow have to be introduced simultaneously in all major economies to stop finance simply migrating to tax-haven states. American opposition to such changes explains why the UK didn't expand its stock trade tax into a more general financial transaction tax, and Britain's opposition in turn explained the reason why the European Union shied away from such a tax despite support for it in France and other large economies.

Baker was having none of it. Yes, he acknowledged, that might be true for small countries. But when a nation with a political footprint and an economy as large as that of the United States took a stance, it had a pretty good chance of bringing other countries along for the ride. Sure, some individuals and corporations could move their trades overseas, but what was to stop the American government from passing laws saying that such transactions, engaged in by U.S. citizens and U.S. companies, were subject to an American financial transaction tax regardless of where the trade occurred? What was to stop the American government putting in place incentives to report these trades, such as, Baker said mischievously, rewarding whistleblowers with a percentage of the taxes owed once they were collected? And what was to stop the government from making it clear in international meetings that it expected as much cooperation from allies in the arena of tax evasion as it did in the realm of anti-terrorism work? "I call this the Incredible Hulk theory of international relations," Baker said drolly. "There're a million things we could do to a country that doesn't go along with us."

In Congress, Senator Tom Harkin from Iowa and Representative Pete DeFazio from Oregon proposed a 0.25 percent financial transaction tax, which would have generated about $60 billion annually. Not surprisingly, in a Congress tilting ever more conservative in the wake of the 2010 midterm elections, the proposal went nowhere, languishing without ever being put up for a vote.

But, outside the halls of power, after the 2008 collapse a grow-ing chorus of voices *did* begin calling for just such a revenue-raising mechanism. National People's Action and a number of trade unions urged a tax of 2 percent on financial transactions and estimated that such a tax could add upward of $350 billion to federal tax rev-enues. An increasing number of economists signed on, embracing the notion of a tax somewhere between the low-end version pro-posed by Harkin and DeFazio and the higher-end one called for by the NPA.

The framework, argued Baker, was already in place: Some stock market transactions were currently taxed, albeit at a miniscule rate, to fund the operations of the Securities and Exchange Commission. Ex-pand this, phase in the new taxes over a couple of years so as not to dis-rupt markets, and the country ends up having available a huge pool of money that it didn't have before. And, as a side benefit, the economist explained, it would, like any other sin tax, lead to something of a re-duction in the harmful behavior being taxed, in this case resulting in the country having fewer destabilizing speculative transactions to worry about, and thus more long-term market predictability.

It was another win-win proposal left to languish not because of overriding economic objections but because of political stalemate.

In addition to embracing the financial transaction tax, a propor-tion of additional funds brought in by increasing the capital gains tax, the top tax brackets for the highest earners, and the estate tax—as of 2012, the first $5 million a person inherits was exempt from estate tax, and beyond that the rate topped out at only 35 percent—could also be dedicated to an anti-poverty fund run by the federal government and allocated either directly to individuals through fed-erally funded and maintained safety net systems or via state and lo-cal programs.

The lesson here should be one of possibility. Taken as a whole, some fairly mild and targeted tax increases could dramatically change the fiscal environment in Washington, D.C., making possible large-scale anti-poverty interventions and infrastructure development projects that in the early years of the century were rendered impossible by a rigid emphasis on cutting top-end tax rates.

After all, it's hard to find money for services for the poor when the Joint Committee on Taxation estimates that because of huge rollbacks in the estate tax less than 0.2 percent of all estates—or only about 3,600 estates per year—are paying so-called death taxes to the federal government. Conversely, a whole bunch of money could be freed up by almost laughably small adjustments to the tax code: In July 2012, *BusinessWeek* reported that merely moving the taxable estate-worth threshold downward from $5 million to $3.5 million and raising the top estate tax rate from 35 to 45 percent (a maneuver that would only result in about 4,000 additional estates being taxed each year) would bring in $9 billion in extra revenue.[4]

Taken as a whole, these tax reforms should generate hundreds of billions of dollars annually.

WHY NIXON WAS A RADICAL AND ALASKANS GET FREE CASH

One can do a lot with that kind of money.

With this additional revenue ear-marked for anti-poverty programs as a cushion, localities and states, funded by the federal government, should be able to get to work building up the assets of the poor rather than, as occurs all too frequently, stripping them down.

Legislators could, for example, set in place a guaranteed minimum income, of the sort advocated by no less a conservative than Richard Nixon, back in the 1970s, as a way to ensure that everyone has at least a few dollars to spend on necessities each month. How would it work? One way would be to design it in a manner akin to the proposal for old age pensions put forward by the Townsendite movement during the Great Depression. That movement called for all seniors to be given $200 a month from the federal government. But, it came with a catch: All $200 would have to be spent each month. If the money wasn't spent, it was forfeited. In the 1930s, such a plan was deemed impractical. How would the government be able to monitor the spending levels of millions of individuals? Today, with modern-day technological advances, such a system would be easy to implement: anyone without work and without income could qualify for, say, a guaranteed subsidy that would take them somewhere between a quarter or halfway toward the poverty line—on the assumption that food stamps and other assistance would bring them up closer to the poverty line itself. It would provide enough income to avoid complete destitution, but not enough to be an attractive long-term alternative to work.

The country could, argued Almaz Zelleke—a Harvard-educated political scientist who worked as associate dean for academic affairs at New York's New School until 2011, when she left to devote more time to campaigning on behalf of the U.S. Basic Income Guarantee Network—set a minimum of $10,000 per adult per year. Come tax time, anyone who had earned less than that amount the previous year would have the difference made up to them in the form of a government check. Or, if policy makers wanted to go down a more ambitious route, she explained, they could establish an annual income floor of between $6,000 and $7,000 per year to every man, woman, *and child* in the country—an idea embraced in the past by Milton Friedman and Martin Luther King Jr.—thus going a long way toward eliminating the huge and growing problem of deep poverty experienced by single mothers and their children. Extending income guarantees to children would move the country into line with most Western European nations, which have long used child allowances, or "milk money," to ensure that kids get basic levels of nutrition and avoid the worst ravages of destitution if their parents' finances collapse.

Zelleke believed this would be relatively easy, and affordable, to set in motion. But she also felt that it was a second-best solution. Ideally, she argued, one would go further down this road, with the government sending monthly checks to *all* Americans, regardless of income. Those who fell below certain income thresholds would get to keep this money; for those above it, the money would be recouped through a series of banded income tax levels at the end of each tax year. Warren Buffett and Mark Zuckerberg would get their checks as regularly as would an out-of-work single mother. But whereas the impoverished lady would keep it, Buffett and Zuckerberg would be expected to pay it back. Do this, she argued, with all the fervor of a convert to a cause, and one could do away with a slew of other bureaucratic, and costly-to-implement subsidies and social programs. There would, for example, be no need for the mortgage interest tax deduction, or for housing assistance, or food stamps, or the Earned Income Tax Credit. How much would it cost? At $6,000 per person, its first year would run to an eye-popping $2 trillion. But, Zelleke hurriedly explained, aware of the almost cartoonish nature of that number, most of that would be recouped through back-end taxes, through the elimination of other costly subsidies, and through the magnifier effects created as money more effectively circulated through some of the country's most vulnerable regions. Think of it like a hybrid car: The starting price is far more expensive than for the gas-guzzling version of the same car, but over the years, most of that difference is recouped via lower annual gas expenditures. It was, Zelleke said, somewhat optimistically, something that libertarians and progressives might one day be able to build an alliance around, its universality, like that of Social Security, protecting it from being whittled away, its simplicity making it easy to administer. "It's a way to provide all Americans with economic security forever," she averred. "A permanent safety net that is truly substantial."

As grist for her argument, Zelleke explained that a handful of cities in New Jersey, Washington, and Colorado had run what were called guaranteed minimum income pilot programs in the 1960s as a part of the War on Poverty. Canada had also experimented with the idea. More recently, some basic income projects had taken root in towns in Brazil, India, and Namibia, with preliminary research suggesting they were effective at lowering rates of malnutrition, boosting local economic activity, and increasing the number of local kids attending schools.

Furthermore, Zelleke added, for more than three decades Alaska, hardly a bastion of radical socialist thinking, had had a variant of this in place, in the form of the Alaska Permanent Dividend Fund. There, every man, woman, and child was entitled to a percentage of the state's oil revenues, an amount that, in recent years, had ranged from a little under $1,000 on up to $3,000 per person. In September 2012, the Associated Press calculated that a resident who had lived in the state since the first checks were issued in 1982 would have received more than $34,000 from the fund during the three decades that followed.[5] Perhaps not entirely coincidentally, despite the fact that the legislature doesn't collect back the dividend from wealthier residents via higher state taxes, Alaska's Gini Coefficient data—Gini being a complex measure used to track inequality—indicated the state had less extremes of wealth and poverty than almost any other state in the union.

Almost certainly, Zelleke's proposal is too big a pill to swallow. But there's no practical reason that an alternative, more limited, model couldn't be developed. It would be easy to distribute a basic guaranteed income to the poorest of the poor via an EBT card—the same sort of card that food stamps recipients currently receive their benefits on; one that would be accepted by any business that accepts credit card payments. And, at month's end, any remaining balance would simply be erased from the card. Such a program, which could be administered either federally or via existing state agencies, would prevent the most extreme cases of destitution while also circulating desperately needed funds through low-income communities and the businesses located in these neighborhoods. In 2012 America, six million people had *no* sources of cash income, relying exclusively on food stamps and the charity of friends, relatives, churches, and nonprofits to survive.

Were such a program to provide each of these men, women, and children with a few thousand dollars a year to get them heading up toward the poverty line, the total cost would be between $20 billion and $30 billion. That's a lot of money, but it would pay dividends through stimulating local economies, increasing sales taxes that cities and states would bring in, and reducing the number of health emergencies experienced and crimes committed by the desperately poor.

It would also go a long way toward eliminating the sort of destitution experienced by Maria, in Phoenix, Arizona, when, at the age of 36, she took her five children and left her abusive, drug-addicted husband. Maria, a high school dropout, had worked for a time in a factory making phone parts, but she had never managed to save anything: What she earned kept her kids fed and clothed. What was left, she said, her husband spent on drugs. When the work ran dry, her car was repossessed; the family was evicted five or six times from different apartments for failure to pay the rent. More often than not, her husband was out of a job too.

"It was destroying my children, destroying me as a person," she said. Without a dime to her name, Maria finally screwed up the courage to leave. But it had taken her years to find that courage. "It was very scary. The uncertainty of where I'm going to live. Are they going to have food to eat? Are we going to be out in the cold? It was scary. I took my kids, a few things we needed. I lost everything. Memories, those are all gone. But I looked at it as new beginnings; we can make new memories."

At first she stayed with her mother. Then she and her five children lived with a friend—but they had to leave after the landlord threatened to evict the friend for housing too many people. "Just the thought of having to take my kids to sleep at a bus stop, that was horrifying. I lost sleep. Somebody told me to call the Contacts Line, that they could help me with somewhere to stay. Every time I called, they had no room." Eventually, she managed to get a spot in an emergency shelter, and the family moved into their new accommodations.

When I met Maria two years later, she and her kids were living in a sprawling transitional housing shelter, home to more than 500 residents, a couple miles from the Phoenix airport in a building that, until recently, had been a low-end hotel in a region of the city long bedeviled by prostitution and crime. The building was full-to-overflowing; from 2009 to 2010 alone, the number of homeless families in Maricopa County had increased by 28 percent.[6] Maria was, finally, fulfilling her dream: She was studying to be a registered nurse. She was getting her life together. Had she had a guaranteed income years earlier, however, she wouldn't have been stuck in a violent, abusive situation for as long as she was. She would have had the means to move much sooner, to start the next stage of her life without worrying that her kids would be out on the street.

WHEN SMALLER IS BETTER

Beyond the guaranteed income, state governments should also experiment more with state-backed micro-credit lending for low-income communities. Such lending seeds startup businesses in much of the developing world, yet, despite its documented success in raising numbers of borrowers out of poverty in countries such as Bangladesh, there has been a paucity of it within the United States.

Yes, the Small Business Administration provides low-interest, long-term loans to organizations such as the Milwaukee-based Wisconsin Women's Business Initiative (WWBI), which then leverage that money to raise additional low-interest loans from private banks, which can then be turned around and loaned at a slightly higher rate of interest to poor Americans looking to start their own companies. Yes, the Treasury Department, the Department of Commerce, and the Department of Health and Human Services's office of refugee resettlement, all have dollars that they provide to micro-lenders. But the numbers have never kept up with the need, and too often the programs simply remain hidden, underutilized and lacking clout.

And that, said Connie Evans, president of the D.C.-based Association for Enterprise Opportunity, the trade association for American micro-lenders, was a shame. If one out of three Main Street businesses each added one employee, she argued, America would rapidly reach full employment again. Many of those businesses, she believed, could use micro-loans to expand; yet the programs that could help them do so were too few and far between. The Aspen Institute's FIELD program estimated that nationwide in the years leading up to 2012 only around 117,000 such loans were disbursed annually.[7] Given that there were more than 20 million micro-businesses in the country, and given the fact that small businesses in the post-2008 environment too often were denied credit by banks, that wasn't nearly enough.

Why not use some of the revenues raised from a financial transactions tax to put the federal government directly into the micro-loan business? Why not open up these loans to employees wanting to buy out retiring company owners and create worker-owned cooperatives? Why not, asked Wendy Baumann, executive director of WWBI, create a national micro-credit lending pool into which the government, as well as private banks, could contribute? In 2008 and 2009, such contributions could have been one of the conditions upon which the feds provided banks with bailout money. These days, such contributions could be one of the requirements for banks wanting the umbrella of FDIC insurance.

Owing to the desperate nature of the times, said Baumann—whose organization lent small amounts of money for a few years at a time, and 95 percent of whose clients met the terms of their loan—in an era of high unemployment and obliterated retirement nest eggs, increasing numbers of people were asking to borrow limited pots of cash to start their own businesses. "There's a large number of individuals 50 or over starting businesses. It's out of necessity." With pilot-program funding from the Department of Labor and the Small Business Administration, Baumann's organization had held workshops, in conjunction with the Milwaukee Jobs Corps, for young men and women and had held similar sessions, in conjunction with the AARP, for older people.

Baumann's organization only lent to people looking to start, or to expand, businesses. But in theory there was no reason why micro-lending couldn't also be used to tide over low-income Americans from one paycheck to the next. According to the Center for Financial Services Innovation, every year fifteen million Americans use payday loans, auto title loans, pawn shops, and other cogs in the low-income debt machine.[8] Micro-loans issued by nonprofits could be used as a short-term alternative to these exploitative products, providing a method for the poor to access credit to tide them over rough patches in a way that doesn't condemn them to endless fees and exorbitant interest rates. That's what the company Progresso Financiero does in California and Texas. Aimed mainly at Hispanics in the two states, the short-term loans are provided at roughly 36 percent—far higher than the long-term loans given out by banks so that people can buy homes and cars, but far lower than those of payday loan companies, the fees and penalties on which can rapidly add up to several hundred percent annually. It's also what the nonprofit Capital Good Fund does in Providence, Rhode Island, using grant money as well as dollars raised from investors to loan small sums to homeless women and those who need to escape domestic violence, so that they can pay a month's rent.

Recall Maria's slide into homelessness in Phoenix after she left her abusive husband. It was an unnecessary coda to her already painful story; federally backed and properly publicized micro-lending systems could have provided reasonable alternatives, allowing her to leave her husband without ending up on the streets.

Such money could be loaned directly from government funds or used as collateral against commercial bank loans, so that banks would be more likely to lend small amounts, at near-equivalent interest rates to that charged their premium clients, to low-income borrowers who don't have decent credit histories. Given the difficulty states have had in legislatively controlling the payday loan industry, developing more attractive alternatives to this industry, and thus depriving it of vulnerable clients, might well be the best way to ensure that it simply withers on the vine.

DOWN PAYMENTS ON THE FUTURE

Revenues from the financial transaction tax should also be used to immediately make more widespread universal child development accounts. The idea behind these is simple but powerful: encourage parents to put money aside for their children's college education by providing state-funded subsidies to bulk up the savings.

When the Labour government in Great Britain set up such accounts in the late 1990s—200 years after the radical polemicist Tom Paine had called for grants to be given to all women upon the birth of their children as part of a universal social insurance system—it argued that the grant would increase poor people's ability to participate in the economy by giving them an incentive to invest either in post-secondary education or in meaningful job training courses.[9] In the years following, the state invested billions of pounds in this, with a considerable degree of support from across the political spectrum. It was seen as a cost-effective investment in the country's economic future, both financially aiding the poor and also, psychologically, encouraging them to believe they have a stake in their own future. Unfortunately, the program fell victim to the austerity budgets of the Conservative-Liberal coalition, elected in 2010, before it could really bear fruit.

A pilot childhood development account (CDA) program *does* already exist in San Francisco. All babies born in the city have a small city-funded education account set up in their name, so as to encourage low-income families to think of higher education as a possibility for their children. Another pilot program is up and running in Oklahoma. And a similar one, funded by philanthropist Harold Alfond, was set up statewide in Maine in 2008, giving $500 to every new-born child in the state, so long as that child was enrolled in the state's 529 college savings plan.[10] Three years after it was created, about four in ten babies born in Maine were being enrolled in the education saving programs and were thus becoming eligible for the $500 gift. That wasn't a great take-up rate, but it was a whole lot better than nothing.

There are roughly four million babies born each year in the United States. Providing each one of these with $500 to kick-start their education accounts would cost $2 billion annually. That's chump change for an economy as large as America's, but it would have huge benefits down the line, encouraging more families to save for college and thus making higher education more affordable, and less of a debt generator, for millions of people.

Implementing a small federal CDA program would be easy and wouldn't need a separate revenue source. But ultimately, any remade social contract ought to have a far more ambitious higher-education component built in. And so we return to the idea of an extra line on our tax forms, to the concept of a dedicated government trust fund, floated by a quarter-percent income tax paid by employees and a quarter-percent tax paid by employers. That's not a large sum: $75 a year for a person earning $30,000. But the payoff would be huge.

The concept is simple: if a family puts aside a few hundred dollars a year into one of the state-run education savings accounts, which is all that most families can afford, they're unlikely to save anywhere near enough to put a kid through college. But if each child has a lump sum of several thousand dollars put into the education account by the government when they are born, over eighteen years that will have grown, through compound interest and other rates of return, into a large nest egg; probably not enough, by itself, to entirely fund a university degree, but certainly enough to fund a good part of that education. A payroll tax of one-quarter of 1 percent on employees and one-quarter of 1 percent on employers would seed a fund that could easily put aside $5,000 for higher education for each child born in the

United States. And because it is payroll-generated, that amount could, like Social Security, have a cost of living component built in legislatively, so that each year the amount set aside increased in line with inflation.

Add into that small additional annual contributions from each family, or the Pell Grant for lower-income students, and one gets closer to the concept of higher education that doesn't saddle students and their families with lifelong debts.

Pooling resources, as is done with Social Security, but at the start of life rather than the end, allows everyone to benefit.

As an interim measure, for those who were born in the years before the tax reform kicked in, and who went to college subsequently, reserves from this fund—my proposal would generate considerably more per year than the $20 billion distributed annually to newborns, thus rapidly building up a reserve—could be tapped to subsidize a portion of their tuition.

And for those who, for whatever reasons, still didn't go to college, despite having the money put into their education account at birth, that additional cash could be added into their Social Security payments upon retirement, to be paid out either as a lump sum once a person starts claiming Social Security, or as an extra annuity for a given number of years. Because people without a degree tend to earn less than their college-educated peers, and because Social Security payments are related to how much one earns over a lifetime, this would have an equalizing effect, ensuring that the non-college-educated retained a degree of financial security in old age. Assuming 3 percent annual growth via the state educational accounts' investments, far more conservative annual rates of return than those that most retirement accounts anticipate, $5,000 left to grow during sixty years would, at the back end, be worth more than $30,000. At 5 percent annual returns, it would grow to more than $80,000.

Done well, such a program could plausibly become an integral part of the modern state, as essential to the financial well-being of

the young, and to the non-college-educated elderly in the twenty-
first century, as Social Security became for the well-being of the old
during the twentieth.

Phased in initially as a 0.25 percent tax, it could be increased, over
a decade, to 1 percent, ultimately providing more than enough money
to allow each child to have $20,000 put aside at birth, to grow over
time either into a near-complete subsidy for higher education, or into
a near-guarantee of economic security in old age for those who don't
attend college. The additional tax burden would cease to intimidate
voters, once it became clear how much they, and their families, stood
to gain from not having to service student debt for decades, and from
not having to worry about economic security in old age.

In the same way as payroll contributions for Social Security and
Medicare came to be accepted by most Americans, so too a phased-in
Educational Opportunity Fund (EOF) tax, if championed by a progressive political party, ought to be as palatable, and, ultimately, as
salable to an electorate. Without a sense of shame, people in the mid-
twenty-first century could say they were on educational opportunity
income, in much the same way as people today say they are on Social
Security or Medicare. They could say that they and their families had
earned the right to be on this program by paying taxes into it over
decades; and that their paying taxes into it now will provide their children and grandchildren the right to access it down the road. It would
be an easy and affordable way to create an inter-generational sense of
common purpose.

To make such a program more attractive to national debt hawks,
who have long argued that the country's largest challenge involves
the size of its national debt, I propose the following: Once the EOF
has fully kicked in, and has been shown to massively reduce student
debt—and to thereby free up many thousands of dollars a year in
income that ex-students would otherwise have had to set aside to
pay down their private, student debts—I propose that the EOF then
be raised to 1.5 percent, on both employees and employers, with *all*

of the additional revenue generated by raising the tax above the one percent level needed to fund higher education being used exclusively to pay down the national debt.

Again, everyone would win: at a relatively low cost, the EOF, phased in over the course of more than a decade, would replace the private risks currently imposed on those seeking higher education with pooled risk; would dramatically expand the long-term financial security of the portion of the population, lacking higher education, currently most at risk of an impoverished old age, and would also eventually generate huge sums of money that could be used to help pay down the national debt. The additional tax burden imposed on Americans by this reform would more than be cancelled out by the long-term financial benefits accrued under an EOF regimen.

All of this is important. In 2000, the total level of student debt nationwide was estimated to be around $200 billion.[11] A mere twelve years later, that number had increased to an astonishing $870 billion— or $24,000 for each graduate who left college having taken out loans. And, while underwater homeowners could use the bankruptcy system to clear their mortgage debts, there was no legal mechanism in place to allow student-loans to be similarly discharged.

In April 2012, when Michigan Congressman Hansen Clarke proposed HR 4170, a Student Loan Forgiveness Act that would allow people to discharge their debt if they had paid at least 10 percent of their discretionary income on student loans for at least ten years, more than 1 million people signed petitions in support of the legislation.[12] Yet the GOP-led House didn't pass it. Despite the passage of other significant student loan reforms during the first Obama administration, the country remained more awash in student debt than in financial obligations built up via credit cards and auto loans. The vast majority of that money was owed by younger graduates, who had attended college during a period of public disinvestment in higher education.[13]

"The total sum is a lot, having to make three separate payments on three separate loans. It seems pretty daunting, like it will take a lot of really careful budgeting. It seems pretty hard to imagine having to pay back large sums of money, with interest accruing, over the next ten, fifteen years, while also having the concerns of a career, a job, a family, things like that," 22-year-old Javier Trejo, who had recently graduated with a political science degree from St. Louis University in Missouri, told me when I interviewed him at the community center in Albuquerque at which he spent his time volunteering, as part of the Jesuit Volunteer Corps, in exchange for a $100 per month stipend. He was back home in Albuquerque because, fearful of ever higher levels of debt, he had deferred attending the graduate program in public policy to which he had been admitted.

All indicators suggest the trends toward ever higher levels of student debt will continue in the years to come—debts that for a growing number of workers will prove not just difficult, but to all intents and purposes impossible to repay—thus undermining the basic economic calculus that a higher education will lead to a lifetime of financial benefits for attending college in the first place.

In part, the growing financial burden placed on students has emerged because cash-strapped public universities are raising their tuition fees by amounts far in excess of the rate of inflation. In the 1990–91 school year, to take just one example, a student attending one of the University of California campuses could have expected to pay $1,820 in tuition; by 2012 that number had gone up to more than $13,000.[14] In part, it's because quality education, be it public or be it private, like quality healthcare, involves ever more emphasis on technology, and technology comes with a price tag. In part, though, it's because Pell Grants and other assistance to lower-income students, as well as the amount of money states pony up to fund their university systems, have taken huge hits in recent years, as conservative rhetoric around budgeting has emerged center stage.

In 1979, Howard Friedman noted in his book *The Measure of a Nation*, a Pell Grant covered three-quarters of the cost of a four-year college; thirty years later, it covered only one-third.[15] Where, two generations ago, the GI Bill sought to use federal dollars to broaden educational access, today federal lawmakers roll back educational assistance to lower-income Americans. In early 2011, Republicans attempted to cut Pell Grants by $20 billion, a move that would have removed approximately 1.7 million recipients from the rolls.[16] They failed. But, a few months later, as Democrats and Republicans jousted over raising the national debt ceiling, Pell Grants *were* restructured in a way that made roughly one hundred thousand families ineligible for them, reducing from $30,000 per year to $23,000 the amount a family could earn without having to pay toward higher education, and limiting the number of semesters students could qualify for the grants.[17] In Paul Ryan's budget plans for 2012 and beyond, the GOP again targeted the education grants, pushing for cuts of approximately 20 percent in the years to come.

At the risk of flogging a dead horse, let me reiterate a key point here: cutting education grants to poor people is utterly counterproductive. *It's stupid, slash-and-burn, public policy.* It burdens families who stay the educational course with crippling levels of debt, and it discourages others from staying in school and going to college in the first place, thus tamping down their income potential for the remainder of their working lives.

It doesn't take a whole lot of imagination to conceive of better alternatives. We could start with education accounts opened for every child at birth, at first relatively small ones funded by existing revenue sources; then larger ones, funded by the newly created Educational Opportunity Fund. We could expand AmeriCorps and other service options in lieu of debt payments. We could modify debt-repayment schedules so that ex-students only have to pay down their debt once their income, averaged over three or four years, rises above a certain amount. And we could enact Representative Clarke's legislation so that low earners aren't burdened with student debt repayments throughout their working lives. Above all, we could elect people willing to go to bat for valuable communal goods such as higher education; willing, and able, to explain to the public the necessity of raising enough taxes to build protective firewalls around proven success stories such as the Pell Grants and to try out new programs, such as the EOF, so as to reduce the crippling levels of debt too many students today leave college with.

LAND BANKS, STATE BANKS, AND THE NORTH DAKOTA WAY

Let's continue thinking about connections. Boosting wages, making higher education more accessible, perhaps setting in place minimum income standards—all are good starting points.

But what about building up public and environmental infrastructure? What if there were ways to kill two birds with one stone, using public funds to improve the commons in a way that simultaneously reduced poverty and stimulated a renaissance of American manufacturing and industry?

The answer is, there are.

Again, to reiterate: Hundreds of billions of dollars of additional government revenues could be generated annually, without grievously damaging the economic dynamism of the country, through the financial transaction tax, profit taxes on energy sales, and a few other eminently practical changes to the tax code. Why not use some of that extra revenue to help establish state banks—similar to Germany's seven *landesbanks*, and to the state bank already in existence in North Dakota—the purpose of which would be to provide funding for local infrastructure projects, small businesses and other community-building projects, and to provide a backstop for a coherent national industrial policy aimed at regenerating good-paying, blue-collar jobs in areas hammered in recent years by outsourcing.

In North Dakota's case, the bank, originally established in 1919, with $2 million of seed money from the state, as a way to shore up investments in local grain farms and agricultural technology, today circulates upwards of $270 million per year through the state's economy and controls assets worth upwards of $4 billion. All North Dakota state taxes and fees are deposited in the bank, and the institution then loans the money out to build up infrastructure: its dollars go toward student loans—the first federally insured student loans in the country were issued by the bank in 1967—small business expansions, responses to weather-related disasters, investments in new farm equipment, and so on. Half of the bank's profits get reinvested in the state's general fund each year.

It's a good system, and one with bipartisan support in the state. "We invest back into the state in economic development type of activities. We grow our state through that mechanism," bank president Eric Hardmeyer told *Mother Jones*'s Josh Harkinson in 2009. "We're using this to spur economic growth for our state, to provide niches where others aren't comfortable, whether it's in-state financing of residential loans or making student loans."[18]

As of 2012, state banks had been proposed by legislators in a dozen other states. Running into ideological opposition—of the knee-jerk sort that deems all things state to be "socialist" and therefore suspect—none of these proposals, so far, has been successful. It's a shame. For a carefully thought-through network of state banks *could* play a powerful role in a national campaign to eradicate poverty and improve public infrastructure.

In fact, with money from the federal anti-poverty fund along with targeted investments by a network of newly created state banks, both the federal government and state governments could begin a decades-long investment in green jobs, helping both to boost the economy and also address serious, and growing, environmental challenges.

Some of these funds could be used to create markets for high-tech green transport, construction, and energy generation methods. Some—as discussed by President Obama's onetime "green jobs czar," the Los Angeles–based community organizer Van Jones, in his book *Rebuild the Dream*—could be used specifically to train people from groups and neighborhoods long blighted by high unemployment and poverty in the skills needed to get jobs in green industries. Such is already being done by the Women's Bureau of the federal

Department of Labor, which set up a green jobs training project in 2009, and also by the Environmental Protection Agency, which has, for the past several years, given out grants to nonprofit groups to train low-income, minority, and unemployed residents in cleaning up contaminated sites in their communities.[19] Such could be the case on a larger scale if legislation that has long sat un-acted on in Congress passed to create a subsidy for low-income Americans to weatherize their often aged, dilapidated, homes, so that they had to spend less money and use less energy heating their homes in winter and cooling them in summer.

Done well, these investments would serve both to boost environmental protections and to intervene against poverty simultaneously. They would, ultimately, set in place a virtuous circle—a have-your-cake-and-eat-it scenario—in which economic and environmental benefits reinforced each other rather than being set up in opposition to each other, as conservative critics of environmental regulations claim is often the case currently. Call it "green neo-Keynesianism," Van Jones explained. Put in money from the state, and, at the same time, utilize people's skills to implement local, environmentally sound, economic investments.

That's what the Mott Foundation was doing in Flint, Michigan, a city long bedeviled by high unemployment and low educational attainment levels, where it worked with local companies to train several dozen workers to be able to repair distressed, foreclosed-on properties, gathered together into what was called a "Land Bank"—which they were then allowed to buy at a discount after the work was completed. It was a great idea: tackling blight, rebuilding the value of properties no one wanted, providing an affordable entry point into a housing market from which too many impoverished families had historically been excluded. In partnership with the Open Society Foundation and the state-run Michigan Works Agency, Mott was also helping run a local Earn-and-Learn program. The program fully subsidized for several months the wages of several hundred employees hired on by local companies. The catch? The employees had to go through rigorous retraining programs so that their skills were matched to the needs of employers.

There was no reason such programs couldn't be replicated, on a larger scale, with an emphasis on training the out-of-work in the skills needed to man a green economy.

Green investment dollars could also be used to encourage the urban gardens movement in Detroit and elsewhere; to create local markets for the fresh produce grown on these miniature farms; and to rehabilitate the land and soil of abandoned lots in struggling cities across the country.

This list is, of course, not comprehensive. But it *does* give an idea of some of the creative anti-poverty strategies that could swiftly be brought to bear were we, as a country, willing to impose small, and entirely manageable, taxes on the money-making transactions of the powerful financial sector as well as the super-profits generated by energy companies and other large-scale multinationals. Again, let me stress a point I made earlier: our problem is not a lack of resources to tackle poverty; rather, it has been a lack of will to enact the legislative and taxation reforms that would free up the necessary dollars for such an effort.

PUTTING THE BRAKES ON HOMELESSNESS

Done well, however, an anti-poverty program would have to recognize that it isn't simply a matter of getting more money into poor people's hands, either through micro-lending or through green job training, through tax reforms or subsidies on low-end wages. For, at the end of the day, many Americans are still going to struggle to pay their bills.

In no area is that more the case than in housing.

And so, if we're serious about rolling back the hardship that has emerged in recent years, investments must be made to render housing more affordable for those struggling at the bottom of the economy. Both through pumping more money into time-tested subsidies such as Section 8, which allow the poor to take part in private housing markets, and also through building more, and better, public housing for low- and middle-income Americans, government must once more acknowledge its power to modify markets for the broader public good.

For some people, those with particular difficulties in accessing housing, new protections will be needed. A case in point here is the enormous difficulty that children in state foster care systems have in navigating the move into adulthood. A 1995 study found that three in ten of America's homeless population had been in the foster care system at one point; other research indicates that about one-quarter of erstwhile foster kids report having spent some time homeless within four years of leaving the system.[20]

"These are the Commonwealth's forgotten children. They come to the state abused and neglected and we house, clothe, feed, educate and provide health care for them until they turn 18. Then, they are sent out to live on their own with minimal, if any, assistance. The cutoff of services at age 18 does not make sense given what we know about child and adolescent development, the impact of trauma and what it takes for youth in the general population (let alone abused and neglected youth) to achieve self-sufficiency," wrote the authors of a 2005 report by the Massachusetts Society for the Prevention of Cruelty to Children.[21] One in four homeless young adults in Massachusetts, the authors noted, had recently left foster care.

It is because of these dismal numbers that Illinois, California, and several other states have moved in recent years toward bulking up their foster systems, staggering the age-out process so that onetime foster care residents can continue to receive state welfare benefits and housing assistance through the age of 21. University of Chicago researchers who have compared Illinois with neighboring states that continue to remove all benefits from foster kids at the age of 18 have found that a lower percentage of ex-foster kids in Illinois end up homeless than is the case elsewhere.[22]

But simply extending the age limit won't solve this crisis. There are, after all, simply too many problems that foster kids bring with them regardless of when they age out: profound feelings of abandonment, oftentimes posttraumatic stress disorder, addiction, insecurity, a complete lack of family resources to fall back on. To deal with this cocktail of crises—each ingredient of which in itself is frequently enough to knock a person off track and into destitution—advocates have long urged an expansion of Section 8 housing, the use of rental vouchers, one-year rent subsidies for those leaving foster care, and, perhaps most significantly, the building of transitional housing units, complete with networks of counselors, specifically to be used by young adults leaving the fragile protections of the foster care system.

"It felt like I was being abandoned, I was the problem," explained Aaron, a 28-year-old ex-foster kid, whom I met in a small, remote town in the far north of California. "My mom *did* abandon me, allowed my dad to convince her to get rid of me." In the group homes in which he was placed, Aaron claimed to have been beaten and physically restrained, leading to a lifetime of back pain.

When I met him, Aaron was picking up casual day jobs to supplement the few hundred dollars a month in Social Security that he was receiving because of his injured back. He was shopping at thrift stores and picking up food at a local pantry. Four or five days out of each month, he estimated, he went without food so as to be able to afford his $475 rent and the roughly $100 that his utilities cost him.

Making it easier for people like Aaron to navigate their worlds isn't just a matter of charity but of simple, common sense: if states can provide a safety net for these young men and women at the start of their move into adulthood, they are far less likely to have to provide emergency interventions, be they shelter assistance, expensive emergency medical care, or the exorbitant cost of housing a person in jail or prison, down the road. There are, after all, over two million prison and jail inmates in twenty-first-century America, hundreds of thousands of whom are serving time for nonviolent crimes; the sorts of relatively low-level crimes—street drug sales, vagrancy, stealing from shops—that down-and-out young men are particularly likely to engage in.

In 2011, the California Senate's Office of Research conducted a study of the state's 171,000 prison inmates: it found that 14 percent had been in foster care.[23] The same University of Chicago study of three Midwestern states that concluded people who received foster benefits until the age of 21 did better than those left to fend for themselves at 18 found that one-third of foster kids ended up with a "high involvement" in the criminal justice system; moreover, upward of eight out of ten males and more than half of all females with a foster care background reported being arrested at some point.[24]

The trend holds up around the country. Nationally, according to a May 2011 report by the Brookings Institution, as of 2004 "there were almost 190,000 inmates of state and federal prisons in the U.S. who had a history of foster care during their childhood or adolescence. These foster care alumni represented nearly 15 percent of the inmates of state prisons and almost 8 percent of the inmates of federal prisons. The cost of incarcerating former foster youth was approximately $5.1 billion per year."[25] This is a large amount of money, much of which could be saved were states to more effectively blend aid to ex-foster kids into their overall anti-poverty strategies.

————————

In bygone years, such carefully tailored programs might have gone a long way toward mitigating homeless numbers. After all, traditionally, large numbers of the country's homeless, the residents of skid rows from New York's Bowery to Los Angeles's Central City East, have come from a handful of demographic groups: foster care kids, drug addicts and alcoholics, the mentally ill, military veterans, ex-prisoners. Set up appropriate assistance programs and treatment clinics, build transitional housing, send caseworkers out into shelters and onto the streets, and one had a fair shot at significantly diminishing America's homeless numbers.

Not anymore. These days, with millions of families having been left homeless or at imminent risk of ending up on the streets by the housing market bust, a far more general anti-homelessness strategy is needed. Of course, treatment for addicts or the mentally ill, and housing for vulnerable groups has to remain a core part of any war on poverty, but these alone won't be enough. Federal and state authorities must step in more assertively to salvage the savings and homes of those millions of families whose financial security was put at such risk by the foreclosure crisis.

In part, the national settlement the Obama administration and state attorneys general negotiated with the five largest banks in 2011 was on the right track, forcing large banks to place $26 billion into funds that states would then channel into mortgage relief programs. In part, however, it was a desperately incomplete project; for it didn't include many slightly smaller lenders, it left many families still paying subprime interest rates, and its provisions were only intended to last a few years, leaving millions of families still vulnerable at the back end of the process.

At a state level, some attorneys-general, most notably California's Kamala Harris, picked up where the national settlement left off, pushing homeowners' bills of rights that restricted how and when banks could foreclose on owners; that made it easier for owners to go through loan modification processes; and that held open the prospect of states and individuals suing banks for more financial damages down the line.

All of this is important; but, taken piecemeal, no state or federal legislation can undo the damage caused by years of predatory loans being handed out like candy, followed by years of declining property values, and waves of robo-signed foreclosures collapsing entire neighborhoods.

And that's why the response has to get more creative.

What happened in Boston is a good starting point. Shortly after the financial collapse, a number of Harvard Law School students signed on to work for a foreclosure legal clinic run by a law professor named David Grossman. The students and their professor would contact foreclosure victims, give them legal advice, sometimes represent them in court, during hearings that would determine whether or not they could remain in their homes. They also put them in touch with anti-foreclosure activist groups, and, perhaps most importantly, with a credit union named Boston Community Capital.

The students worked off of foreclosure lists, knocking on doors to try to connect with owners. At each house on their list, the volunteers, traveling in teams of three, would stop their car, get out, knock on doors, scout to see if the property looked abandoned (broken or boarded up windows, weeks of uncollected mail, trash strewn in the yard, and so on); if it did, they moved on. But if it still looked inhabited—or if there was even a glimmer of a chance that it hadn't yet been abandoned—they would leave a red plastic bag hanging on the doorknob. Inside was information about the foreclosure process; about the Harvard Law School legal aid clinic, which had been working in conjunction with several other regional law schools to offer legal services in Housing Court and beyond to owners and tenants in homes being foreclosed by banks; and about the consortium of lawyers, community groups, and the Boston Community Capital (BCC) credit union collectively known as Project No One Leaves.

BCC, the law students informed owners, had been working to buy distressed properties back from the banks at the new, low market rates, and to then resell them to the original owners at near the newer, lower price, thus providing them the chance to stay in their homes at a lower monthly payment. It was a win-win scenario: the banks got to cut their losses, selling the properties they owned for more than they could sell most similar foreclosed properties; the owners got to keep their homes; neighborhoods that would otherwise end up increasingly abandoned and dilapidated got a shot at staying afloat; and the

BCC locked in a chance at making a profit by selling back to the owners at 25 percent over what it had paid for the property, as well as by getting the owners to sign a profit-sharing agreement in which half of all profits made if the owners flipped the homes got plowed back into the BCC house-buying pool of cash.

"We discovered the average outstanding mortgage amount [in these neighborhoods] was $325,000," BCC head Elyse Cherry explained. "But if you applied any kind of underwriting criteria the average mortgage they could support was somewhere in the region of $150,000. We tried to reinvent the community bank, so we have a service relationship with our borrowers, we underwrite our borrowers."

In 2009–10, the credit union purchased sixty properties, containing a total of ninety family units. The organization's intent, if it could raise tens of millions of dollars in cash on the secondary markets, was to buy back hundreds more homes in the years to come, mostly in impoverished working-class communities of Boston. "We have a zero default rate," Cherry asserted. "Eleven million dollars in lending and about one hundred families. We have no defaults."

The Boston story drew national attention. Law school students from a number of universities around the country came out to Massachusetts to see how it worked. Several other community credit unions were established to provide similar help to homeowners elsewhere. There's no good reason these models shouldn't become a key part of state and federal housing strategy in the near future, with credit unions able to access low-interest federal startup loans in return for guaranteeing to keep given numbers of people in their homes.

More ambitiously, given the amount of toxic mortgage debt that the federal government was forced to buy up in the months following the 2008 collapse, there's no reason that it shouldn't use its status as a de facto lender of last resort to create similar profit-sharing agreements of its own with homeowners underwater on their loans or already skidding along the foreclosure route.

Why not allow these families to stay in their homes on hybrid rental-ownership agreements? They could pay the federal government a monthly rent lower than their original, and ultimately unaffordable, monthly mortgage payment. Temporarily, the government would act as landlord, taking on upkeep responsibilities, making sure the property was insured. The rent money, minus a portion to be used for utilities, insurance, and maintenance, would be put into a dedicated account, administered by the government but in the name of the individual or family associated with the property.

If the newly minted renter wanted to move, he or she could—with no penalties, no outstanding debt. Unlike in a traditional foreclosure process, the government could let the person walk away without the action imploding his or her credit rating. In that case, the government would keep ownership of the property and would rent it out to other low- and middle-income residents. It would, essentially, become part of a growing pool of public housing. But if the ex-owners-cum-renters stayed current on their rent payments for a specified period of time, say five years, they would once more be considered homeowners, and the money in their account would be used to pay down the principal they still owed on the property.

Let's assume that a person owed $100,000 on his home when he went into foreclosure and the government became his landlord. Let's then say that each month, for five years, that person had paid $1,000 in rent, $500 of which was set aside into his dedicated housing account. After five years, there would be $30,000 in the account. If the individual reconverted to being owner of his property, he could immediately apply that $30,000 to paying down his principal, meaning that from that point on he would be making monthly mortgage payments on a $70,000 loan. Or he could pay down a portion of the principal and put the remaining money in trust to subsidize, and make more manageable, his future monthly mortgage payments.

Consider it a mortgage variant on being Born Again: a person who had originally put down almost no cash for a mortgage financed by a predatory loan would essentially spend five years, with the assistance of the government, building up a significant down payment so that he could then reenter the mortgage market to access a smaller loan, payable to the government instead of to a commercial lender, with no predatory conditions attached.

There are many pluses to such a scenario. First, it would take large numbers of underwater properties off the housing market for at least five years, thus tightening the supply of for-sale homes and helping to kick-start local property values again. Second, it would keep homes occupied that would otherwise be abandoned, would prevent communities with large numbers of distressed properties from falling into blight, and would keep residents housed who would otherwise be at risk of homelessness. Third, it would build up a pool of affordable housing maintained by the government and available to low- and middle-income families. Fourth, the dedicated housing accounts would trigger a tremendous burst of enforced savings, moving large numbers of low-income Americans onto a more sustainable financial path for the rest of their lives.

Last, but by no means least, as with the BCC arrangements, and as with an array of profit-sharing housing cooperatives set up by trade unions in New York and elsewhere in bygone decades, when the owner came to sell, a portion of the profits, ranging from, say, 25 to 50 percent, would go back to the government. Out of the ashes of the housing conflagration, a huge reserve pool of money would be created for future investments in affordable housing projects nationwide.

BETTER SCHOOLS, BETTER COMMUNITIES

In addition to housing, the other crucial public investment to expand is that in schools, and, more generally, in the communities within which schools operate.

It might seem strange to have waited so long, within a book such as *The American Way of Poverty*, to tackle a topic so important. In fact, there's nothing strange about it. It's not that education is of less importance than housing and jobs, drug treatment and community safety; clearly, education is of paramount importance. Rather it's that absent a host of other changes occurring either before, or at the same time as, shifts in how schools approach teaching, educational reforms in isolation strike me as disconcertingly Sisyphean in nature: exhausting, and, too often, futile.

If that comes off as pessimistic, it shouldn't. For the flip side of the equation is that with the right support network of reforms in place, with the sorts of holistic school-cum-community environments advocated by reformers such as Richard Rothstein, fixing the education system oughtn't to be nearly as confounding a challenge as it has been portrayed to be.

Stable economic environments tend not to produce gangs, street-level drug markets, hunger, homelessness, and all the other daily facts of life that poor kids have to navigate in their communities. Less hunger, violence, and drug dealing tends to mean less disruptive classrooms. Less disruption inside the classroom means that teachers have more time to actually teach kids and engage with them educationally as opposed to trying to impose discipline on chaotic, and sometimes dangerous, situations. And more meaningful teacher-student interactions tend to lead to higher educational attainments.

In many ways, I believe, educational virtuous circles can be spurred at least in part by non-educational reforms. And many of those reforms are at the heart of the holistic anti-poverty strategy that I have detailed in the pages of this book. Absent those changes, absent the pathways to broader prosperity made possible by investments in job creation, by affordable healthcare, by large-scale changes in housing markets, and so on, the path to a renascent K-12, even with significant infusions of extra cash, is much rockier—which is why I'm not prioritizing a dedicated K-12 trust fund in the same vein as the EOF.

It may still be possible, through creative charter school curricula, and inspiring environments, to improve the classroom setting and students' participation within it. Tennis star Andre Agassi, for example, created an extraordinary academy for low-income children in Las Vegas. The campus is a pastel-hued, airy, architectural masterpiece—built at a cost of $40 million; the students learn music on concert-quality instruments; they travel to places such as Paris on school trips; experience school visits from local Cirque du Soleil troupes; and are all, without exception, expected to attend college after graduation. The results, to date, have been a grand success.[26] Networks of strong charter schools exist in Harlem, in Sacramento—where former basketball star, now mayor, Kevin Johnson was instrumental in creating high-achieving inner-city schools—and in many other locales. But doing all of this takes massive financial investments and, usually, the backing of a celebrity figure such as Agassi or Johnson, or a well-connected business executive with a passion for change, capable of marshaling the support of a network of donors and other supporters.

With more than two million students enrolled in charter schools nationally, according to the National Alliance for Public Charter Schools, and hundreds of new schools opening each year, such institutions *have* earned their place at the table as one part of a broader attempt to improve the educational setting for poorer children. But replicating the successful charter school experience in deeply impoverished communities on a mass scale would be hugely difficult—and would come with an implausibly high price tag.

Moreover, because of all the external problems left untouched, such successes are peculiarly vulnerable to derailment. Navigate a virtuous circle counter-clockwise, and one dysfunction butts up against another. If you're born into wealth, you will have available to you the most cutting-edge educational facilities. But if you're born into poverty—and, increasingly these days, into middle-income families—your options, unless you are one of the lucky few to live near a thriving charter school or a good local public school, are far more limited. Your family will be unable to afford quality preschool—which makes it far less likely that you'll succeed academically once you do enter school. You will suffer the consequences of buzz saws having been taken to programs like Head Start that subsidize early learning opportunities for lower-income kids. You will all too likely attend overcrowded schools reeling from teacher and staff layoffs as a result of endless local and state budget fiascos, in which you use out-of-date textbooks, no longer have access to non-core-requirement courses, and rarely are exposed to music, art, and other vital, culturally enriching, aspects of life. Your school year will be shorter than that students experience in most every other wealthy democracy. And, if and when you manage to get into college despite these obstacles, you will end up heavily indebted and working an array of jobs in a vain attempt to keep up with soaring tuition costs and make up the shortfalls from inadequate Pell Grants.

At every stage of the educational journey, in short, we make it harder on those at the bottom of the economic pyramid. It's as if we set up a one-hundred-meter race, some of the participants in which get to sprint down open lanes, while others have to jump a series of hurdles. No guesses for which group of racers will tend to finish ahead of the pack.

Libraries' worth of books have been written, and reports issued, on how to improve the teaching environment in schools mainly populated by children from poor backgrounds. And that is, of course, a worthy project. It isn't, however, my project.

Not that I don't think it critical that schools give urgent attention to developing ways of improving the education they provide their students. It should, at this point, almost go without saying that schools themselves must be focused on, so as to get the best teachers possible working in the best school environments possible, utilizing the best textbooks available, and holding students to the highest plausible standards. It should go without saying that schools need good, motivated, enthusiastic teachers; they need ways to bring in fresh blood and to get rid of do-nothing teachers on occasion. They need ways of measuring students' academic success that go beyond a series of multiple choice tests, that take into account students' economic backgrounds, their immigration and linguistic status—in

California, for example, according to *Mother Jones* reporter Kristina Rizga, immigrant children still learning English tend to score badly on tests yet often do well on nontimed essay assignments, and frequently respond well to engaged, creative teachers.[27]

Anyone thinking about how to tackle poverty has to have in mind innovative ways to improve the classroom experience for American kids, coming from a multitude of economic, cultural and linguistic backgrounds and too often short-changed by their local schools. They might want to think about expanding programs like the federally funded Race to the Top, in which states compete to create templates for new learning environments that merit the infusion of extra dollars from the feds. They might want to push legislation such as that championed, so far without success, by Denise Juneau, Montana's energetic superintendent of education, mandating that all students remain in high school until they turn 18. They might want to argue the merits of charter schools, or school vouchers, both of which have engendered spirited, frequently overheated, debate in recent years. They might want to emulate Oregon's recent efforts to create an all-encompassing education strategy that goes from preschool to higher education, with an oversight board empowered to shift resources into particular settings as the need demands.

In poorer communities, in particular, they might want to supplement property taxes, which provide a core part of the funds for education in most states, with additional state and federal grants; or intervene with federal emergency funds, as was done in the two years following passage of the 2009 American Recovery and Reinvestment Act, to stop teachers from being pink-slipped during recessions. They might want to think about new funding mechanisms, similar to Medicaid, that mandate more federal spending goes into education in poorer states, while requiring richer states to maintain their own higher spending levels on schools.

But all of this must occur in a way that recognizes that schools, and school problems, are anchored in the broader community.

While taking dollars away from schools is a surefire way to reduce the quality of the learning experience, raising the money spent on schools, while leaving the broader social conditions unchanged, can't in and of itself guarantee improvement.

In recent years, many reform movements, from federal ones such as No Child Left Behind to state efforts such as Louisiana's ill-starred takeover of the New Orleans school system in 2006—when the state tried to fire all the Big Easy's teachers, rehire some of them on different contracts, and convert the system into a network of charter schools—have focused exclusively on teachers and school administrations: those who don't generate good standardized test scores amongst their students are fired, their schools taken over—or, in some cases, even closed.

Such measures sound good, tough, no-nonsense. But in reality, taking the country as a whole they're likely to be as effective as trying to empty a swimming pool with a teaspoon.

Yes, schools need educators in the classroom willing to go the extra mile; but they also need students with at least some community and family resources to fall back on outside of the classroom. They need, for example, parents who care when kids miss school—which is why Kamala Harris, back when she was San Francisco's District Attorney, had set up truancy courts to hold accountable the parents of elementary school kids who routinely failed to show up for school. After all, Harris reasoned, fully 30 percent of homicide victims in her city were high school dropouts; and the kids who weren't finishing high school were, disproportionately, ones who had never had a regular school attendance in the first place. Threaten the parents with fines, even in extreme cases with jail time, and you could nip much of this problem in the bud; back it up with drug treatment programs for addicted, disengaged parents, and you could start making a profound difference. San Francisco's district attorney's office reported, in 2012, that truancy had been reduced by more than 20 percent in one year, as the city moved more aggressively to enforce its anti-truancy initiative.[28]

An anti-truancy program in Milwaukee has reduced truancy rates, amongst those kids who go through the counseling program by nearly half, while also reducing daytime burglaries and other crimes associated with teenage truants.[29]

Trying to fix a school's woes, or the great web of poverty that so many students are trapped within, simply by firing mediocre teachers is destined to only achieve partial results. It might be necessary, but in few instances will it be sufficient. Recall Principal Kuzman's discussion of how hundreds of his North Las Vegas students didn't have homes to call their own; how they came to school without having eaten breakfast and left school knowing there would be no dinner; how many of them had never even been downtown to see the sights let alone on a trip out of the city or out of state; how their worlds had been constricted to a few square blocks in a mean, and violent, enclave.

So long as the broader conditions limit children's learning potential—so long as kids are homeless, coming to school hungry, living in communities broken down by drugs and gangs, attending schools so short of funds that class sizes are soaring and textbooks become a luxury rather than a necessity—good teachers alone will not be sufficient.

"No nation in the world has eliminated poverty by firing teachers or by handing its public schools over to private managers," wrote New York University research professor of education Diane Ravitch in the *New York Review of Books*. "Nor does research support either strategy. But these inconvenient facts do not reduce the reformers' zeal. The new breed of school reformers consists mainly of Wall Street hedge fund managers, foundation officials, corporate executives, entrepreneurs, and policy makers, but few experienced educators."[30]

Ravitch, a onetime assistant secretary of state for education under president George H. W. Bush and author of the book *The Death and Life of the Great American School System*, felt that wealthy reformers were setting up charter schools that, because they could cherry-pick their students, weeded out those who did badly on tests. They provided the illusion of better education while, in reality, oftentimes they were simply being more selective in which students they accepted than could the regular public schools with which they were in competition. "Charters would be fine if they focused on the kids who were the lowest-performing kids. And then [they could] come to the public schools and say, 'Hey, we've learned something new, we want to share this with you because we're part of the same system we want to help,'" she told the *American Prospect*'s Abby Rapoport in the fall of 2012. "Instead, charters have become a competitor to see who can get the highest test scores."[31]

It was one thing improving test scores, Ravitch and fellow critics of the testing mania argued; it was quite another genuinely improving educational opportunity. For Helen Ladd, professor of public policy and economics at Duke University's School of Public Policy, poverty was the elephant in the room all too often ignored in discussions about education reform. "Current policy initiatives are misguided," she told a Washington, D.C., audience in November 2011, "because they either deny or set to the side a basic body of evidence documenting that students from disadvantaged households on average perform less well in school than those from more advantaged families. Because they do not directly address the educational challenges experienced by disadvantaged students, these policy strategies have contributed little—and are not likely to contribute much in the future—to raising overall student achievement or to reducing achievement and educational attainment gaps between advantaged and disadvantaged students."[32]

Instead, Ladd urged legislators to fund pilot programs and block grants that could be used to develop after-school programs for the children of working parents that would be continuations of the classroom experience rather than glorified babysitting operations. Like Richard Rothstein, who believed putting opticians in schools and helping low-income kids get spectacles would serve as one of the

most effective education reforms yet developed, Ladd advocated
integrating schools into local health and mental health service networks, as was being done by several charter schools in New York's
Harlem district and as had been done in the greater-Omaha area
in Nebraska. There, a public-private partnership, started in 2006,
named Building Bright Futures had created a network of health centers in schools. In the few years they'd been open, thousands of kids
had received medical care they otherwise wouldn't have gotten. Not
surprisingly, there were large declines in the numbers of kids missing
ten or more days of school each year. A similar program had also
been started by the Oyler School in Cincinnati, where a medical
center and vision clinic provided services to the mainly low-income
kids who attended the school. It was, proponents explained, a new
model, a "community learning center," intended to bring social and
health services into the educational setting, and, in so doing, to expand kids' educational horizons.[33]

Ladd also wanted to build on a Durham, North Carolina, program, in which schools distributed large numbers of books, tailored
to students' individual needs and abilities, to low-income children at
the end of each academic year, so as to overcome the infamous "summer reading gap," when poor kids, not exposed to books on a daily
basis, routinely regressed several months in their academic abilities.

All of this gelled well with onetime candidate for Mississippi governor Bill Luckett's emphasis on his state's education system. Luckett
had entered politics because he was disgusted with the levels of poverty in his state. He had hoped to run an administration that would
focus, laser-like, on cutting the Gordian knot. And he had concluded
that huge expansions in education investments represented the best
route to success. Schools, he believed, had to serve as the central hub
from which the spokes of reform would emanate. "We're the only
state in the South that doesn't have state-supported pre-K. We have
the most need and we don't have pre-K. I tried to address it from the
educational standpoint. We have a very good system of community

colleges, but they find the students who enroll are so far behind when they come out of high school that they just can't achieve." For the attorney-cum-politician, it made no sense for his state to short-change so many students year in and year out. All it did was lock in place Mississippi's unfortunate status as poorest, and least educated, state in the union.

> We also have to convince parents' of the value of an education. A lot
> of parents need an education and need counseling to appreciate what
> they don't have and what their children are not attaining. Without
> the proper education, the jobs aren't going to materialize. It's a
> many-faceted problem with many different solutions. It's gonna take
> a huge collaboration of people willing to mentor, people willing to
> help parents get the early childhood element in place, partner with
> daycare centers, with Head Start; get the teachers trained, the right
> people in the right places. Break some of the patronage we see so
> much in our school systems. We have the lowest teacher pay in the
> country so that's reflected in the quality we can get to teach here. It's
> a big, big, problem. And we have to address it from so many areas at
> once. There's not a silver bullet, not a single answer here.

Think about these problems in isolation and they appear over-whelming. Think of them as pieces of a whole, and, paradoxically, the problems become more solvable. Fixing America's education system cannot be done simply by focusing on schools; but understand the specific challenges faced by low-income kids who go to school hungry, who lack basic medical attention, who might have never been tested for eye problems, whose parents have lost jobs or landed themselves in prison, and more realistic solutions present themselves. Understand homelessness as simply a personal catastrophe and it is difficult, if not impossible, to fathom why so many millions of Americans lack stable housing options; but approach this crisis as the collateral damage caused by unemployment, by the systemic marketing of bad debt, by underinvestment in mental health and foster care systems, by overinvestment in criminal justice systems, and, again, new and creative solutions can be generated.

As a country, we have the political tools to break both old cycles of poverty and also the new ones produced in the wake of financial collapse. Add in a credible dose of empathy, of moral imagination and indignation, and there's no reason that we couldn't, to deliberately misquote Grover Norquist, shrink the problem of entrenched poverty down to a size at which it could be drowned in the bathtub.

That someone is born poor in a country as wealthy and dynamic as is the United States ought in no measure to determine that they will die poor. And yet, for millions of Americans today, their birth is indeed their destiny. Ensuring that the democratic aspiration of mobility and opportunity for all becomes a reality once more should, I believe, be one of twenty-first-century America's top political and moral priorities.

CHAPTER THREE

BOOSTING ECONOMIC SECURITY FOR THE WORKING POOR

Walmart worker Mary Vasquez, at a union hall in a suburb of Dallas, Texas.

285

The last and in some ways most complex part of the anti-poverty puzzle is about building up security, creating firewalls against recurrent hardship once people have gotten educational qualifications and found employment, and ensuring those people have enough opportunity and economic security to stay out of poverty not just for a while but permanently. After all, it's one thing not to be destitute. It's something else not to be afraid that a single illness or a minor car accident; an arbitrary reduction in the hours your employer allots you one week; or a spike in food, gas, or electricity prices might not send you straight back to financial square one.

In 2011, congressional Democrats in the Progressive Caucus, led by a onetime community organizer from Tucson named Raul Grijalva, pushed a federal budget proposal that, had it been enacted, would have gone a long way toward addressing this challenge. They called it a "People's Budget," in a nod to the radical social reform legislation of that same name passed by the British Parliament 102 years earlier. This budget built in proposals that over ten years would have massively ramped up, to the tune of $1.7 trillion, the nation's commitment to investing in job training, public works, national infrastructure projects, and social safety net programs. At the same time, it carefully accounted for the additional expenditures through reductions in military spending, as well as targeted tax increases, including a series of extra income tax bands topping out at 49 percent for the very wealthiest sliver of the population, higher taxes on capital gains, and higher estate taxes on large inheritances. As a result, despite the expansion of government that it envisaged, analysts with the Economic Policy Institute found that the People's Budget wouldn't further balloon the national debt; rather, they calculated, unlike other suggestions on the table, a budget proposal like this could actually lead to a federal budget *surplus* by the year 2021.

Grijalva, who lives with his wife, Mona, in a Spanish-speaking, working-class neighborhood of Tucson, is in his mid-sixties, with a thick salt-and-pepper goatee and a penchant for wearing jeans and T-shirts to official functions. He has lived by a motto his father used to quote to him: "'Don't hang your hat where you can't reach it.' It meant, 'You're trying to act too big. Don't treat people like that.'"

Grijalva slouched his large shoulders as he talked. He drank a lot of coffee and smoked cigarettes incessantly. "The disparity between those who have and those who are trying to have and those that don't have is just wider and wider," he argued.

> The disparity of wealth, the disparity of income, the shrinking of wages. We find our country moving into the most stratified class distinctions that we have ever seen. And with it comes an increase in poverty. It's a very dangerous social crisis that faces this country. Every time we cut a vital support program the poverty rate goes up and the misery quotient goes up. For us to tolerate a poverty rate and a permanent underclass of poor people in this country goes against everything that we believe we are as a nation in terms of our values.

The People's Budget contained a series of ambitious proposals to counter these trends that, taken as a whole, would have packed a heavy punch. Perhaps that's why it didn't go anywhere. In a politically degraded environment, it actually proposed serious solutions to serious problems.

TAX CREDITS AND LIVING WAGES: WHY PAYING MORE IN ALABAMA IS BAD, BUT PAYING MORE AT WALMART JUST MIGHT BE GOOD FOR THE SOUL

And so, we return to a more piecemeal approach, to using existing programs more effectively, and to pushing new solutions into the forefront of policy debate.

Let's start with the Earned Income Tax Credit.

Once employed, whether it be in newly created private sector jobs or in public works–funded green ones, whether it be in a new factory or on an old farm, many workers are at first likely to earn too little to be able to fully support themselves. So let's again use the Robin Hood pool of cash, garnered by taxing wealthier Americans and their financial dealings at slightly higher levels to bolster the income of these men and women and, in the process, to increase their purchasing power and boost the broader economy. This time around, let's do so by expanding and protecting the extra income generated by the Earned Income Tax Credit.

While the "flat tax" and related proposals pushed by anti–big government conservatives sound superficially fair and in their simplicity seem inherently seductive—everyone pays the same percentage of their income, and all the complexities of a modern tax structure can be put to one side—in reality tax systems work best when they are steeply progressive. In other words, the wealthier one is, the higher percentage of one's marginal income that goes toward taxes; the poorer one is, the smaller the percentage that goes toward taxes.

"Simplifying" the tax code by eliminating all but one or two tax brackets, as most GOP politicians advocate, makes for a snappy sound bite but is bad public policy. A flat tax or a system that significantly reduced the number of tax brackets could not accommodate the needs of the working poor or those who suffer income declines during recessions. In fact, almost by definition, a flat tax reduces the rate paid not by those at the bottom of the economy (as Mitt Romney notoriously pointed out during the 2012 election campaign, the bottom part of the population currently pays either no, or very little, federal income tax) but by those at the top—thus failing political philosopher John Rawls's test for who benefits from significant political decisions. Similarly, a two- or three-tier system, implemented in a climate when anti-tax advocates are on the offensive, probably means poor people will pay what they used to, while the higher up the income scale one goes, the less taxes one will end up paying. And because at least a minimum level of social services and government infrastructure have to be provided for even in the most conservative of states, when income, corporate, and capital gains taxes are limited—either by state constitutional provisions, as in, say, Alabama, Mississippi, and several other states, or by supermajority provisions for raising taxes, as in California, Oklahoma, and elsewhere—the result is that states adopt a grab-bag of other, more regressive revenue-raising measures. Among these are sales taxes, including on food, and fees paid for in equal measure by poor and rich alike.

That's one of the main reasons why a poverty-line resident of Alabama will pay several dollars more each week when she goes to the supermarket to buy her groceries than will people elsewhere in the country. Her food purchases are being taxed. Nationally, it's why the wealthiest Americans only pay about 5 percent of their income in state and local taxes; middle-income Americans pay more than 9 percent; and those at the bottom of the economic heap, who spend most of their income purchasing necessities that are subject to sales taxes, pay more than 10 percent. According to a 2009 analysis by the Institute on Taxation & Economic Policy, in ten states the poorest residents pay state and local taxes that, as a percentage of their income, are six times higher than that paid by the wealthiest residents.[1]

Denude the federal tax system of its remaining progressive elements, and you end up having to hike a whole bunch of fees and sales taxes disproportionately paid by poorer people. Yes, tax forms and tax collecting can and should be streamlined. But taking advantage of computer technologies to make it easier to work out how much different people owe the IRS is very different from "simplifying" the system and eliminating its progressive qualities in a way that only the already-affluent benefit from.

Far better to move in the opposite direction. For the working poor, instead of paying more money in taxes, come the end of each tax year you actually get a credit; the IRS pays you rather than the other way around.

University of Chicago economist Milton Friedman, whose supply-side economics generally won him conservative plaudits and liberal criticisms, argued in favor of a credit that, he hoped, would be palatable across the political spectrum. Conservatives who opposed "handouts" could defend it as being a "hand-up," a benefit that promoted its recipients' independence rather than what they believed the welfare system did—encouraging a do-nothing dependency on the state. Go out and get a job, they could say, and even if it paid a pittance, with a form of negative income tax in place you could make it work for you. Liberals could be sold on the program as one that used government dollars in a sensibly redistributive way, helping poor workers—and helping them even more the poorer they were and the more family members they needed to support.

It was, Friedman argued, in a 1968 television interview with William Buckley in front of a large studio audience, "a proposal to help poor people by giving them money, which is what they need, rather than, as is now, by requiring them to come before a governmental official, detail all their assets and their liabilities, and be told you can spend x dollars on rent, y dollars on food, and then be given a handout." In what Buckley called, in his impossibly aristocratic intonations, a "revolutionary idea," Friedman explained that a family with no income at all would be entitled to get $1,500 back from the government, "available for its personal consumption." But as soon as people within the family started working, until they reached what he called a break-even point in income, the negative income tax they received would increase, and thus they would have an incentive to start earning money. Friedman suggested that it was a way to break the infamous poverty trap created by the then-current welfare system—which penalized people when they began work by immediately cutting their benefits—by encouraging people to find employment rather than to stay at home in exchange for government aid.[2] Ultimately, he hoped, this income-tax-in-reverse would come to replace the entire cash-based welfare system.[3]

Despite President Richard Nixon's sympathy for the idea—at about the same time that the country's thirty-seventh president came out in support of mandatory health insurance, provided by employers or through public subsidies, he also proposed a Family Assistance Plan that, if it had passed, would have essentially created a guaranteed baseline income for all Americans—ultimately Friedman's more ambitious ideas around the negative income tax didn't materialize.[4] It was as politically difficult a sell in the 1960s as Zelleke's updated version of the basic income guarantee would be nearly a half-century later. It smacked of "the dole," of government control, of bureaucracy run amok.

Instead, what emerged a few years after Friedman began floating his concept was a de facto income subsidy for low-wage workers, in the form of the EITC.

In a polarized age, the tax credit was one of the few big institutional developments that could command, if not total, then at least widespread bipartisan support. No less a conservative than Ronald Reagan called it "the best anti-poverty, the best pro-family, the best job creation measure to come out of Congress." From the liberal side, Teddy Kennedy and George McGovern agreed.

Instituted in 1975, a year after Gerald Ford had assumed the presidency in the wake of a disgraced Nixon's resignation, the tax credit was enlarged during both the Reagan and George H. W. Bush presidencies. In 1993, Democratic president Bill Clinton again expanded the program dramatically and used this expansion, in conjunction with welfare reform, to move more poor people into the workforce. Under the Clinton expansion, childless adults were given limited EITC subsidies, and parents heading large families were given larger subsidies. For families with two or more children, the extra money made available was enough to fairly dramatically alter their financial calculus.

In the decades following its introduction, approximately half of the states in America also introduced their own versions of the EITC, as a top-up to the federal one. Today, most Northeastern states already have generous earned income tax credits. In the South, though, politically the polar opposite of the Northeast, EITCs either don't exist, or exist only to cancel out tax obligations rather than to provide actual income subsidies to the working poor. In some parts of the South, money families receive from the federal tax credit is then taxed by the state, reducing the overall value of the benefit. The results, not surprisingly, have been mediocre at best: In states without top-up EITC credits, health outcomes are worse, overall poverty rates are higher, and the prevalence of childhood poverty in particular is far above that of the Northeast.

Studies of the efficacy of the tax credit, both at the state level and also federally, have shown not only that it removes millions of families from poverty, but that in doing so it dramatically improves the health of children born into these families, reducing the numbers of babies born at a dangerously low weight, leading to a reduction in the rate of premature births, and increasing newborns' Apgar scores—all indicative of positive changes wrought by families accessing EITC money.[5]

This is another no-brainer. The EITC does enough good that states without their own version in place are clearly harming their lowest-earning residents.

Expanding the EITC once more and providing states without EITCs of their own, or with only limited programs, a fiscal incentive to expand their tax credits ought to immediately be embraced as federal policy. As with Medicaid spending, for example, the federal government could institute a formula so that richer states bear more of the cost of these tax credit programs, while poorer states would receive larger federal subsidies. It would be an effective, and not terribly expensive, weapon in the arsenal used for tackling poverty in states and regions with some of the most entrenched hardship in America.

————

There is, of course, a flip side to this: What is to stop large companies from simply paying workers scandalously low wages, secure in the knowledge that the state would step in with generous EITC benefits to top-up the incomes of the working poor? Recall the abysmally low wages Walmart was paying Mary Vasquez in Texas. Or, for that matter, in a slack labor market, if more people are tempted into the labor pool by the existence of a tax credit, what is to stop the laws of supply and demand from simply driving down wages—not just for EITC recipients but for all the low-end workers competing for entry-level jobs?

Such a problem isn't entirely speculation. University of California at Berkeley economist and public policy professor Jesse Rothstein has done research that indicates precisely this flaw in the EITC. During a tight labor market, such as that present in the late 1990s, he calculated, companies such as McDonald's were having to woo prospective employees with signing bonuses and relatively high wages. During a slack labor market such as that in the post-2008 period, however, no such incentives were needed. Unfortunately, labor markets are rarely as tight as they had been in the late 1990s. And so, averaged out over thirty or forty years, Rothstein averred, "Wages have gone way, way down. So thinking the solution is to get more people into that labor market, that just doesn't add up."

For sure, the Earned Income Tax Credit could push individuals into employment and help a certain number of individuals navigate their way out of poverty, but what it couldn't do was raise the overall well-being of the entire working-age population. While EITC recipients—especially single mothers at the bottom of the income pyramid—still benefit, despite the driving down of wages, because of the additional dollars sent their way by the government, individuals not eligible for the tax credit actually end up worse off than they would have been without the program in place. The combination of more people competing for their jobs and employers using the tax credit as an excuse to drive down wages has proven disastrous for this group of people.

In 2009, Rothstein published a paper in which he wrote that while each dollar spent on EITC increased the incomes of women with children by $1.07, "this is accompanied by a decline of $0.34 in the net-of-tax incomes of women without children."[6] Overall, because more people benefit than lose—and benefit by *more* than those on the short end of the stick lose—the tax credit still deserves some plaudits for limiting poverty, but, argued Rothstein, not quite in the unqualified manner that its advocates might believe.

The Berkeley economist's calculations suggested that a well-administered negative income tax, which maximized the subsidy to workers earning zero and then gradually was reduced in value as incomes rose, would protect the entire labor pool better. Because workers are given a baseline income in this model regardless of whether they have jobs or not, they have less incentive to accept lower-paid employment, and thus higher wage levels are preserved. *You want me to work? Sure. But you're going to have to pay a wage that I can reasonably be expected to live on.*

In theory, there's no reason that the federal government couldn't create a framework, similar to the ones discussed earlier, for a basic income guarantee nationally. Nor is there a reason that other states shouldn't take Alaska's lead and themselves introduce dividend funds to be distributed from revenues gained by more effectively taxing the use of scarce natural resources and the pollution generated by industries within the states.

Politically, given current rhetoric around taxes and government spending, this would be an extraordinarily hard sell. Even if it proved cost-effective to give everyone a monthly check from the government in lieu of the hodge-podge of programs and non-cash assistance that people currently use and then to reclaim that money from more affluent Americans come April when people file their taxes, convincing people of this in a world of fifteen-second sound bites would be a monumental challenge. The huge initial sticker price would scare many people off, even if the bulk of it could be recouped through back-end taxes and the cutting of programs, such as housing assistance, made redundant by the minimum income safeguard. The loss of familiar perks such as the mortgage interest tax deduction would terrify many voters, even if the net result of the new system was a wash for their families, and the sense that ever more people were coming to rely on handouts would prove anathema to a society long suspicious of what conservatives have come to deride as an "entitlement culture."

Inertia is, as physicists will tell you, a powerful force of nature. If for no other reason than that, it's unlikely that the entire tax code and the massive infrastructure of government programs that distribute benefits to the American populace will be scrapped and replaced with a more holistic anti-poverty framework such as the basic income guarantee anytime soon.

And so we return to the more limited, but politically more sellable, EITC.

Let's assume that this tax credit is too successful to scrap, that it is too embedded in the tax code to be entirely replaced by an alternative income-subsidy model. In which case, it would make a whole bunch of sense to make it better. Let's shore the system up, with the creation of certain baseline minimum income levels ensured via a negative income tax, and with wage protections enacted to prevent employers from diverting much of the benefits of each EITC dollar to themselves rather than their employees.

How could that be done?

One solution would be to implement so-called big box living wage statutes, requiring mid- to large-sized companies to pay hourly wage rates that allow workers to rise out of poverty without government tax refunds having to kick in. Chicago tried to implement such a law in 2006, mandating that large companies with store sizes of above 90,000 square feet and annual revenues in excess of $1 billion, pay at least $10 per hour to employees. But ultimately city leaders were scared off by the threat from Walmart and other big stores that they would simply abandon the city. In the end, Walmart agreed to a starting wage of $8.75 an hour, fifty cents above Illinois's state minimum. Facing a mayoral veto of the higher living wage, proponents were forced to sign on to the deal. Then, to rub salt in the wound, Walmart spokespeople went out of their way to say that this was similar to deals worked out around the country. In other words, according to the Walmart spin-meisters, the living wage

campaign hadn't forced the mega-chain into any financial conces-
sions it wouldn't have agreed to anyway out of the goodness of its
corporate heart. Believe that, dear readers, and you can find me after
you've finished this book for a discussion about a bridge that I want
to sell you in Brooklyn.

The lesson from Chicago: Large corporations *do* respond to public protests about working conditions. But for such an intervention
in the labor market as a living wage law aimed at big box stores to
really work, it would have to be done at least at the state level, and
ideally at the federal one. In this context, bigger is indisputably
better: The larger the area covered by the law, the harder it is for
companies simply to up the stakes and move their business elsewhere in response.

How would consumers be impacted by these laws? In December
2007, researchers at the University of California at Berkeley's Center
for Labor Research and Education calculated that Walmart would
need to increase prices by less than 1 percent in order to fully cover
the cost of the higher wages. "Low-income Walmart workers would
see a raise of $1,020 to $4,640 per year," the authors wrote, "while the
average Walmart shopper would spend an additional $9.70 per year."[7]

When, after years of struggle, tomato pickers in Immokalee,
Florida, won a one-cent increase for every pound of tomatoes they
picked, the *New York Times* reported that it would take their average wages up from roughly $10,000 per year to $17,000.[8] That's
enough to make a huge difference in the lives of some of America's
lowest-paid workers. The cost to the fast food restaurants such as
Burger King and Taco Bell who fought against the pay increase?
Well, Burger King estimated it would cost the company a quarter of
a million dollars annually. Spread out over the 2.4 billion burgers
the chain sells globally each year, and that works out to an additional 0.01 cent per burger for consumers. That's right: If you ate a
hundred Burger King meals each year, your additional costs would
total all of one cent.

Whichever way you spin it, either $10 a year more on one's Walmart purchases or one cent a year more on fast food hamburger purchases, it hardly seems an unreasonable amount to ask consumers to invest in for the broader social good.

———————

For Ai-jen Poo of the National Domestic Workers Alliance (NDWA), finding ways to boost the earnings power of the working poor was long overdue. The NDWA counted among its target audience some of the hardest-working and lowest-paid employees in America: people who swept up other people's dirt, cleaned up their messes, washed their bodies when they were sick, and dressed them when they were old. Frequently, they worked ridiculously long hours that, in practice if not in theory, put them far below the legal minimum wage. Like Maria, the home help in Albuquerque whom we encountered earlier in the book, they were often either undocumented or newly arrived, speaking only a paucity of English, unaware of their legal rights and scared to protest their workplace conditions. And yet as the American population aged and its healthcare needs increased, this was, most analysts agreed, likely to continue to be one of the fastest-growing sectors of the economy.

Faced with this reality, Poo's group, and trade unions such as the Service Employees International Union (SEIU) and the American Federation of State, County, and Municipal Employees (AFSCME), had begun organizing domestic workers. By 2012, Poo had helped launch the Caring Across Generations campaign, designed to convert millions of low-paying, off-the-books, home help jobs into work that was organized and legitimately above-board, paid a living wage, and offered decent benefits. Through giving tax credits to employers and tweaking Medicare so that it would fund more home-care arrangements, the campaign hoped to create two million "industrial-strength" jobs. What did they mean by that? Essentially, jobs with the same prestige, high pay, and solid benefits as those in the car factories, electronics plants, defense production facilities, and other workplaces that defined the heyday of American industrial production in the decades after World War II.

Not that getting there would be easy. Among other challenges would be that of finding ways to increase childcare subsidies for the working poor during tough economic times rather than cutting them, which had been the default position in recent years as states raided childcare funds to prop up other areas of their stressed general funds. That was of particular importance for home-care workers, who put in long and irregular hours, which often reduced to a minimum the time they could spend with their own children. So, too, the campaign would have to convince scared, frequently undocumented workers that they had more to gain than lose by emerging out of the shadows. And they would have to persuade the government to use existing, but too frequently unenforced, labor laws to crack down on employers who had grown used to paying low wages, off the books, for an array of domestic services.

Absent living wage ordinances and related pay increases for vulnerable workers in the fields, in home healthcare, and the like—or acting in tandem with such reforms—legislators could also put state and federal tax codes to work on the side of the poor. In the same way the Affordable Care Act uses tax law to penalize employers who don't provide health insurance to their workers, so the codes could be tweaked to impose penalties on those who don't give their workers a modicum of economic security through paying them a decent wage. As an employer, do you really want to pay your workers so badly that they fall back on state benefits? Fine. But know there are tax consequences to your decision. In San Francisco, a living wage ordinance put a variant of this in place years before the expansion of healthcare kicked in. There, companies were given a choice: They could either pay a higher-level wage, or they could pay a slightly lower wage, in which case they were mandated to provide health insurance for their workers.

At the same time, Congress should immediately increase the federal minimum wage, building in inflation-indexed increases annually, in much the same way that Social Security does. Such a move would not only shore up income levels for bottom-tier workers but would also have a magnifier effect up the next rungs of the economic ladder, as companies seeking to lure workers by paying better-than-minimum-wage rates increase the wages they offer so as to remain attractive to potential employees.

Without such a reform, the minimum wage, like welfare benefits such as TANF, will continue to be set legislatively. We know the consequences of this, and they aren't pretty. Held hostage to political fortune, for years at a stretch the value of the minimum wage, kept constant by legislative inaction, is eroded by inflation. This happened from the mid-1990s through to the mid-2000s. It's happened again during the post-2008 period. As a result, an increasing number of the country's working poor end up either having to be subsidized by the state or falling ever deeper into poverty.

Raise the minimum wage too high, and one stifles employment. Raise it responsibly, however, and many economists believe few jobs are lost as a result. "My view," said Jesse Rothstein, "is the minimum wage does not reduce employment. It would cut off the effect that I'm worried about."

In October 2010, economists with the Political Economy Research Institute (PERI) at the University of Massachusetts at Amherst released a report calling for a significant increase of the minimum wage as well as expansions of the EITC. They argued for a new federal minimum wage of $12.30 per hour and backed their number up with a set of detailed calculations and studies of previous local minimum wage hikes that showed the overall effects on business operating costs of such an increase, even in industries that were extremely labor intensive, to be extremely small and manageable to cover—either through slightly reduced profits or through marginal hikes in the prices of goods sold. As with the Immokalee tomato workers, the poorest of the poor could be provided a measure of economic dignity at a cost that most consumers would not notice.

The new baseline, the PERI team argued, would be below the "tipping point" at which significant numbers of businesses would start laying workers off. As evidence, they quoted from analyses of previous increases. When Florida raised its minimum wage by 19 percent, total costs to businesses statewide, as a percentage of sales, increased by only 0.04 percent. When Arizona raised its minimum wage by 31 percent, fast food operating costs as a percentage of total sales increased by only 1.73 percent. Even if all of that were to be passed along to consumers, a Big Mac would only increase in price by a couple cents. When Santa Monica increased its minimum wage by a whopping 85 percent, hotels—the most labor-intensive industry in the city—saw their labor costs increase by just over 8 percent.

The reason? In most industries, nonlabor costs, such as the buying and maintenance of machinery, energy bills, and real-estate expenses, outweigh payroll costs. Even in industries in which payroll is more dominant, a majority of workers already earn significantly above the minimum wage, meaning that only a small percentage of additional costs are foisted on companies by raising the floor. And, finally, in low-wage industries where more workers are paid at bargain-basement rates, the authors calculated, generally even in those situations many workers were paid somewhere in between the old and new minimum wages, meaning relatively small wage increases for the majority of employers, combined with larger increases for a minority, would bring the company into compliance with the new federal minimums.[9]

Finally, the EITC could be revamped so that it doesn't penalize dual-income households. At the moment, because families lose access to the credit when their *total* income goes above a certain level, it has

the somewhat perverse effect of encouraging many secondary earners, primarily women, to opt out of the workforce. But if each earner
was evaluated individually and able to access the EITC based on his
or her income alone rather than the combined income of all household earners, it would encourage several million more people to
work, and would, Rothstein estimated, help lift millions more families not just out of immediate poverty but into long-term economic
security.

All of this sounds technical, and in some ways it is. But the bottom line is pretty straightforward: *If* the tax system is used to channel money to poor individuals and families, and *if* at the same time
laws protecting and boosting low-end wages and incomes are enacted, an awful lot of Americans could be pulled out of poverty, at
minimal cost to the broader society, and an awful lot of dollars
could be circulated through communities that are currently either
stagnant or in decline.

IF IT WAS GOOD ENOUGH FOR THE NEW DEAL . . .

What to do, though, when the jobs aren't there in the first place?

For communities where a large proportion of the private-sector
jobs have ceased to exist, public works programs ought to be implemented to keep workers employed. Despite the volume of the voices
raised in opposition to such investments, there's actually considerable public support for the idea. In 2011, a Gallup Poll found that
72 percent of those surveyed supported expanding such public
works as school repair programs, and three-quarters wanted to make
available more public funds to hire teachers, police officers, and firefighters.[10] In September 2012, another survey found that more than
half of Americans wanted to increase spending on public infrastructure projects as a way of kick-starting the still-sluggish economy.[11]

For Katherine Newman, this was another no-brainer. "Fundamentally, the problem of poverty is a problem of people either not
having jobs or not having jobs that pay enough," she explained. Yes,

even a healthy economy has a certain level of unemployment, as companies reinvent themselves and people shift between locations and between jobs. The danger occurs when the economy can't regenerate jobs lost, when a pool of ex-workers builds up at the bottom of the economy, and a significant portion of the labor force remains without work for a prolonged period of time. At that point, she believed, even when the jobs return, they tend not to benefit those who have been excluded from the workforce for a long time. Remember those "unemployed need not apply" signs? Employers look at the sparse résumés of these men and women, at their absence of recent references, at their paucity of up-to-date skills, and they go elsewhere. "It becomes so hard for someone who's been unemployed for a long period of time to convince an employer to take a chance on them. They just look like damaged goods."

For these men and women, Newman argued, the federal government ought to create public works programs. It was, she felt, an entirely legitimate function of government to backstop employment when the private sector faltered.

Massive public works investment was done in the early years of the New Deal, to stunning effect—with the large, mechanized infrastructure projects of the Public Works Administration and then the labor-heavy projects of the Works Progress Administration, putting 4 million people back to work within a matter of months and providing those men and women with cash in their pockets that rapidly circulated throughout the entire economy. As a result of this stimulation, private employers then added another 4 million jobs. From 1933 to 1937, unemployment in America declined from 25 percent to 9 percent of the workforce.

What would the price tag for such a program be today? Newman's son, Steven Attwell, a graduate student of the history of public policy at the University of California at Santa Barbara, thought he had some answers. Having crunched the numbers and then, he said, having run his estimates by experts at the American Enterprise Institute and Brookings Institution, he argued that one could have used the $787 billion that the 2009 stimulus package cost to create a large-scale public works program, along the lines of the Works Progress Administration, that would have been able to employ up to 20 million people, thus largely eliminating the huge well of unemployment and joblessness that bubbled up in the wake of the financial crisis and that has so stubbornly refused to go away. In contrast, he reminded audiences, the hodgepodge of investments and employment subsidies that the 2009 legislation unleashed cost a fortune and only created, or saved, between 3 and 4 million jobs.

Obviously, what's done is done. There's no rewinding the clock on how the stimulus package was shaped, and no ability to recoup the hundreds of billions of dollars spent so as to respend them more effectively. But that doesn't mean there isn't room, still, for a more limited public works program. Thirty billion dollars, said Attwell, could create a million jobs. Those men and women could, he argued, get to work on the $2 trillion of repairs that the American Society of Civil Engineers estimates needs to be carried out to bring the country's infrastructure up to par.

How could such a program be funded? One way, Attwell explained, would be to set up a social insurance system, similar to Social Security, based on a small payroll tax—Attwell calculated that it would need to be in the 1 percent range—that all workers and employers would pay into, which would then be put into a reserve fund, initially seeded by a loan from the Federal Reserve, used only for public works programs during periods of high unemployment.

Attwell's Public Works Fund, in combination with the Educational Opportunity Fund that I have proposed and a reinvigorated Social Security trust fund, would go a long way toward re-creating a viable social compact that all Americans felt they had a stake in protecting. It would, as a side benefit, help neutralize Grover Norquist's destructive "starve the beast" argument; after all, why starve a beast that demonstrably improves your and your children's chances to get an education, keep a job during the down times, and retire without fear of destitution?

Yes, these are expensive concepts, but arguably not nearly as expensive as throwing millions of workers into long-term unemployment, ultimately pushing them out of the labor force, and giving them precious few alternatives other than to scramble for any and every method of public assistance they could find. It was no accident, for example, that as the numbers of long-term unemployed rose in the wake of the 2008 collapse, so too did the number of enrollees on the federally funded disability assistance program. It was, quite simply, one of the few welfare institutions with the capacity to provide economic assistance to an increasing number of people. And in many ways, as TANF and other programs shrank, it had been occupying that role for many years before the rug was pulled out from under the broader economy.

As early as 2006, in fact, the economists David Autor of the Massachusetts Institute of Technology and Mark Guggan of the University of Maryland had published a paper in the *Journal of Economic Perspectives* warning that the numbers on disability were growing at an unsustainable rate. They wrote that in 1985, "2.2 percent of individuals between the ages of 25 and 64 were receiving DI [disability insurance] benefits, but by 2005 this fraction had risen to 4.1 percent. If recent entry and exit rates continue in the years ahead, then more than 6 percent of the nonelderly adult population will soon be receiving DI benefits."[12] By May 2012, *Bloomberg News* was reporting that 5.3 percent of the population between the ages of 25 and 64 were on disability; Autor and Guggan's prediction was well on the way to being realized.[13] In four years, the number of enrollees had gone up by 23 percent, causing a massive undermining of the trust fund's viability and a warning to Congress, from the Social Security Board of Trustees, that it would run out of cash and have to start slashing benefits as early as 2016.[14]

Richard Parker, at Harvard's Kennedy School of Government, has termed this massive overuse of disability programs a "refugee camp for people who've been disqualified from welfare."

It's not that the country's able-bodied millions are suddenly, en masse, becoming dramatically sicker. There's absolutely no evidence to support such a scenario. Rather, it's that disability assistance, operating largely under the radar of conservative critics, is one of the few parts of the safety net not to have been shredded in recent decades. If someone's out of work, it's entirely rational to look for any assistance that's available, and if that assistance happens to be there for people who can show that they are disabled, then it makes perfect sense to claim you are too sick to work. Thus the emergence of a large number of ex-workers who have what might be termed a "disability-lite," a problem that previously didn't prevent them from working but that, in an era in which jobs have vanished for millions of Americans, now becomes a core part of that person's identity.

Far better, Parker and Attwell argued, to encourage more people to remain within the labor market, paying them to work and acquire job skills rather than to totally, and permanently, opt out of the labor market. Far better to make the minimum wage more closely approximate a living wage—as has been done in a handful of cities, as well as the state of Washington, in recent years—and ensure that work is accompanied by benefits such as healthcare, child and sick leave, and pensions. Make work available and viable, and the attractiveness for the marginally disabled of parking themselves on the disability rolls at the first sign of recession diminishes. Leave disability for the truly and seriously disabled, and the program's long-term financial viability is increased.

Not that this will be easy. For those on disability, in particular, reentering the workforce, and perhaps taking on less stressful and demanding jobs to meet their diminished physical capacities, is difficult at the best of times. Absent significant societal investments in job retraining programs, oftentimes it is impossible. Yet instead of making more money available to retrain out-of-work Americans, post-collapse Congresses have been busily slashing such funding. In April 2012, the *New York Times* reported that the federal government was spending a mere $1.2 billion per year on job training programs, a decline of 18 percent since 2006—when unemployment was less than half of what it was in 2012. Even more disheartening, the amount of federal money being spent on job training in 2012 was close to $1 billion less than what it had been in 2000, at the tail end of the Clinton presidency.

MISSION "DO RIGHT"

That was a huge shame. After all, job training programs had a long track record of taking poor people from poor communities and getting them into jobs.

For Josephine P. Rhymes, it all began with listening to people: What sorts of job training programs did the poor want? What teaching methods worked best with people taught for years to think that their voices have no power? After all, it was one thing getting someone a job; it was quite another providing them with a ladder to economic success.

Rhymes had worked with the unemployed and partially employed in the Mississippi Delta town of Clarksdale for decades, linking them up with job training via a group called the Tri-County Workforce Alliance.

The alliance ran a nationally recognized program teaching young, unemployed women the basics of carpentry, electricity, and plumbing. "Once they've completed the program, they have to do forty hours of community service with Habitat for Humanity or Council of Aging," she explained.

> The program is free to them; we provide them with the tools they need, transportation, childcare, and training. We have several young ladies who have helped to build their own homes, some who have remodeled their homes, some who have increased their businesses. We have one young lady who has started her own business;

she makes doghouses, screen porches. She told us she did not have a high-school diploma, so we enrolled her in a GED class; she actually got her GED. They also get self-skills training; financial education, what is sexual harassment, conflict resolution, how to choose childcare, how to balance work and stress, how to write a résumé, go to an interview. Those are the survival skills they get in the program.

What made the curriculum of particular interest was the fact that it was generated after a series of focus groups held with out-of-work young adults in the Delta, who explained what skills they felt they needed, and with employers who explained what skills and personal traits they were looking for in new workers. "We brought both groups together. They were both saying basically the same thing. We had ideas of what we needed to do in order to bridge the gap. We chose two unemployed people, two educators, two employers, and two social services people. And they sat down, over a six-week period, and wrote a curriculum. The components were education—how to get the GED, where to go, what does it entail; a lot of things came out about the use of drugs. We put in education, finance, leadership, work ethics, computer literacy, conflict resolution." When Rhymes's clients completed their training, they were given a small stipend. When they stayed with their jobs for three months, they were given a second small amount of cash.

The program was small-scale, but most of its graduates had found long-term employment. "They had low self-esteem coming into the program; and now they are proud workers."

———

On a far larger scale, Focus: HOPE in Detroit, with financial backing from the Open Society Foundation and other organizations, was also working with young adults who had grown up in calamitous economic environments. It was, said CEO Will Jones, one of the biggest games in town. In the thirty years since it had begun workforce development projects, approximately 12,000 people had participated in its Fast Track math and reading programs, followed by intensive job training. Because it was in Detroit, the program emphasized teaching people to be machinists and machine operators.

Six feet, seven inches tall and thin, his graying hair and mustache carefully trimmed, Jones had spent decades working as a financial officer with Chrysler in Detroit and overseas. He knew machines inside out, and he knew the needs of employers. There was nothing halfhearted about the training regimen that he ran, or, as he put it, "There's no jive in our program." Test dirty for drugs, his staff would send you away and tell you to come back when you were clean. Employers, he explained, wouldn't let you near sensitive machinery if you were high. Come to work late, you'd receive a dressing-down. On the other hand, show your skills in the basic program, prove you could use the machines to make precision parts, and you'd be moved into the Center for Advanced Technologies, a converted Ford Tractor plant with soaring sheet-metal walls and shiny green floors. There, you would work on a project coordinated by the National Science Foundation and several local universities. You'd be put on a path to getting an associate's degree, possibly even a bachelor's in engineering. You would make components for the much-touted Chevy Volt car, use robotic manufacturing methods, and even do some specialized welding work for the Department of Defense.

Over the years, Jones said, he'd put through the program people who had come to him from devastated neighborhoods, lacking even high school diplomas, some with prison terms behind them. And they had ended up getting bachelor's degrees from the University of Michigan, followed by good, secure employment. "Career-sustaining wages, family-sustaining wages. Not simply a job," explained Jones. "We believe in the redemptive powers of education, training. When you believe in people, you can encourage them to believe in themselves. We don't take shortcuts here. A lot of us in the senior management team have been in industry before. We know what it takes in order to be successful."

What made Focus: HOPE stand out was its holistic approach. Trainees were given enviable access to state-of-the-art machining equipment, laboratories, and computers. Also, the program had contracts both with car manufacturers and with defense industry contractors to produce precision parts. But none of that would have worked without the support infrastructure. On the sprawling campus was a food pantry, in an old industrial building that was several blocks long. It was one of the biggest in the city, storing thousands of tons of food, and feeding 40,000 locals. There were education classes, and the program went out of its way to cultivate relations with nearby schools. There were basic training programs in CPR and customer service skills, all designed to make the young adults who came through more attractive to employers. Childcare services were offered, and transportation vouchers were given out to make attendance more affordable—after all, said Jones, some of the students were homeless, and many of them traveled by bus two hours each way just to get to the center. Social workers were available to counsel trainees if they were having a bad day.

There was even the Hope Village initiative, designed to turn the hundred square blocks surrounding the campus into a more vibrant community. Students were trained in crime prevention; they held regular block meetings, staffed arts programs for residents, and distributed school supplies to neighborhood kids. And, to round out the circle, Focus: HOPE had recently sold some of its buildings to manufacturing companies that had come into the area and in exchange hired on Focus: HOPE graduates. Step by step, a part of the city long given up on by the powers-that-be was coming back to life.

———

Around the country, businesses were being developed with precisely this sort of community-building raison d'être. Increasingly, they were codifying these missions, using so-called Benefit Corporation Statutes—as of mid-2012 on the books in Illinois, Louisiana, Maryland, New Jersey, Vermont, and Virginia, and talked about in several other states. What are these statutes? They are essentially state laws that protect businesses with a proven commitment to social justice—to environmental sensitivity in their practices, to decent pay for workers, to the provision of affordable housing, and to concern for the communities in which they operate—from being sued for not maximizing their profits. Why is that important? Because, absent such laws, the legal assumption is that companies are obligated to maximize the bang they provide for their shareholders' bucks. Pay workers more than your competitors and lower your profits, there's a chance you'll be sued by an irate investor. Accept a buyout offer from a company offering less than a rival but guaranteeing to, say, keep your workers' pensions and other benefits intact; again, there's always that risk the courts will find you liable for your investors' losses.

Write a social justice mission into your business's articles of incorporation, however; qualify it as a benefit corporation; submit to third-party evaluation from the Pennsylvania-based B Lab nonprofit organization episodically to make sure your company is maintaining its progressive commitments; and that risk dissipates. Put simply, it gives businesses, otherwise operating in a cutthroat economic environment, legal cover to do the right thing. That's why National People's Action and other activist groups have championed these laws. And it's why expanding the number of states using such legislation ought to be a core part of our expanded War on Poverty.

As of September 2012, B Lab listed 603 benefit corporations nationwide, with total revenues of more than $4 billion.[15] That was, however, just the tip of the iceberg. A couple months earlier, *Forbes* magazine had estimated that there were at least 50,000 companies nationwide with the sorts of social justice commitments protected by the statutes.[16]

Harness that energy, provide the companies with legal protections behind which they can pursue goals other than simply maximizing their profits, and you fill in one more gigantic piece in the anti-poverty puzzle. You also go a long way toward redefining value and recalibrating workplace priorities.

KEEPING THE WELL FROM RUNNING DRY

If enough effort were put into all of these changes—to how we pay workers, how we protect workers' jobs during down times, and how we use the power of government to boost the income of the most insecure parts of the labor force—America would look very different from how it does now.

Yet, while all of these reforms are important, none of them will be enough if, at the end of the day, elderly Americans, after a lifetime of hard work, are then left to fend for themselves.

And so we come to the final great challenge.

The three major reforms of the twentieth century that limited the poverty of America's elderly were the creation of Social Security and Medicare and the rise of defined benefit company pensions. As a result, the percentage of the elderly population living in poverty declined from upward of one-third of the population in the post–World War II period to roughly 10 percent a few decades later. Yet in recent years, most defined pensions—the sort that give you a monthly payment, based on a formula that factors in how long you worked and how much you earned, from the day you retire until the day you die—have gone the way of the dodo. Using Department of Labor data, Alicia Munnell, director of the Center for Retirement Research at Boston College, calculated that in 1980 six in ten private employees who had a pension coming their way had defined benefits awaiting them upon retirement, and another 23 percent had a mixture of a traditional pension alongside a 401(k). In other words, more than eight out of every ten private-sector workers who qualified for a pension a generation ago had at least a modicum of financial predictability and stability awaiting them in their golden years. Fast-forward a quarter-century: In 2006, Munnell calculated, only one in ten had pensions entirely based around defined benefits, and slightly under a quarter had a combination of defined benefits and 401(k)s.[17]

In the public sector, one city and state after another was rethinking the pensions that they offered new employees, replacing defined benefits with 401(k)s, or making employees pick up more of the tab for the annual retirement contributions. Firefighters, police officers, correctional staff, teachers, and civil servants all saw their pensions attacked by legislators desperate to save scarce dollars from beleaguered budgets.

Making matters worse, where once already-promised pensions were considered a sacred bargain, increasingly companies are heading to bankruptcy court to argue their need to renege on promises made to their workers and to reduce the amounts they will pay retirees down the road. Such has been the fate in recent years of pension promises at United Airlines, Bethlehem Steel, Delphi—which manufactured electronic systems for GM cars—and many other major companies. Bankrupt, these giants turned over their pension obligations to the government-run Pension Benefit Guarantee Corporation (PBGC), which pays out only a small portion of the value of the original pension—enough to keep retirees from ending up homeless, but not nearly enough to maintain the quality of life they had assumed their pensions would allow them to have. The bankrupt companies also ended their health and life insurance coverage for ex-workers.

In 2011, American Airlines also went to bankruptcy court to argue its right to dump its pension obligations. In a scathing response, the PBGC reminded the company that it had successfully lobbied Congress to allow it to defer paying contributions into its pension fund for several years, thus saving AMR, the parent company of the airline, more than $2 billion over the six years leading up to its bankruptcy filing.

Were the company to shed its pensions, the PBGC warned, retirees stood to lose all their healthcare benefits as well as $1 billion worth of pension payments.[18] Many of them would, as a result, end up no better off than the people I had interviewed around the country who lived paycheck to paycheck and couldn't imagine ever having the option of retiring. For example, the ex-aluminum workers in Longview, Washington, whose company had gone into bankruptcy and left large numbers of workers in their late '50s and early '60s without healthcare and too young to qualify for Medicare.[19] Also, the erstwhile middle-class men and women who had lost their jobs and burned through their IRAs and 401(k)s.

"I honestly see myself working till at least 73, 75 years old," Luann Prokop, the onetime accountant in rural Pennsylvania averred at the end of our conversation. She no longer had retirement savings and no income that could come close to replenishing what she had lost. "I just get up every day and keep going. And try to stay focused."

Remember Hacker's theory about the Great Risk Shift? In no aspect of our lives has that shift occurred faster, and with more ferocity, than it has around retirement. Start early; invest well; have decades of good luck both in terms of individual affluence and in terms of avoiding macro-crises such as stock market collapses; and if you're an average earner, you may just about be okay once you're too old to work. Wait a few years to begin saving, though, make a few mistakes in how you invest your money, or simply have the bad luck to live through a couple big economic meltdowns, and chances are your retirement won't be nearly as comfortable as was that of your parents.

———

If you're counting on state-paid benefits to make up the shortfall, don't get too comfortable. Unlike in Great Britain, say, there is no baseline, universal old-age pension in America. Many workers, including hundreds of thousands of government employees who were promised good, reliable retirement packages, have not had Social

Security taxes deducted from their paychecks over the decades and thus qualify for no Social Security at the end of their careers. Take away their pensions, and they have nothing. There *is* Supplemental Security Income (SSI) for old people who don't qualify for Social Security or whose Social Security checks are miniscule and would otherwise be destitute. But the amount SSI gives to individuals tops out at a few hundred dollars a month—providing recipients with income well below that needed even to get near the poverty line.[20] And, to qualify for that top-up, you have to prove your destitution through a series of means tests. Have any assets, and you're not going to get that particular government check.

As for the vast trust funds administering the broader Social Security and Medicare systems, there's an all-too-real risk of them coming apart at the seams. Both face daunting odds as their yearly numbers worsen in the face of increased longevity; an explosion in the cost of medical care; and above all, a national reluctance to increase taxes enough to improve these programs' financial footing.

By some calculations, without additional revenues and reforms around what services are covered and how they are paid for, the Medicare Trust Fund will run dry as early as 2016. Others estimate the problem can be kicked down the road a few more years, perhaps until 2024. At that point, having burned through its assets, it would have only enough money on hand from existing taxes to pay about 87 percent of its obligations. And, from that point on, its annual situation would only worsen.[21]

Whatever the exact date of insolvency, on current trajectories all agree that at some point soon either benefits will have to be cut, or more money will have to be injected into the fund. Held hostage to an unbending anti-tax rhetoric, the program's stability looks increasingly precarious.

Were Medicare's funding model to collapse, that by itself would be calamitous for tens of millions of elderly Americans. But compounding the crisis—adding to Hacker's Great Risk Shift—is the fact that the Social Security trust fund is in almost as unhappy circumstances.

In 2012, the fund's trustees concluded that it was likely to head into insolvency in 2033, just a little shy of a century after it had been created. From 2033 on, they warned, absent new money being injected in, Social Security would only be able to pay out about seventy-five cents on the dollar.[22]

The point needs to be made once more: These are artificial crises, caused not by any impending bankruptcy on a national scale but by an insane reluctance to tax those individuals and companies at the top of the economy enough to sustain the civic structures upon which the vast majority of the population either already rely or one day will. They are crises triggered by a collapse in the very notion of a common good.

Social Security and Medicare were carefully designed to build up huge financial reserves. They were, in a sense, a vast pool of communal wealth, into which everyone contributed, from which everybody could gain. Had we tended these funds well, they ought never to have come close to running dry. Instead, we have treated them like the huge Ogallala aquifer, deep under the country's plains states: as things so big, so inexhaustible, that we could tap them with impunity. And now, just like the Ogallala aquifer, a reserve of groundwater built up over millions of years, is rapidly running dry—so too are these great financial commons.

———————

There is still time to reverse this risk shift, but we need to do so soon. Unlike the Ogallala, into which it is impossible to pump large amounts of new freshwater reserves, the Social Security and Medicare trust funds *can* still be replenished.

In fact, given the amount of ink that has been spilled on the enormity of this problem, it turns out that the solutions, at least for Social Security, are actually fairly simple. We could, for example, modestly raise the Social Security tax burden on high earners. Simply opening up income above a quarter of a million dollars to the Social Security tax would, many analysts believe, keep the system solvent almost into the twenty-second century.[23] It's as close to a painless fix as one could hope for. Or we could very modestly increase the Social Security tax imposed on workers at all income levels. Alternatively, we could perhaps gradually increase the retirement age to meet the realities of our newly expanded life expectancies. For those without higher education, who tend to earn less over a lifetime than do their better-educated peers, we could shore up Social Security with the additional moneys detailed in my EOF proposal. And if the political will isn't there to raise the Social Security tax on the most affluent, or to implement something akin to the EOF, at the very least we could have a calm national conversation as to whether it makes sense to reduce the Social Security payments sent out each month to wealthy seniors so as to preserve benefits for the rest of the population.

While Medicare presents a somewhat thornier set of problems, given the huge advances in medical technology and the expenses accompanying the uses of these new diagnostic procedures, medicines, surgeries, and so on, in essence the same set of solutions holds. Because this is a program that benefits virtually *all* elderly Americans, it ought not to be impossible to convince American workers that they have a self-interest in paying slightly higher payroll taxes to ensure that when they retire, they have healthcare available to them.[24] Framing that issue in a way sellable to voters is a *political* challenge more than an economic one. Nor ought it to be beyond our collective capacities to work out a way to rein in costs—after all, most advanced democracies have found a way to adequately deliver quality healthcare to their elderly populations.

That there is even the possibility of Medicare heading toward insolvency, or the $2.6 *trillion* Social Security reserve fund being depleted over a twenty-year period, is testament not to the bankruptcy of the funds themselves, but to the straitjacket that anti-tax politics have wrestled the country into in recent years.

When it comes to how we protect the economic security of aging Americans, we need a Social Security system with protected, and properly funded, benefits and cost-of-living adjustments. We need more portable retirement accounts to fully meet the needs of a mobile, flexible workforce. Given the number of self-employed workers, we need something like the 401(k) model to be extended to these workers, perhaps with the government serving to meet matching fund commitments in lieu of the employer. And, above all, we need to protect and expand the web of defined benefit pensions rather than run roughshod over the few that remain. Yes, these changes would come with a cost attached, but if done smartly, perhaps in tandem with raising the retirement age to meet twenty-first century life expectancies, they would be affordable. And, to repeat a point I have made elsewhere in this book, to not act would, in the long run, be even more costly.

PUTTING DEPOSITS IN THE EMPATHY BANK

To sum all of this up, if we want to break long-term, ingrained, vicious cycles of poverty, if we want to create a society in which opportunity is widely dispersed and economic dignity is the norm for the vast majority of Americans from the time they are born until the time they die, we need far more policy deposits in what I'll call an empathy bank. We need a societal commitment to share the pain during hard times and a willingness to think through the long-term consequences on one's community of not so doing. It's not too dissimilar from a strategy that Germany embraced a few years back, when it began increasing the unemployment insurance contributions it required of companies that laid off workers during recessions before first seeing if they could trim their costs while keeping their workforce intact by reducing the number of hours worked by *all* employees.

The central idea is simple: As a community, we strengthen ourselves when we find ways to protect our most vulnerable. When we work out mechanisms to boost the wages of earners trapped at the bottom of the economy. When we think up creative solutions to keep poor people housed and with access to healthcare. We bolster the country when we invest in educational infrastructure in a way that makes it possible for poorer children to have as much opportunity in life as their more affluent peers, and when we make sure that pension systems are strong enough to keep the elderly out of poverty. We enrich ourselves as a society when we reinvigorate our sense of the common good.

As our journey comes to a close, let's return, briefly, to college lecturer Jim Miller, and his walk through California's Central Valley to highlight the hardships faced by so many of the state's residents and the cost to the social fabric of letting basic public services crumble.

"The march forced you to slow down; the act of walking itself forced you to come face to face with people," he recalled, months after he had returned home to his wife and son in San Diego.

> We were in a small town called Planada, and we pulled into town, a tiny town mostly of farm workers. The school was so devastated; the principal came out and told us that 80 percent of the kids who were in his school were on some kind of state aid. They said, "Come onto campus," and so we drove the truck on. The entire elementary school emptied out and joined us, came out cheering. This one guy came out with tears in his eyes. He'd marched with Chavez. They impromptu scheduled a community dinner. The parents came. They did a dance, fed us, and we told our stories and listened to their stories about what was happening in their communities. Dozens of small stories like that, day after day. They weave together into a mosaic. How is it that the lives of people who frequently don't even think of each other are connected in some way? How are most people's interests interconnected?

ATTENTION MUST BE PAID

New Mexico colonias.

In a renovated Victorian-era Unitarian church just north of Detroit's downtown, a young African American community organizer named Charity Hicks held forth on the problems facing her city.

Hicks had arrived in town in 2002, she said, to work with a team that had been awarded a National Institutes of Health grant to study the impact of deep poverty on the lives of the Motor City's residents. She had encountered what she called a below-the-radar economy, based around barter, casual labor, and groups of marginal people moving from one part of the city to the next in search of scraps: scrap metal, scavenged recyclables, the leftovers of a decayed industrial behemoth. Since the 1960s, she argued, neither industry nor government had invested in what she called "The Commons."

Education was a ramshackle, haphazard affair at best—half of the people Focus: HOPE tested in its workforce development program couldn't survive a ninth-grade math class or tenth-grade reading tests, Will Jones had announced during our meeting. Unemployment was endemic. Crime rates were bad enough that for some residents it could cost upward of $5,000 annually to insure a car in the city—but public transport was so dilapidated that not having a car often meant having no way to get to what little work there was available. To cap off the indignity, tens of thousands of impoverished residents were living in homes without running water and without electricity. Officially, there were only about 12,000 homeless people living in Detroit. Unofficially, if you factored in all the people squatting in abandoned buildings, Hicks estimated, you had to multiply that number at least four-fold. Meanwhile, tens of thousands of these abandoned properties had recently been put up for sale by the Wayne County treasurer.

Charity was a community organizer and advocate for environmental justice. But that didn't pay the bills. When I met her, she had been unemployed for four years, had run out of cash, and had recently lost her home to foreclosure. She called hers "the downsized generation." In Detroit, she explained, thousands of outcast residents had almost become a "sovereign" people: too poor to survive in the economic mainstream, and too forgotten by government to have their lives ameliorated by social programs. For food, they farmed their subsistence plots. For shelter, they slept wherever empty buildings beckoned. They neither paid taxes nor received assistance. They expected nothing from the state, and they weren't disappointed.

"The only people who can solve poor people's problems," Hicks had concluded, "is poor people. We have to develop agency and participation—and think of ourselves not as consumers but as human beings. How do we flip the frames, to see everybody as important, as an asset?"

Hicks was young, African American, and urban. Luann Prokop, by contrast, was in her mid-fifties, white, and from a small town in Appalachia. On the surface, their worlds were far apart. Yet in many ways, Prokop's experiences of the past few years were similar to those of Hicks. She felt abandoned, betrayed, and forgotten, resting as firmly atop the communal trash heap as was Willy Loman, the battered Joe-Everyman in Arthur Miller's play *Death of a Salesman*.

"When I picked up the phone to call for unemployment benefits, I broke down crying with the woman—because I was never unemployed in my life, worked solidly for twenty-five years, felt capable in what I was doing. I just really felt alone. It's created this chip on my shoulder; I don't think a day goes by that I can't believe the amount of bad luck that just seems to keep rolling my way. It's very frustrating. A lot of days I'm very anxious, very nervous. But I try to keep my head up. Keep going."

So, too, in Prokop's daily scramble to survive, to pay her bills, to keep her house her own and her utilities on, and to retain her sense of hope while so doing, was her story related to that of Cruzanta Mercado and Paul Abiley, in their Heath Robinson plywood cabin in Hawaii, a continent and half an ocean away from Appalachian Pennsylvania. The young couple were still struggling to make ends meet and to navigate basic daily rituals that most Americans had long since been able to stop worrying about: making sure they could keep a few naked bulbs lit with electricity provided by a small generator; running down the unpaved road they lived on at the edge of the jungle in Hawaii's Puna district to Paul's uncle's house when they needed to use the toilet.

It was also, in its desperation, similar to the story of the 65-year-old restaurant owner I met an hour's drive from Prokop, who had had to drop her and her husband's health insurance several years earlier because the cost had risen to an unaffordable $16,000 per year. They had then been hit with a $30,000 bill when her husband lost an eye following a carpentry accident. For the rest of their lives, they would be playing an unwinnable game of financial catch-up.

And Luann's story shared key points with that of Matthew Joseph, the out-of-work steel worker and cathedral deacon from Stockton, California, who had found himself curled up in the fetal position on his bed, "thinking that life was over," wondering how he and his wife could avoid losing their beautiful suburban home to the bank.

I had to look for a cheaper phone; "I'm not going to use the Internet, have cable TV. I'm canceling the gym membership." That extra $75, $80 a month, that was what was going to save things. "What can I get out of this meal, what can I make that will last us two meals?" I need to be able to thin everything: thin what we're doing in life, thin what we're doing with the house, even when it gets down to the point of a simple drive in the country costing me gas that I may need to use to do a job interview. Where do I come up with money for PG&E [the local utility company], garbage, water? Where do I come up with that? I was making a late payment, or I'd say, "This is the situation. What bill is the most important? Can I make a deal with PG&E to make a payment to keep the lights on?" Some people work with you, some don't. Whatever's the most important. Heating for your house—or you turn off the heater and wear a lot of sweaters, blankets.

Joseph talked about his erstwhile middle-class neighborhood being pockmarked with dozens of garage sales, at which desperate residents sold off personal possessions for pennies on the dollar to pay their bills. Other common sights included vagrants picking through garbage bins in front of homes, scrappers going into abandoned houses and stripping them of copper wires, and others stealing catalytic converters from underneath parked cars.

The leftovers of the new poor, in their misery, were being scavenged by an ever more desperate old poor. These are the denizens of what the journalist Chris Hedges termed America's sacrifice zone.

"Is it ever going to turn around? Somebody has to have a plan for something else," Joseph questioned. At the beautiful old red brick cathedral in which he was a deacon, the unemployed metal worker encountered parishioners who told him, "'I cannot afford to go to the hospital; I can't afford the ambulance ride. I can't afford to feed my family.' The amount of people at Thanksgiving and Christmas, not looking for gifts but looking for food. It's the ordinary people, the old, doing things they never had to do before. People are stealing more. My neighbor got his gas syphoned. I haven't heard about that in a long time."

And so we return to the challenge that Michael Harrington laid down in 1962: How should the world's wealthiest nation respond to the vast levels of poverty that lie, hidden in plain view, just below the country's affluent surface?

A half-century after Harrington wrote *The Other America*, poverty remains in many ways as deep and as intangible as ever. As I write this concluding chapter, we do not have the luxury of saying "We didn't know." For the truth is that we did. We knew because of the work that journalists such as Jacob Riis did more than a century ago. We knew because of the exposé that Harrington himself penned in 1962. And we knew because, if we were honest with ourselves, as the twenty-first century unfolded we saw the effects of poverty on a daily basis: in the dilapidated trailer parks alongside freeways that we passed on the way to work or while traveling on family vacations, in the lines for free food that we routinely witnessed in our cities and suburbs, and in the stories of jobs lost and homes foreclosed on that we encountered every day in our newspapers and on our television news shows. We knew then, and even more so, we know now.

We know why so many people are born poor, why so many people become poor, and why so many people remain poor. We know how different problems affect people's economic well-being at different stages of their lives. And, as I have detailed in these pages, we know if not how to entirely eliminate these scourges, then certainly how to limit their scope and mitigate their damage.

The cost of such an effort would be large—many hundreds of billions of dollars—but for a nation as wealthy and as blessed with natural and human resources as is America, not unaffordable. More to the point, the cost of inaction is far larger, in terms of potential wasted, lives truncated, and communities corroded. For raging levels of poverty have, once again, become the spanner in the American works.

The necessary big-picture changes include how we fund and maintain our safety net programs, from the smallest of local systems to the largest of federal ones. How we subsidize, through the tax system and through cash benefits, the incomes of both the out of work and the lowly paid. How we regulate the wages and benefits employers provide their employees—including those who lack legal documentation to live and work in America. And how we ensure that the federal government steps in with public works programs during deep recessions and periods of prolonged mass unemployment. They must encompass how we educate children, from the preschool years through high school graduation—and how we extend the opportunity of college education to more young adults. How we provide healthcare to more Americans, protect pension systems, build up affordable housing stocks for those who can't afford market rents or mortgages, and open up job training opportunities for those left unemployed or jobless by long-term economic shifts. Other changes will determine how, and why, we use our criminal justice systems, what help we provide to the addicted and the mentally ill, and what resources we send to young men and women leaving foster care.

How do we pay for such an ambitious set of projects?

Partly through targeted, sensible, fair tax increases: raising the capital gains tax, increasing the income tax on the wealthiest Americans, eliminating the upper limit for Social Security contributions, reintroducing an oil windfall profit tax, creating a viable financial transactions tax, and imposing estate taxes on large inheritances that are more in line with the taxes levied by countries such as England and Germany. We un-starve the beast that Grover Norquist's acolytes have spent three decades gratuitously depriving of nutrients. The creature that is social assistance for the poor, the young, and the elderly is, after all, a far less harmful beast than that of the new plutocracy—which has spent the past several decades fattening itself at the public's expense; insulating its monies from taxation; and ensuring the uninterrupted transfer of wealth, privilege, and power down the generations.

Voters recognized that reality on November 6, 2012, reelecting a president who campaigned on a pledge to increase taxes on the wealthy; voting in a slew of senators, such as Elizabeth Warren of Massachusetts, who openly talked about the positive role that government should play; and passing state initiatives, such as Proposition 30 in California, that raised sales taxes and income taxes on top earners so as to better fund schools, universities, and departments responsible for overseeing public safety.

Partly, we fund such programs through paring other areas of the budget—for example, limiting defense spending increases and restricting the percentage of healthcare dollars that can be used to feather the nests of insurance company executives. And by asking consumers to pay marginally more—for goods bought at big box stores and fast food restaurants, for example—so as to provide mechanisms to boost the wages of the working poor.

And partly, through designing them well, we make sure that these programs help fund themselves: Increasing the EITC, for example, by providing low-income families more money to spend on nutritional food and on preventive healthcare, reduces the medical costs associated with large numbers of low-weight and premature babies. Creating a guaranteed minimum income, using taxes imposed on the extraction of states' natural resources to distribute annual checks to residents of specific states, or seeding businesses in poor communities through an expansion of micro-credit—all would help circulate money through depressed neighborhoods. Boosting employment through public works would lead to a virtuous circle of economic growth.

How do we generate the political will for such an overarching, and holistic, project? We educate. We empower people. We convince enough Americans that no matter how much money from big-dollar donors floods the political system, a democracy as vibrant as America's can, *and should*, respond to the fundamental needs of its populace. If there is one single message to be learned from the election results of November 2012—the first presidential election to be held in the wake of the *Citizens United* Supreme Court decision—it is that ordinary voters don't like seeing elites trying to lock them out of the political process. They don't respond well to the assumption that wads of cash thrown into political races by shadowy political action committees and irate billionaires can determine a country's destiny.

Those election results present a tremendous political opportunity over the coming years: They provide room for progressive political leaders in Washington, D.C., and organizers on the ground to embrace the language of economic and social justice rather than continually to run from it. Explain the connections between political democracy and economic opportunity, between empowerment at the ballot box and empowerment economically, and a host of previously out-of-reach goals suddenly seem reachable.

As did Pericles two and a half millennia ago, when he warned that raging economic divides threatened the Athenian citizen democracy, and as did Polanyi sixty years ago, we detail the dangers to freedom that necessarily accompany a stampede toward ever greater levels of inequality. And we highlight a set of values and a slate of policies that can block that journey into plutocracy.

All of this is doable. All of it is pragmatic. And all of it would increase the quality of life for tens of millions of people who have somehow been allowed to fall outside of the American Dream.

If, in the year 2062, another journalist has to revisit this issue again, to comment on poverty's stubborn presence on the American landscape a century after Harrington's *cri de coeur*, it will be because of a failure of wills far more than a failure of intelligence or a lack of resources. We know the challenges that we face, we know the byways of the American Way of Poverty. To deny them is to thumb one's nose at an unpleasant reality.

And now, knowing the challenges, and hearing the demands of conscience, our task is to act.

Note on Sources and Book Structure

Researching *The American Way of Poverty* was a project that took me around America, interviewing people living in poverty and people working on poverty-related themes. Although I did not get to every state, over an eighteen-month period I did conduct interviews in more than half of the states in the country.

To avoid cluttering my text with footnotes, I decided not to footnote these individual interviews. Endnotes are, thus, reserved for written sources and secondary sources. Where no sourcing is given, readers should assume that the interview was conducted by me, either in person or via telephone. At times, I have quoted both from the works of published authors and also from personal interviews with them. Where their work is being quoted, I cite with endnotes; where there is no endnote, readers should assume the quote is from an interview.

Many of the interviews for this book are archived in an oral history audio archive that I set up in 2011. Titled *The Voices of Poverty*, it is accessible online at www.thevoicesofpoverty.org.

The website contains detailed geographic information on poverty, as well as thematic lists of stories, thus allowing audiences to gain detailed information on such topics as housing and poverty, healthcare and poverty, and unemployment and poverty. Though most of the stories on the site are in the form of recorded interviews between me and interviewees, some are user-submitted stories. In my book, with one exception, I have only used the *Voices of Poverty* stories that I myself conducted the interviews for.

The American Way of Poverty is divided into two parts. Broadly speaking, the first part of the book tells the stories of the impoverished people I met around the country, whereas the second part of the book maps out a broad set of policy discussions and connections between issues that any meaningful national-level attempt to tackle poverty will have to include. Themes include tax reform, the welfare system, wages, access to healthcare, changes that could be made in the criminal justice system, changes in how America deals with addiction and mental illness, reforms in the foster care system, and many other areas that overlap with poverty. My intent in this section was not to write a complete, in-depth policy analysis of all of these themes—such a project would run to many volumes and would, I fear, scare off most of my readers. Rather, my aim was to draw a series of sketches, first drafts of what I hope will develop out of this book as far more detailed conversations.

The two parts of the book are somewhat self-contained; readers who want to viscerally experience American poverty via stories from the poor themselves may read only the first section; those more interested in the policy side of the story might read the second part instead. My hope, of course, is that many of my readers will end up reading both.

Notes

PROLOGUE

1. Michael Harrington, *The Other America: Poverty in the United States* (New York: Touchstone, 1997).

2. Richard Parker, *John Kenneth Galbraith: His Life, His Politics, His Economics* (New York: Farrar, Straus and Giroux, 2005), 481.

3. See http://www.federalreserve.gov/releases/housedebt/.

4. Peter Edelman, *So Rich, So Poor: Why It's So Hard to End Poverty in America* (New York: The New Press, 2012), 29.

5. Jeannette Wicks-Lim, "The Great Recession in Black Wealth," Amherst, Massachusetts, Political Economy Research Institute, January 29, 2012.

6. See http://www.kpbs.org/news/2011/aug/22/imperial-valley-unemploy ment-rate-tops-30-percent/. For a good discussion of Imperial County's economic condition and the prevalence of low-wage employment, see also http://www .rohan.sdsu.edu/~jgerber/docs/Explaining_low_income.pdf.

7. Patricia Lesko, *Huffington Post*, August 22, 2012. Available at http:// www.huffingtonpost.com/patricia-lesko/detroit-childhood-poverty_b_129 9269.html.

8. See http://louisianajusticeinstitute.blogspot.com/2011/10/poverty-sky rockets-in-new-orleans-65-of.html. For a more general display of New Orleans's poverty data, see http://www.nationofchange.org/blogs/bill-quigley/katrina-pain -index-2012-7-years-after-1346013999.

9. For a discussion of Philadelphia's child poverty rates, based on U.S. Census Bureau data, see work done by Witnesses to Hunger: http://www.witnesses tohunger.org/News-Highlights/News-Highlights/72/vobId__285/.

10. See http://www.in.gov/legislative/igareports/agency/reports/CCP02.pdf.

11. American Community Survey estimates, 2010. Northern St. Louis corresponds to Missouri's Congressional District 1.

12. Peter Adamson, UNICEF, *Measuring Child Poverty*, 2012. Available at http://www.unicef-irc.org/publications/pdf/rc10_eng.pdf.

13. Harrington, *The Other America*, 159.

PART ONE, CHAPTER ONE

1. See http://www.pusd.org/education/components/scrapbook/default.php ?sectiondetailid=3188&.

2. Howard Friedman, *The Measure of a Nation: How to Regain America's Competitive Edge and Boost our Global Standing* (Amherst, NY: Prometheus Books, 2012), 34. Friedman footnotes reports from the OECD and UN statistics to boost his case.

3. Friedman credits this information to C. J. L. Murray et al., "Eight Americas: Investigating Mortality Disparities Across Races, Counties, and Race-Counties in the United States," *Public Library of Science Medicine* 3, no. 9 (2006): e260. For lists of life expectancy rates by race, gender, and state, see: http://www .worldlifeexpectancy.com/usa/life-expectancy-African American-male.

4. See http://www.nytimes.com/2008/03/23/us/23health.html.

5. For one example of the media coverage on this, see http://www.ny times.com/1992/04/21/science/black-scientists-study-the-pose-of-the-inner -city.html?pagewanted=all&src=pm.

6. S. Jay Olshansky, "Differences in Life Expectancy Due to Race and Educational Differences Are Widening, and Many May Not Catch Up," available at http://content.healthaffairs.org/content/31/8/1803.abstract. Olshansky is a professor of public health at the University of Illinois, Chicago.

7. Kristin Lewis and Sarah Burd-Sharpes, *The Measure of America 2010–2011* (New York: NYU Press, 2010), 63.

8. 2010 U.S. Census Bureau data.

9. Credit Suisse Research Network, *Global Wealth Report 2011*, 17.

10. Merrill Lynch and Capgemini, *World Wealth Report*, 2011. Available at http://www.us.capgemini.com/services-and-solutions/by-industry/financial -services/solutions/wealth/worldwealthreport.

11. See http://www.huffingtonpost.com/2011/10/20/us-incomes-falling-as -optimism-reaches-10-year-low_n_1022118.html.

12. This has been widely documented. For particularly good discussions of the problem, see http://www.pbs.org/wnet/need-to-know/the-daily-need

/unemployed-need-not-apply/10736/, and also http://www.nytimes.com/2011
/07/26/business/help-wanted-ads-exclude-the-long-term-jobless.html.

13. John Rawls, *A Theory of Justice* (Cambridge, MA: The Belknap Press of Harvard University Press, 1971).

14. Taskforce on Economic Growth and Opportunity, Chamber of Commerce, *The Concept of Poverty* (Washington, D.C., 1965), 2–3.

15. Ibid. For the purposes of the Chamber's study, 1929 incomes were translated to correspond to their value in 1963 dollars.

16. See http://www.cbsnews.com/8301-201_162-57343397/census-data-half
-of-u.s-poor-or-low-income/.

17. Inflation calculators show that a dollar in 1963 converts to $7.52 in 2012, during the writing of this book. For Census information, see http://www.census
.gov/compendia/statab/2012/tables/12s0692.pdf.

18. Edelman, *So Rich, So Poor*, 25.

19. See http://www.census.gov/compendia/statab/2012/tables/12s0692.pdf.

20. See http://www.vanityfair.com/society/features/2011/05/top-one-percent
-201105.

21. Thomas Picketty and Emmanuel Saez, "The Evolution of Top Incomes: A Historical and International Perspective," *Working Paper* 11955, National Bureau of Economic Research, January 2006. Available at http://unpan1.un.org
/intradoc/groups/public/documents/APCITY/UNPAN027111.pdf.

22. See http://elsa.berkeley.edu/~saez/saez-UStopincomes-2010.pdf.

23. See http://www.cbsnews.com/8301-201_162-57343397/census-data-half
-of-u.s-poor-or-low-income/.

24. See http://www.commondreams.org/headlines05/0908-06.htm.

25. Associated Press, "Labor Productivity Rises 1.6%," August 8, 2012. Productivity numbers are calculated by the Bureau of Economic Analysis.

26. See http://stats.oecd.org/Index.aspx?DatasetCode=POVERTY.

27. See http://msnbcmedia.msn.com/i/MSNBC/Sections/NEWS/A_Politics
/October_Poll.pdf, particularly questions 29b and 30. Also se http://www.cbs
news.com/8301-503544_162-20125515-503544/poll-43-percent-agree-with
-views-of-occupy-wall-street/.

28. See http://www.americanprogress.org/issues/2012/03/americans_inequality
.html.

29. See http://www.foxnews.com/on-air/hannity/2011/07/26/sen-lee-obamas
-class-warfare-wont-solve-debt-problem.

30. See http://www.foxnews.com/politics/2011/09/18/rep-ryan-accuses-obama
-waging-class-warfare-with-millionaire-tax-plan/#ixzz1oCX81VoC.

31. See http://www.newshounds.us/2011/09/21/multimillionaires_hannity_
and_palin_lecture_warren_buffett_over_tax_increases_for_the_wealthy_.php.

PART ONE, CHAPTER TWO

1. See http://www.census.gov/population/www/pop-profile/poverty.html.

2. See http://www.census.gov/prod/2002pubs/p60-219.pdf.

3. The poverty rate was 22.4 percent in 1959; it began to go down in the early 1960s, as President Kennedy began implementing modest anti-poverty efforts. The decline accelerated under both Lyndon Johnson and Richard Nixon, reaching an all-time low of 11.1 percent in 1973.

4. Randy Albelda, "Different Anti-Poverty Program, Same Single-Mother Poverty," *Dollars and Sense*, February 2012.

5. In 1991, Harvard University economist Juliet Schor reported that U.S. manufacturing employees worked, on average, 320 hours more per year than did their peers in Germany and France. *The Overworked American: The Unexpected Decline of Leisure* (New York: Basic Books, 1992).

6. See http://www.census.gov/prod/2005pubs/p60-229.pdf.

7. See http://www.fas.org/sgp/crs/misc/RL33069.pdf.

8. See http://www.politico.com/news/stories/1111/68729.html#ixzz1oIK1iA5Y.

9. See http://www.mediaite.com/online/rush-limbaugh-is-upset-about-romney-not-caring-about-the-very-poor-but-for-a-different-reason/.

10. See http://www.rushlimbaugh.com/daily/2011/11/28/ny_times_democrats_not_interested_in_voters_who_work_target_losers_instead.

11. See http://www.usnews.com/news/washington-whispers/articles/2011/10/18/tea-party-budget-cuts-9-trillion.

12. See http://www.americanprogress.org/issues/2011/11/house_pell_grants.html.

13. See http://www.mcclatchydc.com/2011/12/19/v-print/133530/sen-demints-deficit-cutting-plan.html.

14. David Cay Johnston, *Free Lunch: How the Wealthiest Americans Enrich Themselves at Government Expense (and Stick You with the Bill)* (New York: Penguin, 2007).

15. Ibid., 277.

16. For a fuller discussion of Detroit's poverty rate, see http://www.nytimes.com/2012/02/18/opinion/blow-santorum-exalts-inequality.html.

17. See Economic Hardship Reporting Project, interview with Peter Edelman, May 29, 2012.

18. I first wrote about the situation in Longview here: Sasha Abramsky, "No Country for Middle-Aged Men," *Mother Jones*, May/June 2009.

19. See http://livinglies.wordpress.com/2012/08/01/3-million-more-on-the-brink-of-foreclosure/.

PART ONE, CHAPTER THREE

1. Charles Booth, section on "The Church of England," *Life and Labour of the People in London: Volume on Inner South London* (London: MacMillan, 1902), 65.

2. For a broader discussion of Southern poverty and its implications for the tax system, see Katherine Newman and Rourke O'Brien, *Taxing the Poor: Doing Damage to the Truly Disadvantaged* (Berkeley, CA: University of California Press, 2011).

3. Ibid., 141–142.

4. Kaiser Family Foundation, "Where Are States Today? Medicaid and CHIP Eligibility Levels for Children and Non-Disabled Adults." July 2012. Report available at http://www.kff.org/medicaid/upload/7993–02.pdf and http://www.census.gov/compendia/statab/2012/tables/12s0155.pdf.

5. For more information on this, see Daniel Levine, *Poverty and Society: The Growth of the American Welfare State in International Comparison* (New Brunswick, NJ: Rutgers University Press, 1988).

6. The speech is quoted in Wallace's 1944 book *Democracy Reborn*. It is also available at http://newdeal.feri.org/wallace/haw04.htm#8.

7. For details of annual SNAP expenditures, see http://www.fns.usda.gov/pd/SNAPsummary.htm.

8. See http://www.nal.usda.gov/ric/ricpubs/foodstamps.htm.

9. See http://www.digitalhistory.uh.edu/learning_history/children_depression/depression_children_menu.cfm.

10. See Newman and O'Brien, *Taxing the Poor*.

11. Physicians Task Force on Hunger in America, *Hunger in America: The Growing Epidemic* (Middletown, CT: Wesleyan University Press, 1985), 176.

12. See http://www.cms.gov/Research-Statistics-Data-and-Systems/Statistics-Trends-and-Reports/TheChartSeries/Downloads/35chartbk.pdf.

13. See http://www.lbjlib.utexas.edu/johnson/archives.hom/speeches.hom/640108.asp.

14. See http://www.jfklibrary.org/Research/Ready-Reference/RFK-Speeches/Remarks-of-Robert-F-Kennedy-at-the-University-of-Kansas-March-18–1968.aspx.

15. Martin Luther King Jr., *Where Do We Go From Here: Chaos or Community?* (New York: Harper & Row, 1967). The text was based on a speech King gave at the Southern Christian Leadership Conference in Atlanta, Georgia, on August 16, 1967.

16. For an in-depth discussion of shifting public attitudes around welfare and poverty, see Jeffrey Will, "The Dimensions of Poverty: Public Perceptions of the Deserving Poor," *Social Science Research* 22 (1992): 312–332. Available at http://

www.unf.edu/uploadedFiles/aa/coas/cci/publication%20Dimensions%20of%20 Poverty.pdf.

17. See http://www.huffingtonpost.com/dave-johnson/plutocracy-ge-doesnt -pay_b_840936.html.

18. I am grateful to Kathryn Sklar, distinguished professor emerita of history at the State University of New York at Binghamton, for explaining to me the different ways in which the polity responded to male and female poverty in the late nineteenth and early twentieth centuries.

19. Michael Katz, "The American Welfare State and Social Contract in Hard Times," *Journal of Policy History* 22, no. 4 (2010): 508–529.

20. Richard Parker cites this in his book *John Kenneth Galbraith: His Life, His Politics, His Economics* (New York: Farrar, Straus and Giroux, 2005), 481. His footnote attributes the information to historian Irving Bernstein's book *Guns or Butter*, 84.

21. See http://www.youtube.com/watch?v=XcFDF87-SdQ.

22. See http://politicalcorrection.org/blog/201012100003.

23. See http://www.youtube.com/watch?v=r79-Za5tj9E.

PART ONE, CHAPTER FOUR

1. Data provided by the affordable housing advocacy group, the Community Tool Box, available at http://ctb.ku.edu/en/tablecontents/sub_section _main_1305.aspx.

2. See http://www.businessweek.com/stories/2007–08–05/the-pet-economy and http://www2.wkrg.com/news/2012/mar/02/how-much-do-americans-spend -their-pets-ar-3339130/. Also, for TANF spending, see http://www.acf.hhs.gov /programs/opre/other_resrch/tanf_ccdf/reports/broader_safety.pdf.

3. See http://www.bloomberg.com/apps/news?pid=newsarchive&sid=atW bvxYV3vVk&refer=culture.

4. See http://thebodyproject.bradley.edu/industires/index.shtml.

5. These data are from Gina Kolata, "Liposuction Study Finds That Lost Fat Returns," the *New York Times*, April 30, 2011. Available at http://www .nytimes.com/2011/05/01/weekinreview/01kolata.html.

6. Bob Woodruff, "Life on Ice: The World of Crazy Cryogenics." *Good Morning America*, July 27, 2011. Available at http://www.nytimes.com/2011 /05/01/weekinreview/01kolata.html.

7. *Business Wire*, "Paradise Tan Increases an Overall Funding Package to $24 Million," November 26, 2003. Available at http://www.businesswire.com

/news/home/20031126005019/en/Paradise-Tan-Increases-Funding-Package-24-Million.

8. This number is based on information contained in a report by the Harvard Law School's Berman Center for the Internet and Society. See http://cyber.law.harvard.edu/vaw02/mod2–3.htm. The data are from the early 2000s. In all likelihood, that amount has increased considerably in the years since this study was released.

9. See http://www.epi.org/publication/child_poverty_rises_dramatically/.

10. See http://www.census.gov/prod/2011pubs/acs-16.pdf.

11. See http://scjusticewatch.org/2012/01/10/another-legislative-session-more-scapegoating-of-the-poor/.

12. Center on Budget and Policy Priorities, *State-By-State Fact Sheets*. Available at http://www.cbpp.org/files/1-25-11tanf-methodology.pdf and http://www.cbpp.org/files/8-7-12tanf-factsheets/8-7-12tanf-FL.pdf.

13. This information is in the CBPP report, *TANF Benefits Fell Further in 2011 and Are Worth Much Less Than in 1996 in Most States*. The report attributes this information to HHS Poverty Guidelines as well as various state sources and is valid through July 1, 2011.

14. Center on Budget and Policy Priorities, *State-by-State Fact Sheets on TANF*, based on data collected from state agencies and DHHS.

15. U.S. House of Representatives Ways and Means Committee, *Green Book*, Table 8–15, 1996. Available at http://frwebgate.access.gpo.gov/cgi-bin/getdoc.dgi?dbname=104_green_book&docid=f:wm014_18.pdf.

16. Information on summer employment program and murder rates in Flint provided during author interview with Alicia Booker, of the Mott Foundation, June 23, 2012.

17. Peter J. Hotez, "Tropical Diseases: The New Plague of Poverty," the *New York Times*, June 19, 2012.

18. Ibid.

19. For a full discussion of state TANF time limit reductions, see http://voices.yahoo.com/safety-nets-go-bust-over-15-million-welfare-risk-10128845.html?cat=31.

20. See http://crooksandliars.com/karoli/rush-limbaugh-hungry-children-are-wanton-li.

21. See http://www.speaker.gov/News/DocumentSingle.aspx?DocumentID=240370.

22. See http://www.politicalruminations.com/michele-bachmann-quotes/.

23. See http://www.humanevents.com/article.php?id=42693.

PART ONE, CHAPTER FIVE

1. See http://www.pewtrusts.org/uploadedFiles/wwwpewtrustsorg/Reports /Philadelphia_Research_Initiative/Philadelphia-City-Data-Population -Demographics.pdf.

2. See http://www.city-data.com/poverty/poverty-Philadelphia-Pennsylvania .html.

3. For disability data, see the following report by the Center for Independence of the Disabled, New York: http://www.cidny.org/resources/News /Reports/Disability%20Matters.pdf.

4. This paragraph uses research generated by the Community Service Society in a December 2010 report titled *Unemployment in New York City During the Recession and Early Recovery: Young Black Men Hit the Hardest*, by Michelle Holder. See http://b.3cdn.net/nycss/ea8952641d08e68fbb_c4m6bofb0.pdf.

5. Don Terry, "Where Work Disappears and Dreams Die," *American Prospect*, special issue on poverty, July/August 2012.

6. See http://voices.yahoo.com/most-dangerous-cities-america-murder -rates-7293190.html?cat=54.

7. These data are generated by the USDA and publicized by FRAC. For the chart, modified each month, used by the author here, see http://frac.org/pdf /2012_05.pdf.

8. See http://www.nytimes.com/2012/02/26/us/support-grows-for-idea-of -drug-tests-for-welfare-recipients.html?_r=1&ref=welfareus.

9. See http://www.thenation.com/blog/167487/week-poverty-georgia-tries -get-zero-welfare-recipients.

10. For a good discussion of Mettler's work, see Ezra Klein's column, available at http://www.bloomberg.com/news/2012–03–01/middle-class-welfare -state-invisible-by-design-commentary-by-ezra-klein.html.

11. This is from the draft of an unpublished paper that Katz showed the author in summer 2012. The New America Foundation has also done research on these subsidies.

12. Buchanan is referencing the Heritage Foundation's report, Robert Rector, *Understanding Poverty in the United States,* available at http://townhall.com /columnists/patbuchanan/2012/02/24/creators_oped/page/full/.

13. Philip Stern and George de Vincent, *The Shame of a Nation* (New York: Ivan Obolensky, 1965), 130.

14. See http://www.rentjungle.com/average-rent-in-new-york-rent-trends/.

15. Information provided in conversation with JoAnne Page, executive director of the New York City–based Fortune Society.

16. See http://www.pewcenteronthestates.org/report_detail.aspx?id=8589 9372244.

17. See http://www.reuters.com/article/2011/12/24/us-usa-health-psychiatric -idUSTRE7BN06820111224.

18. See http://abcnews.go.com/blogs/health/2011/11/10/will-budget-cuts -threaten-mental-health-in-your-state/.

19. Liz Schott and Clare Cho, "General Assistance Programs: Safety Net Weakening Despite Increased Need," Center on Budget and Policy Priorities, updated December 19, 2011. Available at http://www.cbpp.org/cms/?fa=view &id=3603.

20. See http://money.cnn.com/2010/09/16/news/economy/Americas_ wealthiest_states/index.htm; http://xfinity.comcast.net/slideshow/finance-worst paidteachers/mississippi/; http://www.worldlifeexpectancy.com/usa/mississippi -life-expectancy; and http://www.census.gov/statab/ranks/rank17.html.

21. Kaiser Family Foundation, *State Health Facts*, available at http://www .statehealthfacts.org/profileind.jsp?rep=130&cat=4&rgn=26.

22. A year later, the Kaiser Family Foundation reported that "chronic condi- tions were [also] widespread, with over four in ten (41%) adults responding that they had been told by a doctor that they had hypertension, diabetes, asthma or other breathing problems, or other chronic health conditions."

23. See http://www.kff.org/kaiserpolls/upload/7659.pdf.

24. See http://www.urban.org/publications/900921.html.

25. See http://www.huffingtonpost.com/2009/08/28/four-years-after-katrina _n_270944.html.

26. See http://articles.latimes.com/2010/aug/29/nation/la-na-katrina-201 00829.

27. Estimates of Hurricane Katrina's cost range from approximately $90 billion up to $125 billion; approximately $41 billion of this was covered by in- surance company payouts. See http://useconomy.about.com/od/grossdomestic product/f/katrina_damage.htm, and http://www.naic.org/cipr_topics/topic _catastrophe.htm.

28. See http://www.huffingtonpost.com/2010/11/02/bp-oil-spill-costs-hit -40_n_777521.html.

29. See http://articles.cnn.com/2011–08–29/opinion/kohn.conservatives .fema_1_fema-federal-emergency-management-agency-disaster-relief?_s=PM: OPINION.

30. See http://www.thedailybeast.com/articles/2011/09/10/fema-more-federal -disaster-response-programs-alarming-cuts.html.

PART ONE, CHAPTER SIX

1. Jacob Hacker, *The Great Risk Shift: The New Economic Insecurity and the Decline of the American Dream*, 2nd ed. (Oxford: Oxford University Press, 2006), 5.

2. See http://articles.orlandosentinel.com/2008–02–15/business/bernanke 15_1_bernanke-fiscal-stimulus-package-economy-more-resilient.

3. See http://money.cnn.com/2008/02/14/news/economy/bernanke_paulson /index.htm.

4. See http://politicalticker.blogs.cnn.com/2008/04/22/bush-denies-us -economy-in-recession/.

5. See http://www.huffingtonpost.com/2008/09/15/mccain-fundamentals -of-th_n_126445.html.

6. See http://articles.cnn.com/2008–09–24/politics/bush.transcript_1_markets -financial-assets-economy?_s=PM:POLITICS.

7. Rakesh Kochhar, Richard Fry, and Paul Taylor, *Wealth Gaps Rise to Record Highs Between Whites, Blacks, Hispanics*. Report released by Pew Research Center, July 26, 2011. Available at http://www.pewsocialtrends.org /2011/07/26/wealth-gaps-rise-to-record-highs-between-whites-blacks -hispanics/.

8. See http://news.yahoo.com/documents-show-fed-missed-housing-bust -022039343.html.

9. Elise Gould and Kathryn Anne Edwards, "Another Look at Poverty in the Great Recession," Economic Policy Institute, January 5, 2011. Available at http://www.epi.org/publication/ib293/.

10. The author wrote about these laws in "Reversing 'Right to Work,'" the *Nation*, February 27, 2006.

11. These numbers, generated by the federal government, have been widely reported. For a particularly good analysis, see http://www.hightower lowdown.org/node/1568.

12. For Texas poverty data, see *Spotlight on Poverty and Opportunity*, available at http://www.spotlightonpoverty.org/map-detail.aspx?state=Texas. For information on Texans without health insurance, see http://www.washingtonpost.com /blogs/ezra-klein/post/why-texas-has-the-highest-percentage-of-uninsured-people -in-the-us/2011/08/02/gIQA1wIdHJ_blog.html. For data on hunger in Texas, see figures provided by the Texas Hunger Initiative: http://www.baylor.edu/texas hunger/index.php?id=85493. For job creation numbers, see http://www.politi fact.com/texas/statements/2011/may/29/texas-public-policy-foundation/texas -public-policy-foundation-says-texas-created-/.

13. See http://www.cppp.org/research.php?aid=1133&cid=3&scid=5.

14. See http://www.bls.gov/lau/.

15. See http://www.bls.gov/cps/minwage2010tbls.htm#3.

16. See http://www.nbcdfw.com/news/business/Number-of-Walmarts-in-Dallas-to-Double-116711789.html.

17. See http://www.glassdoor.com/Hourly-Pay/Walmart-Stores-Hourly-Pay-E715.htm.

18. See http://walmartwatch.com/wp-content/blogs.dir/2/files/pdf/walmart_unions.pdf.

19. See http://walmartwatch.com/wp-content/blogs.dir/2/files/pdf/walmart_unions.pdf.

20. See http://www.walmartstores.com/sites/AnnualReport/2011/financials.aspx.

21. See http://www.wptv.com/dpp/news/national/walmart-black-friday-2012-strike-walkout-update-group-of-dallas-walmart-workers-protest.

22. Howard Friedman, *The Measure of a Nation: How to Regain America's Competitive Edge and Boost Our Global Standing* (Amherst, NY: Prometheus Books, 2012), 18.

23. For a full transcript of Santorum's speech, see http://www.freep.com/article/20120219/OPINION05/202190367/Transcript-GOP-primary-candidate-Rick-Santorum-s-speech-Detroit-Economic-Club.

24. See http://cbsdetroit.files.wordpress.com/2011/05/basicskillsreport_final.pdf.

25. For a good overview of the current literature on social mobility in the United States, see *The Economist*, December 29, 2004. Available at http://www.economist.com/node/3518560.

PART TWO, INTRODUCTION

1. Randy Albelda, "Different Anti-Poverty Program, Same Single-Mother Poverty," *Dollars and Sense,* February 2012.

2. Richard Rothstein, *Class and Schools* (Washington, D.C., and New York: Economic Policy Institute and Teachers College Press, 2004), 9.

3. Ibid., 10.

4. See http://thinkprogress.org/climate/2012/07/31/615661/big-5-oil-companies-going-for-the-gold/.

5. For a fuller explanation of this act, see the congressional report issued by the Joint Committee on Taxation, available at https://www.jct.govpublications.html?func=startdown&id=2388.

PART TWO, CHAPTER ONE

1. See Albelda, "Different Anti-Poverty Programs, Same Single-Mother Poverty."

2. In 2008, the *New York Times* quoted estimates that varied from $12.5 billion per month up to $25 billion. See http://www.nytimes.com/2008/03/23/opinion/23kristof.html.

3. These numbers were provided by the Center on Budget and Policy Priorities, available at http://www.cbpp.org/cms/?fa=view&id=3625. To put in perspective: America was spending more each second funding the Iraq War than most welfare recipients in America receive in a year, according to numbers generated by the Center on Budget and Policy Priorities.

4. Edelman, *So Rich, So Poor,* 2–3.

5. See http://www.citylimits.org/news/article_print.cfm?article_id=4463.

6. Hoynes and her colleagues have written several articles on this. The author also talked about these findings with Hoynes several times during the research for this book.

7. Albelda, "Different Anti-Poverty Programs, Same Single-Mother Poverty." Albelda's information came from the Department of Health and Human Services, Office of Assistant Secretary for Planning and Evaluation, Table 4.3 of TANF, 6th Annual Report to Congress (November 2004), and Table 4.2 of TANF, 8th Annual Report to Congress (June 2009).

PART TWO, CHAPTER TWO

1. See http://www.childrenshealthwatch.org/upload/resource/MRVP_CHIA.pdf.

2. See http://blogs.justice.gov/main/archives/1950.

3. See http://www.cepr.net/documents/publications/economists-letter-ftt-2009–12.pdf.

4. See http://www.businessweek.com/news/2012–07–25/billionaires-may-win-as-dems-split-on-estate-tax.

5. See http://news.yahoo.com/alaskans-878-yearly-oil-wealth-payout-1910 45917.html.

6. Information provided to author by United Methodist Outreach Ministry staff during visit to the site.

7. See http://fieldus.org/Stories/FastFacts.html.

8. See http://cfsinnovation.com/content/complex-portrait-examination-small-dollar-credit-consumers.

9. For details of Paine's plan, see Gareth Steadman Jones, *An End to Poverty?* (London: Profile Books, 2004).

10. Known as the Alfond Challenge, the program is administered by the Finance Authority of Maine. The $500 grants were awarded starting on January 1, 2009. For more details, see Margaret Clancy and Terry Lassar's May 2010 report for the Center for Social Development, at the George Warren Brown School of Social Work, Washington University, St. Louis, available at http://csd.wustl.edu/Publications/Documents/PB10–16.pdf.

11. See http://www.nytimes.com/2011/04/12/education/12college.html.

12. This was written about extensively. For a good overview, see the *U.S. News & World Report* article available at http://www.usnews.com/education/best-colleges/paying-for-college/articles/2012/06/28/1-million-people-show-support-for-student-loan-forgiveness-act.

13. This information was generated by researchers with the Federal Reserve Bank of New York. Available at http://libertystreeteconomics.newyorkfed.org/2012/03/grading-student-loans.html.

14. See http://forbestadvice.com/Education/Articles/2011_0721_University_of_California_CAL_Tuition_Fee_History.html.

15. Friedman, *The Measure of a Nation*, 122.

16. See http://www.dailyfinance.com/2011/03/25/pell-grants-face-cuts-in-congress/.

17. See http://thinkprogress.org/economy/2011/12/16/390751/spending-deal-cuts-pell-grants/.

18. Josh Harkinson, "How the Nation's Only State-Owned Bank Became the Envy of Wall Street," *Mother Jones*, May 27, 2009. Available at http://www.motherjones.com/mojo/2009/03/how-nation's-only-state-owned-bank-became-envy-wall-street.

19. See http://www.epa.gov/brownfields/job.htm.

20. N. P. Roman and N. Wolfe, *Web of Failure: The Relationship Between Foster Care and Homelessness* (Washington, D.C.: National Alliance to End Homelessness, 1995); and R. Cook, *A National Evaluation of Title IV-E Foster Care Independent Living Programs for Youth, Phase 2* (Rockville, MD: Westat, 1991).

21. "18 and Out: Life After Foster Care in Massachusetts," 7. Available at http://www.chapa.org/pdf/18andOut.pdf.

22. See http://www.chapinhall.org/research/inside/does-keeping-youth-foster-care-beyond-age-18-help-prevent-homelessness.

23. See http://www.sor.govoffice3.com/vertical/Sites/%7B3BDD1595–792B-4D20-8D44-626EF05648C7%7D/uploads/Foster_Care_PDF_12-8-11.pdf.

24. Mark E. Courtney, et al., "Midwest Evaluation of the Adult Functioning of Former Foster Youth: Outcomes at Age 19," Chapin Hall Center for Children at the University of Chicago, May 2005.

25. Nicholas Zill, *Adoption from Foster Care: Aiding Children While Saving Public Money* (Washington, D.C.: Brookings Institution, 2011).

26. The author wrote about this school as a point of contrast to the surrounding financial gloom in Nevada, in "Nevada Goes Bust," the *Nation*, September 20, 2010. Available at http://www.thenation.com/article/154482/nevada-goes -bust.

27. Kristina Rizga, "Everything You've Heard About Failing Schools Is Wrong," *Mother Jones*, September/October 2012. Available at http://www.motherjones .com/media/2012/08/mission-high-false-low-performing-school.

28. See http://www.sfdistrictattorney.org/index.aspx?page=3.

29. See data provided by the Office of Juvenile Justice and Delinquency Prevention at http://www.ojjdp.gov/dso/Truancy%20Abatement%20and%20 Burglary%20Suppression%20(TABS)-DSOProgramDetail-800.aspx.

30. Diane Ravitch, "Schools We Can Envy," *New York Review of Books*, March 8, 2012, 19–20.

31. Abby Rapoport, "Diane Ravitch on the 'Effort to Destroy Public Ed,'" *American Prospect*, October 2, 2012. Available at http://prospect.org/article/diane -ravitch-effort-destroy-public-ed.

32. Ladd said this during a presidential address that she gave to the Association for Public Policy Analysis and Management, November 4, 2011. The speech was subsequently published in the *Journal of Policy Analysis and Management*.

33. National Public Radio's "Marketplace" reported on the Oyler School in an October 2012 report, available at http://www.marketplace.org/topics /wealth-poverty/one-school-one-year/leading-change-oyler-school/. The report provides a good summary of the premises behind the Community Learning Center movement.

PART TWO, CHAPTER THREE

1. "Who Pays? A Distributional Analysis of the Tax Systems in All Fifty States," *Institute on Taxation and Economic Policy*, 3rd ed. (Washington, D.C., 2009). Available at http://www.itepnet.org/whopays3.pdf.

2. See http://www.youtube.com/watch?v=xtpgkX588nMa.

3. For a good, concise discussion of Friedman's idea, see the *New York Times* business section article on it that followed Friedman's death in 2006: http://www.nytimes.com/2006/11/23/business/23scene.html.

4. I am grateful to University of Pennsylvania historian Michael Katz for pointing this out to me. It is briefly referenced in a draft paper of his, and is more generally written about in Brian Steensland, *The Failed Welfare Revolution: America's Struggle Over Guaranteed Income Policy* (Princeton, NJ: Princeton University Press, 2009).

5. This information is detailed in the June 2012 unpublished paper, "Income, The Earned Income Tax Credit, and Family Health," by University of California at Davis economists Hilary Hoynes, Douglas Miller, and David Simon. Hoynes also talked through her findings with the author during a series of in-person conversations.

6. Jesse Rothstein, "Is the EITC as Good as an NIT? Conditional Cash Transfers and Tax Incidence," Princeton University and NBER, May 5, 2009.

7. See http://walmartwatch.com/wp-content/blogs.dir/2/files/pdf/walmart_livingwage_policies07.pdf.

8. See http://www.nytimes.com/2011/01/19/us/19farm.html.

9. Jeannette Wicks-Lim and Jeffrey Thompson, "Combining Minimum Wage and Earned Income Tax Credit Policies to Guarantee a Decent Living Standard to All U.S. Workers," Political Economy Research Institute, October 2010. Available at http://www.peri.umass.edu/fileadmin/pdf/published_study/PERI_MW_EITC_Oct2010.pdf.

10. See http://www.gallup.com/poll/149567/americans-favor-jobs-plan-proposals-including-taxing-rich.aspx.

11. See http://www.americanprogress.org/issues/public-opinion/news/2012/09/04/35992/public-opinion-snapshot-public-supports-infrastructure-spending-to-create-jobs/.

12. "The Growth in the Social Security Disability Rolls: A Fiscal Crisis Unfolding," *Journal of Economic Perspectives* 20, no. 3 (Summer 2006): 71–96.

13. Alex Kowalski, "Disabled Americans Shrink Size of U.S. Labor Force," *Bloomberg News*, May 3, 2012.

14. Press release, "Social Security Board of Trustees: Project Trust Fund Exhaustion Three Years Earlier Than Last Year," April 23, 2012.

15. See http://bcorporation.net/.

16. See http://www.forbes.com/sites/annefield/2012/07/26/louisiana-about-to-become-a-benefit-corp-state-with-illinois-close-behind/.

17. Munnell's data are sourced in Catherine Rampell, "Pensions 1980 Versus Today," the *New York Times*, September 3, 2009. Available at http://economix.blogs.nytimes.com/2009/09/03/pensions-1980-vs-today/.

18. See http://www.pbgc.gov/wr/other/pg/american-airlines-pensions-get-the-facts.html.

19. Sasha Abramsky, "No Country for Middle-Aged Men," *Mother Jones*, May/June 2009, available at http://www.motherjones.com/politics/2009/05/no-country-middle-aged-men. I also told this story in my book *Breadline USA: The Hidden Scandal of American Hunger and How to Fix It* (Sausalito, CA: PoliPoint Press, 2009).

20. SSI formulas are extremely technical. For an overview of how the system works, see http://www.ssa.gov/policy/docs/ssb/v67n3/v67n3p29.html.

21. See http://www.treasury.gov/resource-center/economic-policy/ss-medicare/Documents/TR_2012_Medicare.pdf.

22. See http://www.ssa.gov/oact/trsum/index.html.

23. See, for example, Politifact's analysis of Rhode Island senator Sheldon Whitehouse's "Keeping Our Social Security Promises Act," which proposed making income of greater than $250,000 per year subject to Social Security taxes. Available at http://www.politifact.com/rhode-island/statements/2012/aug/26/sheldon-whitehouse/us-sen-sheldon-whitehouse-says-proposal-would-keep/.

24. For an interesting analysis of the problems confronting Medicare, and the possibility of saving the system without eviscerating it, see Center on Budget and Policy Priorities, "Medicare Is Not Bankrupt," available at http://www.cbpp.org/cms/index.cfm?fa=view&id=3532. To get a sense of the scale of the challenges facing Medicare, see reports by the Kaiser Family Foundation, including: http://www.kff.org/medicare/upload/7731-03.pdf.

Index

The Nation Institute

Founded in 2000, **Nation Books** has become a leading voice in American independent publishing. The inspiration for the imprint came from the *Nation* magazine, the oldest independent and continuously published weekly magazine of politics and culture in the United States.

The imprint's mission is to produce authoritative books that break new ground and shed light on current social and political issues. We publish established authors who are leaders in their area of expertise, and endeavor to cultivate a new generation of emerging and talented writers. With each of our books we aim to positively affect cultural and political discourse.

Nation Books is a project of The Nation Institute, a nonprofit media center dedicated to strengthening the independent press and advancing social justice and civil rights. The Nation Institute is home to a dynamic range of programs: the award-winning Investigative Fund, which supports ground-breaking investigative journalism; the widely read and syndicated website TomDispatch; the Victor S. Navasky Internship Program in conjunction with the *Nation* magazine; and Journalism Fellowships that support up to 25 high-profile reporters every year.

For more information on Nation Books, The Nation Institute, and the *Nation* magazine, please visit:

www.nationbooks.org

www.nationinstitute.org

www.thenation.com

www.facebook.com/nationbooks.ny

Twitter: @nationbooks